高职高专商务英语、应用英语专业规划教材

欧美概况与跨文化商务交际视听说

编著　郑张敏　陆金英
顾问　都建明　陆金仙
审稿　郑智杰　张丽敏

European and
American Studies
and Intercultural
Business
Communication

ZHEJIANG UNIVERSITY PRESS
浙江大学出版社

编者说明

　　本书旨在帮助 21 世纪的英语学习者在国际交往日益频繁的今天，进一步增强文化意识和跨文化意识，发展跨文化交际能力，以便在已成为"地球村"的世界上，在与他人的交往中能够如鱼得水、应付自如。选取的大部分试听材料体现了与时俱进的教学理念，尽可能体现教材的"时代感、新鲜感、成就感"。如奥巴马总统访华时在上海对话中国青年大学生的视频听力材料和当今世界形势的各种英语新闻等，让学生学到原汁原味的地道的英语口语。同时选取了一些名人英语演讲，从大学生创业的角度，激发他们的拼搏精神和积极向上的精神，如苹果电脑总裁在斯坦福大学的演讲所叙述的坎坷经历和成功的案例对当今大学生的创业有很好的启发作用。

　　第一章的内容以英国历史为主线。在英国历史上有"条条道路通罗马"之称。为了阐述英国的历史渊源，我们讲到了"罗马帝国"、凯撒大帝日记等史料，这是标志英国有文字历史记载的开始。英国本土民族凯尔特人除了被古罗马人征服融合外，还经历了北欧海盗和丹麦人的入侵，以及 1066 年诺曼人的征服。这些事件对英语语言和社会文化各方面均产生了深远的影响。近代英国对美国、加拿大、澳大利亚、中国、印度等国家的海外扩张促进了英国经济的快速发展。

　　第二章美国历史以美国的"大熔炉"文化为主要特色。本章阐述了美国在短暂的历史时期内的发展和崛起的过程。正如某些西方经济学家的断言："When the United States coughs, the rest of the world catches cold."（美国咳嗽时，全世界都感冒了。）由此可见它在世界经济中的地位。

　　近几十年来，经济的全球化(globalization of economy)、商业的国际化把分布在世界不同角落的人与产品聚集在了同一时空之下。因此第三章以 2010 年上海世博会作为其中的一个切入点，略述了各国经济文化的异同以及和中国的跨文化商务交际。如：荷兰国家展示馆中呈"8"字形的人行道迎合了中国文化中的民俗意识和某种文化底蕴；卢森堡国家展示馆的周围森林和堡垒(forest and fortress)的设计迎合了国名的中文音译，融合了中国文化；奥地利国家展示馆的设计为红、白色相间，红色体现了中国文化的喜庆色彩；沙特阿拉伯国家展示馆以沙漠为主题，他们的领导人声称：希望和中国人民共享并展示他们的生活经历，跨越时空则令人联想到中国唐代兴起的"丝绸之路"途经沙漠，将丝绸传播给了遥远的欧洲，供达官贵人享用。在第一章欧洲历史部分提到：

silk 为 emperor's clothes，英国历史部分提到：take silk 为地位的升迁之意，在整篇的布局上力求历史的连贯性和延续性。

本书的大部分材料选自伦敦 Kingfisher 出版社发行的历史百科全书 *The Concise History Encyclopedia* (London: Kingfisher Publications Plc, 2001)和英国大英博物馆出版社出版的 *The British Museum Book of Chinese Art* (Edited by Jessica Rawson. London: British Museum Press, 1999)等权威的著作。对有争议的历史事实有更加公正的立场和评判。例如：对"茶叶"间谍罗伯特·福钧(伦敦园艺会领导人、英国著名植物学家)在武夷山进行物种资源窃取等行为在书中用了"steal"(偷窃)一词。由于中国红茶的俏销，导致英国白银外流，英国政府指示东印度公司派遣间谍。1842年后在中国的三年采集行程中，他学习中文并穿中国人的服饰，按照中国人的方式理了发，加上了一条长辫子，冒着生命危险乔装打扮成当地中国人。在回国时带回了100多种西方人没有见过的植物。他窃取了2万株茶树至印度的大吉岭，结束了一直为中国茶垄断的茶市场。由于英国"偷窃"并合理利用了中国博大精深的工艺和技术，原本是中国财源的茶叶工艺却变成了英国人致富的摇钱树。同样，在知识产权特别受到保护的今天，在当今纷繁复杂的跨文化商务交际活动中的竞争也是信息和技术的较量，因此上海世博会期间各国的文化展示和商务交往是中国和世界沟通的桥梁。

在第四章"跨文化商务交际和我国在商贸领域取得的成就"中，以大量简洁实用的统计图表展示了我国对外交流活动的成就。全国口语大赛、写作大赛和剑桥商务英语(BEC)中高级考试的题型也是以根据图表写作为主要形式，因此本章的学习可以让学生既了解到当今的商务形势，又培养了学生的英语使用能力。

每单元后面附有详细的注释，既适合高校课程教学，又便于广大自学者学习之用。

本教材共四章，分为61课时，并配有61个 PowerPoint 的教学课件。四套相关试卷针对相关章节，并配有试卷的电子稿。同时听力视频材料等也刻录成 DVD 光盘，赠送给使用本教材的兄弟院校老师，以供教学参考之用。

在此告慰为我做出了最大牺牲、无私关心支持我的父亲——文博专业研究员、上海国际拍卖行的文物古玩鉴定专家张梅坤先生。同时向给予我孜孜不倦教诲的硕士导师、浙江大学外语学院朱炳强、顾明华、徐至立、王之光等教授表示最诚挚的谢意。

本教材和上海海洋大学外语学院的郑智杰等老师合作编写。正是与该校在学术上互相交流、互相探讨，更新教学理念，才有了这本别具特色的教材。

郑张敏

2010 年 6 月

CONTENTS 目　录

CHAPTER Four　　**Intercultural Business Communication and Commercial**

　　　　　　　　Achievements·······························187

CHAPTER ONE

History of Great Britain

Unit 1   The Origin of the English Nation

Lead-in: Listening (PPT-1)

Listen to the video "Stonehenge decoded" carefully, and answer the following questions:

1. What did archaeologists newly-find in the remains of the Stonehenge?

_____

2. Do you agree with the hypothesis that ancient people greeted the summer solstice Sunday at the ancient stone circle of the Stonehenge?

_____

3. Why did Mr. Pearson suspect the Stonehenge was once a lost city and what evidence did he provide us?

Reading

1.1   The Native Celts

The **Celts** were a loose grouping of tribes living in southern Germany from around 1500 BC. By Roman Times the Celts **dominated** much of Europe.

Around 500 BC, the Celts were the dominant European power. They had expanded from in what is now southern Germany. They were not a nation but more a

confederation of individual tribes with a shared culture. Their influence eventually stretched from Spain to Britain, Germany and northern Italy and as far as central **Anatolia**.

Celtic roundhouses were made of **timber and thatch**, with **wattle-and-daub** (or sometimes stone) walls. Smoke floated out through the thatched roof, but rain was unable to seep in. Sleeping space was around the inside of the wall, while cooking and washing went on around the central fire.

1.1.1 The Celtic Life

The Celts traded with Rome, Greece and other countries, but they were not much influenced by these civilizations.

The Celts were tribal farmers who gathered around their chiefs' **strongholds**. These were often hill-forts, and some of them later became villages and towns. Most Celts were **homesteaders** and small farmers, living in a variety of tribes.

The Celtic **stag-god Cernunnos or Hurn** was **hammered and chiseled** onto the side of this large bronze **cauldron** around 1,900 years ago. Cernunnos was an important **deity** of the Celts, essentially a nature god associated with produce and fertility.

1.1.2 Power and Law

Each Celt was a free person with individual rights. Druidic justice was famous, and bonds of loyalty within each tribe was strong. The chiefs were elected by tribespeople, and the high kings by the chiefs. Both could be **deposed** if they did not do a good job.

1.2   Celtic Warriors

Known as fierce warriors (the women fought too), the Celts used iron to make their weapons and tools. In 390 BC they sacked Rome and in 280 BC they raided Greece and Anatolia, seeking booty. Sometimes they even fought among themselves. The Roman exploited this when conquering Gaul (France) and Britain. The British Celtic leader, Caradoc was betrayed by other Celts. Disunited, the British warriors lost their independence in 43—80 AD. The Celts came to accept Roman rule and later fought with the Romans against Germanic barbarians. The Celts were also the first European Christians. After the fall of Rome, Celtic ways in Europe survived only in Ireland, Cornwall, Brittany and parts of Wales and Scotland.

Boudicca[1] was the queen of the Iceni of the east of England. She headed a rebellion against the occupying Romans in Britain in 60 AD, in which 70,000 Romans were

Boudicca was the queen of the Iceni of the East of England. She headed a rebellion against the occupying Romans in Britain in A060 in which 70,000 Romans were killed. However, the rebellion was eventually crushed, and Boudicca committed suicide.

killed. However the rebellion was eventually crushed, and Boudicca committed suicide.

1.3   Ancient Celtic Civilization

Stonehenge is a prehistoric monument located in the English county of Wiltshire, about 3.2 kilometres (2.0 mi) west of Amesbury and 13 kilometres (8.1 mi) north of Salisbury. As one of the most famous sites in the world, Stonehenge is composed of earthworks surrounding a circular setting of large standing stones and sits at the centre of the densest complex of **Neolithic and Bronze Age** monuments in England, including several hundred burial mounds. Archaeologists had believed that the iconic stone monument was erected around 2500 BC.

1.4   Celtic Religion—Druidism[2]

1.4.1 Ancient Druidism

There is no evidence of **druids** predating the 2nd century BC. Greek and Roman writers on the Celts commonly made at least passing reference to Druids, though before Caesar's report merely as "barbarian philosophers". These writers were not concerned with ethnology or comparative religion, and consequently our historical knowledge of druids is very limited.

Demigod of magic, prophecy and illusion. Originally an ancient Welsh druid, priest and great magician who went mad after seeing his chief killed. He escaped to Caledon Forest, lived there and gained the gift of prophecy. He once grew feathers so he could leap from tree to tree.

Julius Caesar's Commentarii de Bello Gallico, book VI, published in the 50s or 40s BC, gives the first surviving and the fullest account of the druids.

1.4.2 Modern Druidism

Neo-druidism or **neo-druidry** (referred to simply as **Druidry** by some adherents) is a form of modern spirituality or religion that generally **promotes harmony and worship of nature**, and respect for all beings, including the environment. By other modern druids it is considered to be a philosophical movement that includes religious tolerance,

allowing its followers to be adherents of other religions, or to be **atheists**.

New Words and Expressions

Celt [kelt; selt]	*n.* 凯尔特人
dominate ['dɔmineit]	*v.* 支配，占优势
confederation [kənˌfedə'reiʃən]	*n.* 结盟
Anatolia [ˌænə'təuljə]	*n.* 安纳托利亚(亚洲西部半岛小亚细亚的旧称)
timber and thatch	木料和茅草
wattle-and-daub	*n.* 抹灰篱笆墙
stronghold ['strɔŋhəuld]	*n.* 要塞，据点
homesteader ['həumˌstedə(r)]	*n.* 农场所有权人，自耕农
stag-god Cernunnos or Hurn	牡鹿(Cernunnos 是凯尔特人的神祇，是掌管林野以及狩猎的神灵)
hammered and chiseled	铸打并凿刻成的
cauldron ['kɔːldrən]	*n.* (=caldron)大锅炉
deity ['diːiti]	*n.* 神，神性
deposed [di'pəuz]	*vt.* 免职，废(王位)
Stonehenge ['stəunhendʒ]	*n.* (英国 Salisbury 平原上的)史前巨石柱
Neolithic [niːəu'liθik] **and Bronze Age**	新石器时代和铜器时代
Druid ['druːid]	*n.* 德鲁伊教团员
demigod ['demigɔd]	*n.* 半神半人
neo-druidism	新德鲁伊教
atheist ['eiθiist]	*n.* 无神论者

Notes

[1] Boudicca：或者是 Boadicea，意指胜利，是东英格兰 Iceni 部落的女王。 西元 60 年时，她领导叛变以反抗罗马人，摧毁 Colchester、St. Albans 的城市，攻下伦敦，可是最后她仍然败给罗马人，她不愿受异族凌辱，所以毒死自己以求了断。——Roma Ryan，专辑《凯尔特人》CD 中的小册子。

恺撒大帝在公元前 55 年就开始了对英国的入侵，但他从未在英国实现他的统治。那是在公元 43 年，Claudius 皇帝下令征服英国，在这第二次入侵时发生了女王 Boadicea 的故事。Boadicea 被描述为一个可怕的、强有力的女人。一个罗马作家这样描述了她："她非常高，她的眼神好像会刺伤你，她的声音洪亮刺耳，她那浓密、红褐的头发垂到腰下，她总是戴一个巨大的金色颈环，穿一件用胸针固定的飘拂的格子斗篷。"——Cassius Dio，Terry Deary 引自《腐朽的罗马人》)。

[2] Druidism and Neo-druidism：德鲁伊教在不列颠的母系社会时代就已存在。但经过与罗马人的战争，以及基督教的竭力打压，公元 6 世纪到 16 世纪这千年中，很多德鲁伊教的传统渐渐融入人们的日常生活，甚至被基督教吸收消化，但教团本身却已销声匿迹。直到 16 世纪，随着早期德鲁伊宗教研究著作的翻译和印刷传播，欧洲人开始意识到他们的祖先并非愚昧无知的野蛮人，"德鲁伊教复兴"运动才逐步展开。时至今日，已有数个德鲁伊团体(Order)活跃在世界各地，他们将**环保主义**和**泛爱主义**融合到自己的信仰中，**崇尚人与自然的和谐**，使这个根植于古老传统的神秘宗教焕发出了前所未有的清新与活力。(图"当今德鲁伊组织 OBOD 对德鲁伊教的诠释——带有泛爱主义的意味")

For more information, you can check out the following links:

http://www.baidu.com/s?wd=The+Native+Celts&ch=&tn=baofengyingyin_cb&bar=11

http://www.baidu.com/s?wd=Neo-druidism&ch=&tn=baofengyingyin_cb&bar=11

Unit 2　Britain and Roman Empire

Lead-in: Listening (PPT-1)

Listen to a movie clip, Shakespeare's famous tragedy—*Julius Caesar* carefully, and answer the following questions:

1. Why did Brutus and other alarmed Republicans assassinate Julius Caesar when Caesar became dictator for life?

2. What did Brutus say to persuade the Romans?

Reading

1.1　Roman Britain (55 BC—410 AD)

1.1.1　The Rise and Fall of Roman Republic

Rome was by then run by patricians (the ruling class). They expanded Rome's interests, first in Italy and later throughout the Mediterranean. There followed a struggle between the patricians and plebeians (ordinary people), which led to the writing of a legal code and to plebeian influence in government. This formed the backbone of the Republic.

When attacking a fortress, legionnaires would form a protective shield like this – a *testudo* (tortoise), that advanced slowly under fire from stones and arrows.

The Romans soon established new cities, building order and prosperity and giving conquered peoples a form of Roman citizenship if they cooperated. By 44 BC the Romans ruled Spain, France, Europe south of **Danube**, Anatolia and Northern Africa. They dominated the Mediterranean—in less than 200 years, the Romans became the controlling force in the West.

When attacking a fortress, **legionnaires** would form a protective shield like this—a **testudo** (tortoise), that advanced slowly under fire from stones and arrows.

1.1.2　Julius Caesar's Influence upon English History

The Roman army, commanded by Julius Caesar, invaded England in 55 BC. During the invasion of England, Julius Caesar kept a diary in which he wrote what he said and experienced in England. **His diary marked the beginning of English recorded history**.

The successful invasion of England by the Romans did not take place until a century later, in **43 AD**, and it was headed by Roman Emperor **Claudius**. The Romans left Britain around 410 AD.

1.1.3 Shakespeare's Famous Tragedy—*Julius Caesar*[1]

In 44 BC, Julius Caesar became dictator for life. Alarmed Republicans assassinated him, and soon after the Republic broke up.

Here is an **excerpt** from *Julius Caesar*:

Brutus: Be patient till the last. Romans, country-men, and lovers! Hear me for my cause, and be silent, that you may hear; believe me for mine honour, and have respect to mine honour, that you may believe: **censure** me in your wisdom, and awake your senses, that you may be the better judge. If there be any in this **assembly**, any dear friend of Caesar's, to him I say that Brutus' love to Caesar was no less than his. If then, that friend demand why Brutus rose against Caesar, this is my answer: —Not that I loved Caesar less, but that I loved Rome more. Had you rather Caesar were living and die all slaves, than that Caesar were dead, to live all free men? As Caesar loved me, I weep for him; as he was fortunate, I rejoice at it; as he was **valiant**, I honour him: but, as he was ambitious, I slew (kill) him. There is tears for his love; joy for his fortune; honour for his valour (bravery); and death for his ambition. Who is here so base that would be a **bondman**? If any, speak; for him have I offended. Who is here so rude that would not be a Roman? If any, speak; for him have I offended. Who is here so vile (hateful, shameful) that will not love his country? If any, speak; for him have I offended. I pause for a reply.

All: None, Brutus, None!

Brutus: Then none have I offended. I have done no more to Caesar than you shall do to Brutus.

The Appian Way, a major road from Rome to the southeast coast, was built in 312BC. For the first time, soldiers, traders and travellers travel to these places quickly.

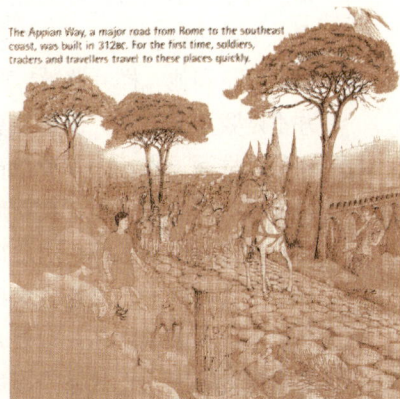

1.3   Britain under Roman Empire

The final conquests, in the century following Augustus, had been in **Britain**, Syria, Palestine and Egypt. The Jews and the British had been difficult to beat, and the **Parthians** impossible. However, most of the conquered people adapted.

People in Gaul, North Africa, Syria, Britain and Hungary adopted Roman ways and thought of themselves as Roman citizens. Running a huge empire was difficult, and it was united by business, not religious or **ethnic** ties. Provincial peoples were allowed to get on with their lives, as long as they obeyed the rules set by Romans.

As the English proverb goes: "All roads lead to Rome."[2]

New Words and Expressions

Danube [ˈdænjuːb]	*n.*	多瑙河(欧洲南部河流)
Legionnaires [liːdʒiˈnɛə(r)]	*n.*	罗马集团军
testudo [tesˈtjuːdəu]	*n.*	龟甲阵, 龟甲形大盾
Claudius [ˈklɔːdiəs]	*n.*	克劳迪亚斯(罗马执政官)
excerpt [ˈeksəːpt]	*n. & vt.*	摘录
censure [ˈsenʃə]	*v.*	责难
assembly [əˈsembli]	*n.*	集会
valiant [ˈvæljənt]	*adj.*	勇敢的, 英勇的
bondman [ˈbɔndmən]	*n.*	奴隶
Parthian [ˈpɑːθiən; -θjən]	*n.*	帕提亚(Parthia)人
ethnic [ˈeθnik]	*adj.*	种族的

Notes

[1] 背景知识：布鲁图演说出自莎士比亚所写悲剧《裘力斯·恺撒》。布鲁图是古罗马政治家，与卡西乌合谋刺杀恺撒，图谋恢复共和政体。汉语译文是在朱生豪译本基础上修改的(个别地方参照梁实秋的译本)。

布鲁图：请耐心听我讲完。

各位罗马人，亲爱的同胞们！请你们静静地听我解释。为了我的名誉，请你们相信我；尊重我的名誉，你们就会相信我的话。用你们的智慧批评我；唤起你们的理智，给我一个公正的评断。要是在今天的集会中，有什么人是恺撒的好朋友，我要对他说，布鲁图也是和他一样爱恺撒。要是那位朋友问我为什么要起来反对恺撒，这就是我的回答：并不是我不爱恺撒，而是我更爱罗马。你们宁愿让恺撒活在世上，大家做奴隶而死呢，还是让恺撒死去，大家做自由人而生？因为恺撒爱我，我为他哭泣；因为他幸运，我为他高兴；因为他英勇，我崇敬他；但因为他有野心，我杀死他。我用眼泪回报他的爱，用欢乐庆祝他的幸福，用尊敬纪念他的英勇，而用死亡制止他的野心。这里有谁愿意自甘卑贱去做奴隶？要是有这样的人，请说出来，因为我已经得罪他了；这里有谁愿意自居粗俗，不愿做罗马人？要是有这样的人，请说出来，因为我已经得罪他了；这里有谁愿意自处下流，不爱他的国家？要是有这样的人，请说出来，因为我已经得罪他了。我等待回答。

众市民：没有，布鲁图，没有。

布鲁图：那么我没有得罪什么人。我怎样对待恺撒，你们也可以怎样对待我。

[2] All roads lead to Rome：英语谚语"条条道路通罗马"源自于罗马人对英国的统治的史实。

For more information, you can check out the following link:

http://en.wikipedia.org/wiki/Roman_Britain

Unit 3　Anglo-Saxon Britain

Lead-in: Listening (PPT-3)

Listen to the movie clip *King Arthur* carefully, and answer the following questions:

1. What kind of hero was King Arthur?

2. Why was he an important figure in the British history, and what contributions did he make?

Reading

1.1　Angles, Saxons and Jutes

The arrival of Angles, Saxons and Jutes in Britain in the 5th and 6th centuries created a new people, the English, who were to dominate Britain.

The Romans left Britain around 410. There was a brief revival of power for the now-Romanized Britain. In 446, the British high-king, **Vortigern**[1], invited some German Saxons from the Rhineland to enter Britain as **mercenaries** to support him in his struggle with the **Picts**[2]. The Saxons gained a foothold in the southeast, but they were held off between 500 and 539 by the British under their leader, **Arthur**. After a major battle in 552, the Saxons began to take over southern and central England, and many Britons were killed or lost their lands, emigrating to Wales, Cornwall, Ireland, Scotland, Brittany in France and northwest Spain.

1.2　The Birth of England

Vortigern, the British high-king, hired **German Mercenaries**, but failed to pay them. In revenge, they started to conquer Britain. Settlers followed, beaching their boats and wading ashore with cattle and sheep.

In the wake of the German invaders, many of their countrymen emigrated to England. During the 6th and 7th centuries, they slowly populated the country. British towns, villages and farms were abandoned, and the Celtic Christian church retreated with them. The Germans brought new farming and ownership patterns, and their **pagan** tribal groupings gradually took the shape of kingdoms. Eventually, **seven kingdoms** were formed.

In 597, Augustine was sent from Rome to convert the Saxons to Christianity but, by 620, the Saxons had reverted to paganism. They were later converted back by the Celtic Christians.

New Words and Expressions

mercenary ['mə:sinəri]	n. 雇佣兵
Pict [pikt]	n. 皮克特人(古代部落)
Arthur ['ɑ:θə]	n. 亚瑟(中世纪传说中的不列颠国王，圆桌骑士团的首领)
German Mercenaries	德国雇佣军
pagan ['peigən]	n. 异教徒 adj. 异教的
seven kingdoms	七大王朝

Notes

[1] Vortigern (不列颠王沃蒂格恩)：这个时期皮克特人及斯科特人对不列颠的严重威胁，在历史中也有不少记述。"他们就像收割庄稼一样，横冲直撞，砍杀和践踏眼前的一切"，"可怜的不列颠人被敌人(皮克特人和斯科特人)砍得血肉模糊，就像绵羊被野兽活活撕裂那样"。在不列颠王沃蒂格恩的邀请下，亨吉斯特带领朱特人渡海而来，在肯特和萨尼特岛建立拓殖地。盎格鲁-撒克逊人得以征服不列颠的第二个有利条件是不列颠人的内部分裂，正是旷日持久的内部分裂，使得不列颠人不能集中力量抗击盎格鲁-撒克逊人的入侵。

[2] Pict：皮克特人指数世纪前，先于苏格兰人居住于福斯河以北的皮克塔维亚，也就是加勒多尼亚(现今的苏格兰)的先住民。最早的文献中的皮克特(Pict)是出现在西元 297 年，古罗马时期的创作者 Eumenius 所著作的颂词里。此外，依照字本身的拉丁文含意，"Picti"常被认为有"被彩绘者"或"背刺青者"。

For more information, you can check out the following links:

http://www.google.com.hk/search?hl=zh-CN&source=hp&q=Picts&meta=&aq=f&aqi=g2g-ms1g-m2&aql=&oq=&gs_rfai=

http://www.baidu.com/s?wd=Arthur&ch=&tn=baofengyingyin_cb&bar=11

Unit 4　Rise and Fall of Danish Rule in Britain

Lead-in: Listening (PPT-4)

Listen to the movie clip *Alfred the Great* carefully, and answer the following questions:

1. "The greatest Anglo-Saxon hero who fought against the invasion of Vikings was King Alfred. He was respected as 'the Father of the British Navy'." Do you agree with this statement after listening?

2. What details impressed you most in the movie clip?

Reading

1.1　Alfred the Great against the Vikings

1.1.1　The Invasion of the Vikings

In England the Viking Age began dramatically on June 8, 793 when Vikings destroyed the abbey on Lindisfarne, a center of learning famous across the continent. Monks were killed in the abbey, thrown into the sea to drown or carried away as slaves along with the church treasures. Three Viking ships had beached in Portland Bay four years earlier, but that incursion may have been a trading expedition that went wrong rather than a **piratical raid**. Lindisfarne was different. The Viking devastation of **Northumbria's** Holy Island shocked and alerted the royal Courts of Europe. "Never before has such an **atrocity** been seen," declared the Northumbrian scholar Alcuin of York. More than any other single event, the attack on Lindisfarne cast a shadow on the perception of the Vikings for the next twelve centuries. Not until the 1890s did scholars outside Scandinavia begin seriously to **reassess** the achievements of the Vikings, recognizing their artistry, the technological skills and the seamanship.

Until Victoria's reign in Britain, Vikings were portrayed as violent and bloodthirsty. The chronicles of medieval England had always portrayed them as **rapacious** "wolves among sheep". During the nineteenth century, public perceptions changed.

The first challenges to the many anti-Viking images in Britain emerged in the 17th century. Pioneering scholarly works on the Viking Age began to reach a small leadership in Britain. Archaeologists began to dig up Britain's Viking past. Linguistic enthusiasts started to work on identifying Viking-Age origins for rural idioms and proverbs. The new dictionaries of the **Old Norse language** enabled the Victorians to grapple with the primary Icelandic **Sagas**.

1.1.2   Alfred the Great

The greatest Anglo-Saxon hero who fought against the invasion was King Alfred. When Alfred the Great was king of Wessex in 871, the Vikings were threatening to overrun his kingdom. Alfred fought nine battles against them in one year alone. To prevent the new invaders from landing, Alfred built Britain's first naval force, and because of this, he later became known as "**the Father of the British Navy**." He finally defeated them in 878 and made them sign the Treaty of Wedmore, which divided England in two—the Saxon west and Danelaw in the east. King Alfred, however, was even greater in peace than he was in war. Alfred was a lawmaker, a scholar and a just king. In his time, texts were translated into English and The Anglo-Saxon Chronicle, an important history book, was begun.

1.2   Relationship between Danes and Saxons

1.2.1   Canute the Great[1]

After the death of King Alfred, Vikings invasions renewed, and the invaders set about taking possession of the entire country.

By 940, **Danelaw** had been won back from the **Danes**. England was reunified under Edgar, but in 1013 the Danes returned. In 1016, the Witan had no alternative but to choose the Canute, the Danish leader, as king of England. England was ruled until 1035 by the Dane.

Canute the great was a wise ruler. Under his rule, England became part of the Scandinavian empire, which also included Norway and Denmark. He secured the Northern border of England by compelling the king of the Scots to recognize him as **overlord**.

1.2.2　Edward the Confessor

After the death of Canute and his sons, the crown was passed to a man of English origin known as Edward. King Edward (1042—1066) had spent most of his early years in Normandy. After becoming king, he filled important positions with people from Normandy and appointed a Norman priest Archbishop of Canterbury. Edward was a devoted believer of Christianity and known as **Edward the Confessor**. He built Westminster Abbey in which he was buried after his death. Edward was the last Anglo-Saxon king in English history. There was better co-operation between the Danes and Saxons under Edward the Confessor. He was childless and soon after his death England was conquered by the Normans from France.

1.2.3　Harold Was Defeated in Hastings[2]

When King Edward was on his death-bed, three men laid claim to the English throne. They were King of Norway, William who was Duke of Normandy and Edward's cousin, and **Harold** Godwinson who was Edward's brother-in-law. After Edward passed away, the English Witan chose Harold as king of England. William strongly opposed the decision and claimed that Edward had promised the crown to him before his death.

Harold knew that William would come to measure swords with him. He placed an army on the southern coast of England to prevent William's invasion. Several months later the harvest time in England came, many of Harold's soldiers went back home to gather in crops. The coast was thus left undefended. William seized the chance and landed his army in southeast England in September 1066. Harold, who had been fighting rebels in north England, hurried to the southern coast with his exhausted troops. On October 14, 1066, the two armies met near **Hastings**, not far from the coast. The Norman cavalry, armed with bows and arrows, easily defeated the Anglo-Saxon troops who fought on foot and with battle-axes. Harold was killed (see the picture above-1.2.1) and the English troops were put to flight. The Normans then crossed the Thames River and established their camps around London, cutting its connection with other parts of the country. Finally London was forced to give in, and a group of Noblemen and church leaders came out to welcome William. He was crowned in Westminster Abbey on Christmas Day, 1066 and became known as William the Conqueror. The Norman line of kings began to rule England.

New Words and Expressions

Viking ['vaikiŋ]	*n.* 海盗，北欧海盗；<口>斯堪的纳维亚人，维京人
piratical [pai'rætikəl]	*adj.* 剽窃的，海盗的，盗版的
raid [reid]	*n.* 袭击，搜捕
	v. 奇袭，搜捕
Northumbria [nɔː'θʌmbriə]	*n.* 中世纪时在英国北方的王国
atrocity [ə'trɔsiti]	*n.* 残暴，暴行，凶恶
reassess ['riːə'ses]	*v.* 再估价，再评价
rapacious [rə'peiʃəs]	*adj.* 掠夺的，贪婪的
Old Norse language	古斯堪的那维亚语
saga ['sɑːgə]	*n.* 传奇
Alfred ['ælfrid] **the Great**	阿尔弗雷德大帝
Danelaw ['deinlɔː]	*n.* 丹麦律法，丹麦律法施行地区
Dane [dein]	*n.* 丹麦人
overlord ['əuvəlɔːd]	*n.* 最高统治主，霸王
Edward the Confessor	忏悔者爱德华三世
Harold	哈罗德

Notes

[1] Canute the Great (克努特大帝)：克努特(995—1035 年)，英格兰国王(1014—1035 年在位)，丹麦国王(1018—1035 年在位)，挪威国王(1028—1035 年在位)。 丹麦历代王者所发展起来的海盗帝国，终于在克努特手里达到了顶峰。

克努特是个有手段的统治者，他制定了《克努特法典》，曾因自己违反纪律而当众处罚自己。有一个故事流传很广。克努特的一个臣下谄媚说，克努特是海洋的统治者，连海洋也会听克努特大帝的命令。克努特于是下令将椅子放在海边，命令海水不准打湿椅脚，结果申斥了大臣的胡说，称上帝才是大海的统治者，国王的权力只是很小的一点点。(见上面 1.2.1 图示)

1035 年，克努特去世，他的北海大帝国很快就分崩离析，他的统治是北欧海盗最后的辉煌。

[2] Hastings ['heistiŋz]：黑斯廷斯(英国港市)，1066 年威廉大帝在此彻底打败 Harold，并取得决定性的胜利，奠定了诺曼征服的基础。

For more information, you can check out the following link:

http://en.wikipedia.org/wiki/Viking_Age

Unit 5   Norman Conquest

Lead-in: Listening (PPT-5)

Listen to the passage carefully, and answer the following questions:

1. What kind of people were the Normans, and where did they come from?

_____

2. When and how did they conquest England?

_____

Reading

The Normans invaded England in 1066 and soon ruled over the Saxon and Viking English, the Welsh and the Irish. They also **wielded influence further afield**.

1.1   The Normans and William the Conqueror

The Normans were Danish **overlords** who lived in **Normandy** from 900 onwards. There were not many of them, yet they were tough warrior-lords. **William the Conqueror** was crowned on Christmas Day 1066— he had been only a French duke, but now he became the English king.

1.2   The Influence of Norman Conquest

After the Norman invasion of 1066, many of the English protested. Williams put down rebellions brutally, taking English land and giving it to his Norman Nobles, for them to rule the local areas. He gave land to the church in order to gain its support, replacing English with French **bishops** and

encouraged French traders and craftsmen to settle in England. The Normans built large castles, churches, monasteries and great **cathedrals**, and many towns grew up around them. The nobility spoke French while the ordinary people spoke early English.

The **Bayeux Tapestry** was made to **commemorate** the Norman invasion of England in 1066. **Halley's Comet**, shown clearly on the tapestry, came close to the Earth in that year, and it was taken as an **omen** that the invasion was justified.

A central administration and tax system was established, and a tax assessment of the country's land and wealth, the **Domesday Book**, was made. Norman rule was harsh. They cared mainly about wealth and power, and used England as a base for foreign adventures, which the English had to finance. However, England developed economically, and within 100 years, the Normans began the invasion of Wales, Ireland and Scotland. England was changing—its landscape, towns and culture were all influenced by the Normans.

The Castle of William, Château Guillaume-Le-Conquérant, in Falaise, Calvados, France.

1.3   Plantagenet Dynasty (1154—1458)

By 1140 there was a disagreement over who should rule the country. This weakened the king and strengthened the nobles' power. A new Norman dynasty called the Plantagenet was founded in 1154 and their first king, Henry II, ruled England and half of France. During this time, the English class system, dominated by nobles, began to develop.

Henry of Anjou became Henry II, the first Plantagenet king of England, in 1154. With his land in France he became one of the most powerful rulers in Europe. He was William the Conqueror's **great-grandson**.

Henry's empire was a family possession, not a country, and he planed to divide it between his four sons. They **squabbled** over this and then revolted against him. Two of them died, leaving **Richard (the Lionheart)** and John. Richard became king of England in 1189, and was followed after his death in 1199 by John.

New Words and Expressions

wield [wiːld] **influence further afield**　在战场上有深远的影响力
overlord ['əuvəlɔːd]　　　　　　　　*n.* 最高统治主，霸王
Normandy ['nɔːmənˈdi]　　　　　　*n.* 诺曼底(法国西北部一地区，北临英吉利海峡)

William the Conqueror	征服者威廉
bishop [ˈbiʃəp]	n. 主教
cathedral [kəˈθiːdrəl]	n. 大教堂
Bayeux [baiˈjəː] **Tapestry**	贝叶挂毯(可能制成于 12 世纪，长 231 英尺，宽 20 英寸，上绣诺曼人征服英格兰的历史场面，收藏于法国贝叶博物馆)
commemorate [kəˈmeməreit]	vt. 纪念
Halley's [ˈhæli] **Comet** [ˈkɔmit]	哈雷彗星
omen [ˈəumen]	n. 预兆，征兆
Domesday [ˈduːmzdei] **Book**	英格兰土地清账书册；末日审判书
Plantagenet [plænˈtædʒinit] **Dynasty**	[英史]金雀花王朝(1154—1458 年)
the Castle of William	威廉大帝城堡
great-grandson [ˌgreitˈgrædsʌn]	曾孙
squabble [ˈskwɔbl]	v. 争论
Richard (the Lionheart)	狮心王理查德

For more information, you can check out the following link:

http://en.wikipedia.org/wiki/Norman_conquest_of_England

Unit 6   The Crusades and Richard the Lionheart

Lead-in: Listening (PPT-6)

Listen to the movie clip *King Richard the Lionheart* carefully, and answer the following questions:

1. What kind of king was Richard the Lionheart?

_____

2. In 1191 on the Third Crusade, **Richard I of England**, known as the **Lionheart**, led an army to the Holy Land. What's their purpose?

_____

Reading

Palestine, once ruled by **Byzantium**, had been conquered by the **Muslim** Arabs in 637. From Rome, the **Pope** called on Christian leaders to fight for the **Holy Land**.

1.1   Conflicts between Christians and Muslims

To Christians and Muslims, Palestine was the Holy Land, a place of **pilgrimage** for hundreds of years. After the Arabs conquered Palestine in 637, Christian pilgrims were still able to visit **Jerusalem** safely, but this changed with the arrival of the **Seljuk Turks**. In 1095, Pope Urban II called on Christians to free Palestine from Muslim rule.

The Crusader army captured Jerusalem, **massacring** its **inhabitants**. Some of the Crusaders behaved badly towards the Muslims.

1.2   Seige of Jerusalem

In 1099, throughout the siege, attacks were made on the walls, but each one was repulsed. The **Genoese** troops, led by commander Guglielmo Embriaco, had previously dismantled the ships in which the Genoeses came to the Holy Land; Embriaco, using the ship's wood, made some **siege towers**. These were rolled up to the walls on the night of July 14 much to the surprise and concern of the **garrison**. On the morning of July 15, Godfrey's tower reached his section of the walls near the northeast corner gate, and according to the *Gesta* two Flemish knights from Tournai named Lethalde and Engelbert were the first to cross into the city, followed by Godfrey, his brother Eustace, Tancred, and their men. Raymond's tower was at first stopped by a ditch, but as the other crusaders had already entered, the Muslim guarding the gate surrendered to Raymond.

1.3   Massacre the Muslims

Many Muslims sought shelter in the Al-Aqsa **Mosque**, the Dome of the Rock, and the Temple Mount area generally. According to the ***Gesta Francorum***[1], speaking only of the Temple Mount area, "...[our men] were killing and slaying even to the Temple of Solomon, where the slaughter was so great that our men waded in blood up to their ankles..." According to Raymond of Aguilers, also writing solely of the Temple Mount area, "in the Temple and porch of Solomon men rode in blood up to their knees and bridle reins." "In this temple 10,000 were killed. Indeed, if you had been there you would have seen our feet coloured to our ankles with the blood of the slain. But what more shall I relate? None of them were left alive; neither women nor children were spared."

The eyewitness Gesta Francorum states that some people managed to escape the siege unharmed. Its anonymous author wrote, "When the pagans had been overcome, our men seized great numbers, both men and women, either killing them or keeping them captive, as they wished." Later the same source writes, "[Our leaders] also ordered all the **Saracen** dead to be cast outside because of the great **stench**, since the whole city was filled with their corpses; and so the living Saracens dragged the dead before the exits of the gates and arranged them in heaps, as if they were houses. No one ever saw or heard of such slaughter of pagan people, for funeral pyres were formed from them like pyramids, and no one knows their number except God alone."

1.4   Richard I of England, the Lionheart

In 1191 on the Third Crusade, **Richard I of England**, known as the Lionheart, led an army to the Holy Land. He took **Cyprus** and the city of Acre, but was unable to recapture Jerusalem. Saladin respected Richard, and they

eventually both signed a five-year peace treaty sharing the Holy Land, including Jerusalem—the Crusaders founded a "Second Kingdom" of the holy city, with its heart at Acre. This allowed European pilgrims to visit the holy places again.

1.5　The Influence of the Crusades

1.5.1　Contact with the East Widened the Scope of the Europeans

The returning crusaders came back to Europe with new tastes in dress and diet, such as peaches and **spinach**. They gave up the custom of wearing a load of heavy armor at nearly all times and appeared in the flowing robes of silk or cotton which were the traditional habit of the Muslims.

The crusades failed to achieve the permanent control of the Holy Land. However, their influence was wide and deep. Much of the crusading **fervor** carried over to the successful fights against the Moors (Muslims) in Spain and the pagan Slavs in Eastern Europe. Politically the crusades weakened the **decrepit** Byzantine Empire, but temporarily kept the Muslims away from it. The First Crusade strengthened the moral leadership of the **papacy** in Europe, but the failures of the later crusades weakened both the crusading ideal and respect for the papacy. **Contact with the East widened the scope of the Europeans, ended their isolation, and exposed them to a rich civilization**. The economic effects of the crusades were modest, but they did reopen of the eastern Mediterranean to Western commerce, which itself had an effect on the rise of great cities such as Venice and the emergence of a money economy in the West.

1.5.2　Trade between East and West—Commerce and Economy

The merchants of Venice and other Italian cities gained the most profit. They amassed considerable income in payment for the services they rendered the crusaders and were enriched by the commercial rights they obtained throughout the Near East. Genoa, Pisa, and Venice gained special monopolies throughout the eastern Mediterranean. Their merchants used these privileges to introduce into the Western world such **oriental** luxuries as silks, spices, and pearls, whose transportation and sale made the cities rich. The demand for these products encouraged explorers to seek out new and more direct routes to the East—most famously in the discovery and exploration of the Americas by Columbus and others starting in 1492. The crusades helped create a moneyed aristocracy and encouraged the growth of capitalism in the Italian cities. Silks and spices not only raised the standard of living of the rich, they stimulated the entire urban economy, although cities remained small.

1.6 Emblems of the International Red Cross and Red Crescent Movement

The emblems of the International Red Cross and Red Crescent Movement, under the **Geneva Conventions**, are to be placed on **humanitarian** and medical vehicles and buildings to protect them from military attack on the battlefield.

Red Crescent is an additional official protection symbol for **non-Christian countries**. The Red Crescent was formally recognized in 1929 when the Geneva Conventions were amended (Article 19). Originally, the Red Crescent was used by Turkey and Egypt. From its official recognition to today, the Red Crescent became the organizational emblem of nearly every national society in countries with majority Muslim populations. The national societies of some countries such as Pakistan (1974), Malaysia (1975), or Bangladesh (1989) have officially changed their name and emblem from the Red Cross to the Red Crescent. The Red Crescent is used by 33 of the 186 recognized societies worldwide.

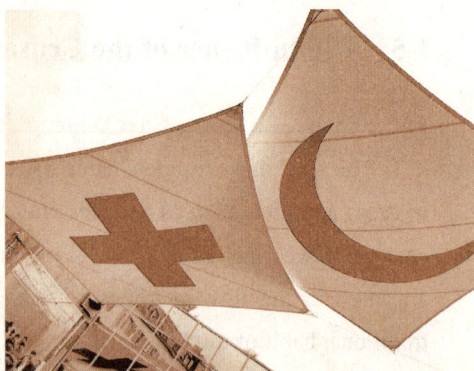

New Words and Expressions

Crusade [kruːˈseid]   *n.* 十字军东侵

Palestine [ˈpælistain]   *n.* 巴勒斯坦(西南亚一地区)

Byzantium [biˈzæntiəm]   *n.* 拜占庭

Muslim [ˈmuzlim; *(US)* ˈmʌzlem]   *n.* 穆斯林，穆罕默德信徒

Pope [pəup]   *n.* 罗马教皇

Holy Land   圣地(巴勒斯坦)

Pilgrimage [ˈpilgrimidʒ]   *n.* 朝圣

Jerusalem [dʒeˈruːsələm]   *n.* 耶路撒冷(巴勒斯坦著名古城)

Seljuk [selˈdʒuːk] **Turks**   (土耳其的)塞尔柱王朝

massacre [ˈmæsəkə]   *n.* 残杀，大屠杀

inhabitant [inˈhæbitənt]   *n.* 居民，居住者

Seige of Jerusalem   血洗耶路撒冷

Genoese [ˌdʒenəˈiːz]   *adj.* 热那亚的

                                  n. 热那亚人

siege tower   楼车，攻城塔楼

garrison [ˈgærisn]   *n.* 卫戍部队，驻军；卫戍地，要塞

mosque [mɔsk]   *n.* 清真寺

Saracen [ˈsærəsn]   *n.* 撒拉逊人(阿拉伯人的古称)

stench [stentʃ]   *n.* 恶臭，臭气

Cyprus [ˈsaiprəs]   *n.* (地中海东部一岛)塞浦路斯

spinach [ˈspinidʒ; (*US*) ˈspinitʃ]   *n.* 菠菜

fervor [ˈfəːvə]   *n.* 热情，热烈；炽热

decrepit [diˈkrepit]   *adj.* 衰老的

papacy [ˈpeipəsi]   *n.* 罗马教皇职位，教皇的在位期间

oriental [ˌɔ(ː)riˈentl]   *n.* 东方人

                          adj. 东方诸国的，东方的

emblem [ˈembləm]   *n.* 象征，徽章

Geneva [dʒiˈniːvə] **Conventions**   日内瓦会议

humanitarian [hju(ː)ˌmæniˈtɛəriən]   *n.* 人道主义者

Red Crescent   *n.* 红新月会(穆斯林国家中相当于红十字会的组织)

Note

[1] *Gesta Francorum*：《赫斯塔 Francorum》系中世纪拉丁文著作，It gives the story of the First Crusade. 它描述了第一次十字军东侵的故事。Its actual author is unknown. 它的实际作者不详。

For more information, you can check out the following links:

http://en.wikipedia.org/wiki/Siege_of_Jerusalem_(1099)

http://www.the-orb.net/textbooks/eccles/crusades.html

http://www.conservapedia.com/Crusades

http://en.wikipedia.org/wiki/Emblems_of_the_International_Red_Cross_and_Red_Crescent_Movement

Unit 7　Charter and Parliament (1215—1485)

Lead-in: Listening (PPT-7)

Listen to the passage carefully, and answer the following questions:

1. What kind of disease was Black Death?

2. What sufferings did it cause? When did the Peasant Uprising happen?

Reading

1.1　Conflicts between Kings and Lords

In 13th century England there was a growing struggle between the kings and lords. The absolute power of rulers was being questioned by those they ruled.

King John of England, the youngest son of **Henry II**, was given to violent outbursts of temper. Not surprisingly, he soon fell out with his barons in English-ruled Anjou and Poitiers, and he lost those lands to France. In England, he taxed his barons heavily and ruled so harshly that they rebelled. The barons threatened John, and demanded that he accept their traditional rights and obey the law.

1.2　The Magna Carta[1]

In 1215, the barons met King John in a meadow called Runnymede, beside the Thames River. There, they forced him to put his **seal** to the Magna Carta, which means "**great charter**". This charter covered many important areas, including weights and measures, the powers of sheriffs, and the legal rights of freemen and boroughs (towns). The king agreed to obey the law himself and he was not allowed to raise taxes without the agreement of his

Great Council of nobles. No sooner had John agreed to the charter then he went back on his word. A civil war broke out, but John soon died, leaving the throne to his young son who became **Henry III**. The charter was reissued, and in 1225, it became the law of England. Henry III was **incompetent** and he spent large sums of money, so the barons got together again, this time led by Simon de Montfort. They forced Henry to agree to consult the Great Council in all major matters. Like his father, Henry III went back on the deal, but de Montfort defeated him in battle at Lewes. Simon de Montfort and the Council then ruled England in Henry's name.

1.3   The Power of Parliament

In 1265, Simon de Montfort called a new Parliament of two chambers, the House of Lords (previously the Great Council of nobles and bishops) and the House of Commons. The House of Commons was made up of two knights from every shire and, representing the people, two burgesses from every borough. Later, Edward I (1272—1307), a successful ruler, reformed England's law and administration, creating a Model Parliament which included even more representatives from the country. However, the king still held power. In 1388, there was a major **clash** and the "Merciless" Parliament removed some of King Richard II's rights.

As time went on, Parliament's powers gradually grew. The House of Commons slowly gained greater power, though Parliament still represented mainly the richer classes. Only in the 20th century did full-scale democracy arrive.

1.4   The Black Death (1347—1351) and the Peasant Uprising in 1381

1.4.1   The Black Death in England

The Black Death was one of the worst disasters in history. It resulted in the death of around a third of the population of the Middle East and Europe.

It started in Italy and soon spread to other parts of Europe. Those who were stricken with it usually died in two or three days. A careful estimate shows that in England about one half of the population died of the disease.

1.4.2   The Peasant Uprising in 1381

The Hundred Years' War was still going on. To fund the war, the government in 1381 started to collect **a flat rate poll tax** of one shilling a head. Most of the peasants had no money to pay the tax and therefore rebelled. **Watt Tyler**[2] was the most important military leader of the uprising. Many merchants supported the uprising because they wanted free laborers. They opened the city gate of London for the rebel peasants to get in. The king and the ministers were scared and they took refugee in the tower of London, leaving London in confusion. A number of big nobles were killed by the rebels, and some places were sacked.

New Words and Expressions

seal [siːl]	*n.* 印，图章
Great Council ['kaunsil]	大议会
incompetent [in'kɔmpitənt]	*adj.* 不胜任的
	n. 无能力者
clash [klæʃ]	*n.* 冲突，抵触
Black Death	黑死病，鼠疫
a flat rate poll tax	人头税

Notes

[1] Magna Carta：即 great charter，大宪章运动。

[2] Watt Tyler：瓦特·泰勒，1381 年英国农民起义领袖。

For more information, you can check out the following links:

http://en.wikipedia.org/wiki/Black_Death

http://www.bbc.co.uk/history/british/middle_ages/black_01.shtml

Unit 8   The Hundred Years' War (1337—1453)

Lead-in: Listening (PPT-8)

Listen to the movie clip *Joan of Arc* carefully, and answer the following questions:

1. Joan of Arc was a heroine in the Hundred Years' War, but why she was burned at the stake as a witch in 1431?

2. "Six hundred years later, in 1920, Joan of Arc was made a saint." Please give some comments.

Reading

The Hundred Years' War was a series of short, costly wars in which the English kings tried to dominate France, but met great resistance from the French. The war continued **intermittently** for more than 100 years with ups and downs for both sides, but it ended in victory for the French.

1.1   Real Causes of the Hundred Years' War

The war was caused by both territorial and economic disputes. After the Anglo-Normans conquered England, they continued to hold Northern France, called Normandy, as their territory. Anglo-Norman king Henry II possessed about half of what is now France, reducing France almost to an inland country, but his son king John lost almost all these possessions except a tiny spot. King John's successors and the English nobility all desired to get back all the territory on the continent. With the establishment of Parliament in the 13th century, the English economy developed remarkably, and the English **bourgeoisie** (middle class) grew rapidly. Since trade was still the main source of wealth for the bourgeoisie, the new class wanted to expand foreign markets. As a big power in western Europe, France also wanted to enlarge its **spheres of influence**. Meanwhile, the English king tried to establish his dominant influence in Scotland, but he suspected that France was giving aid to the Scots in their struggle with England. These conflicts between the two countries were the real causes of the Hundred Years' War, but the war was directly caused by dispute over succession to the French throne.

1.2　Wars between England and France

In 1328, Charles IV of France died without a direct heir. The French barons gave the throne to his cousin, Philip VI, but Charles's nephew, Edward III of England, challenged him, because Edward III's mother was a sister of the late French King, and Philip confiscated Edward's French lands. In 1337, war broke out. At the start of the conflict, which actually lasted 116 years, the English defeated a French fleet in the English Channel at Sluys, then invaded France, winning a major battle at Crécy and capturing Calais. Both sides ran out of money and had to agree to a **truce**, which lasted from 1347 until 1355. In 1355, a fresh English invasion took place, led by Edward's heir, Edward, nicknamed the Black Prince. He won a resounding victory at Poitiers. The Treaty of Brétigny in 1360 gave England large parts of France. But a new campaign followed and England lost most of her French possessions.

1.3　The Child Kings and a Truce

In the late 1360s, the French and English thrones were inherited by children, Charles VI of France and Richard II of England. Richard's uncle, John of Gaunt (1340—1399), ruled for him. In 1396, Richard II married Charles VI's daughter, Isabelle, and a 20-year truce was agreed.

1.4　Joan of Arc[1] and the End of a Costly War

After a long truce the war began again in 1415. **Henry V** (1387—1422), England's adventurous king, revived his country's old claim to the French throne. England still held Calais and parts of Bordeaux. Henry captured Harfleur in Normandy and heavily defeated French at Agincourt. Henry next occupied much of northern France. Charles VI made him heir to the French throne in 1420. He also married Charles' daughter, Catherine of Valois. Henry died just 15 months later, leaving the throne to his infant son, Henry VI. Charles VI died soon after.

In support of the claim, Henry's uncle, John, Duke of Bedford, besieged **Orléans**. The French forces, led by a 17-year-old peasant girl, **Joan of Arc** (Jeanne dÁrc), successfully defended the town. Joan claimed she saw visions and heard voices telling her to free France. She escorted the new but uncrowned king, Charles VII, to Reims to be crowned. However, Joan was soon defeated at Paris and captured by the Burgundians. They sold her to the English, who burned her **at the stake** as a witch in 1431. Six hundred years later, **in 1920, she was made a saint**.

There was sporadic fighting for some years after. The French recaptured their lands by 1453, ending the war. Only Calais remained English. This had been a kings' war, but it was the people who had paid the price.

New Words and Expressions

intermittently	*adv.* 间歇地
bourgeoisie [ˌbuəʒwɑːˈziː]	*n.* 资产阶级
spheres of influence	势力范围
truce [truːs]	*n.* 休战，休战协定
Orléans [ɔːˈliənz, ˈɔːl-]	奥尔良(法国中部城市)
at the stake	炮烙之刑，火刑

Note

[1] Joan of Arc (1412—1431)：贞德，英法百年战争时期法国女民族英雄。1415 年英军占领了法国北部广大地区，法国人民与英军开展游击战争。宗教虔诚和爱国热忱使贞德自幼关心抗英战争的进程。1429 年 5 月初，贞德击败英军，解奥尔良之围。8 月，在巴黎城下受创。1430 年春，兰斯西北的军事重镇贡比涅告急，贞德前往救援。5 月 23 日傍晚，贞德带领少数队伍偷袭敌军失利，撤退时城门已关闭，贞德被勃艮第军俘虏。勃艮第人以高价把贞德卖给英国人，查理七世坐视不救，英国人把她押到鲁昂，交给异端裁判所审判。贞德在关押期间，经受轮番审讯，坚贞不屈，最后被异端裁判所以女扮男装、妖术惑众等罪名判为女巫，处以火刑。1431 年 5 月 30 日，贞德在鲁昂广场英勇就义。

贞德是同胞心目中最伟大的民族英雄，她的功绩成为激励法国民族意识的决定性因素。1456 年，罗马教廷撤销对她的判决。1920 年 5 月 16 日被列为圣女。1920 年 6 月 24 日巴黎高等法院规定每年 5 月的第二个星期日为全国贞德节。

For more information, you can check out the following links:

http://en.wikipedia.org/wiki/Hundred_Years'_War

http://en.wikipedia.org/wiki/Joan_of_Arc

Unit 9　The Wars of Roses and the Tudor Monarchy

Lead-in: Listening (PPT-9)

Listen to the passage carefully, and answer the following questions:

1. How did the English army defeat the Spanish **Invincible Armada**?

2. Why did the defeat of Spanish fleet lay the foundation of the British Empire?

Reading

During the Tudor period, England grew great and powerful, throwing off the past and the influence of Rome, and sowing the seeds of an imperial future.

1.1　The Wars of Roses (1455—1485)

Two years after the ending of the Hundred Years' War, England was thrown into another series of civil wars, generally known as the Wars of the Roses. The wars between the **two branches of the Plantagenet** family: the House of Lancaster and the House of York, were known as the Wars of the Roses, because the **badge** of the House of Lancaster was a red rose and that of York was a white one.

1.2　The Tudor Monarchy (1485—1603)

The Tudors, a Welsh family, rose to power after the confusion of a long civil war, the Wars of the Roses (1445—1485). The first Tudor king, Henry VII, banned private armies and put down any lords who opposed him. He strengthened and enriched both the Crown and England. In 1509, when the young **Henry VIII** became king, England was an important power in Europe. Henry married Catherine of Aragon, a Spanish princess and widow of his later elder brother, and spent 15 years as a pleasure-seeking Renaissance-style ruler, while Thomas Wolsey ran the government. After wars against France and Scotland in 1513, Henry became more politically aware. He and Catherine had only one living child, Mary, and Henry wanted a male heir, so he asked the pope's permission to **divorce** Catherine. He was refused

because the church forbade a husband to divorce his wife and remarry without the Pope's approval. At this time, new religious ideas and demands for church reform were common, so Henry broke away from Rome. He made himself head of the Church in England in 1534, divorced Catherine to marry Anne Boleyn and closed the monasteries, selling their lands to pay for wars and other ventures.

1.3   Henry VIII, the Frivolous King and His Successors

Henry married six times one after another, and during his reign, strengthened English control of Wales and Ireland, established a large navy and planned various colonial and commercial ventures. He was succeeded in 1547 by his only son, **Edward VI** (1537—1553), who died at the age of 16. During his reign, the Church of England grew stronger. He was succeeded by his half-sister **Mary I** (1516—1558), Henry's eldest daughter, who reigned for five years and tried to restore Catholicism. When Mary died, her sister **Elizabeth I** came to the throne. Elizabeth was popular and intelligent. She refused to marry and made her own decisions. The Catholic Mary Queen of Scots, Elizabeth cousin, was found guilty of plotting against her, yet Elizabeth resisted pressure to have her executed for many years.

1.4   Mary Stuart, Queen of Scotland

Mary Stuart became queen of Scotland in 1542 when she was just one week old. Her father, James V, was the nephew of Henry VIII and this encouraged the Catholic Mary to claim the English throne. She was educated in France and married the heir to the French throne in 1558. After his death in 1560, Mary returned to Scotland where she was unpopular. She **abdicated** and fled to England in 1568. As a focus for Catholic **dissent** against Elizabeth, Mary became involved in plots and was imprisoned in Fotheringay Castle, where she was executed in 1587 on a charge of **treason**.

1.5   Reign of Elizabeth I

1.5.1   Achievements during Elizabeth's Reign

Elizabeth I became queen of England and Ireland in 1558. She ruled for 45 years and, due to her active involvement in government, England went through a period of stability, and cultural and economic expansion.

Elizabeth aided European Protestants and sent out English pirates against Spanish ships and colonies. She made a settlement between English Catholics and Protestants, and fought a war with Spain, defeating the **Spanish Armada**. England began to develop overseas ventures, and at home its industries and economy grew. This was Shakespeare's time, when English culture and society flowered, preparing the ground for an English period of imperial greatness.

1.5.2   The Virgin Queen Had No Belief in Romantic Love

On 2 May 1536, her mother, Anne Boleyn was arrested and imprisoned. Hastily convicted on **trumped-up** charges, she was beheaded on 19 May 1536.

Elizabeth, who was 2 years 8 months old at the time, was declared **illegitimate** and deprived of the title of princess. Eleven days after Anne Boleyn's death, her father, Henry VIII married Jane Seymour, who died 12 days after the birth of their son, Prince Edward.

Much to the despair of many people, Elizabeth decided to stay single. Reasons for this decision are not known. Most likely, she just did not wish to compromise her power. This, however, didn't stop her from conducting marriage "negotiations" as part of political strategies.

1.5.3   Elizabeth Was Genuinely Respected by Her Subjects

Elizabeth received a royal education. Her studies included Greek, Latin, French, Italian, history, rhetoric, philosophy and **theology**. The tutors were impressed by her intellect and wit.

Elizabeth's half-sister Mary I was a ruthless Catholic who persecuted Protestants. During Mary's reign a rebellion was put down and Elizabeth became one of the suspects. She was imprisoned in the Tower of London for two months, but no evidence was found of her involvement.

Elizabeth learned from an early age when to keep her thoughts concealed, and how to make her opinions known in a **diplomatic** way. Later she turned the disadvantage of being a woman ruler into an advantage and promoted a regime motivated by sincere love of her subjects. She was genuinely respected.

1.5.4   Elizabeth Was Succeeded by James VI of Scotland

Her successor was the son of Mary Queen of Scots, James VI of Scotland, who became James I of England and thus the Stuarts succeeded to the throne of England.

1.5.5   War with Spain

Encouraged by the pope, Catholic Spain, led by **Philip II**, launched their fleet of 130 ships, the **Invincible Armada**, in an attempt to defeat Protestant England.

Mistakenly, the planned land reinforcement did not arrive in time. The exposed fleet was driven to the north and hit by vicious storms.

The Spanish fleet had to retreat via Ireland's west coast. During this withdrawal, most ships and their crews were lost.

In all, 63 Spanish ships were lost, only 4 in battle.

1.5.6 Achievements in Literature

Elizabeth's reign is known as the Elizabethan era, famous above all for the flourishing of English drama, led by playwrights such as William Shakespeare and Christopher Marlowe, and for the seafaring prowess of English adventurers such as Francis Drake.

Elizabeth is acknowledged as a **charismatic** performer and a dogged survivor, in an age when government was ramshackle and limited and when monarchs in neighbouring countries faced internal problems that jeopardised their thrones. Such was the case with Elizabeth's rival, **Mary I, Queen of Scots**, whom she imprisoned in 1568 and eventually had executed in 1587. After the short reigns of Elizabeth's brother and sister, her 44 years on the throne provided welcome stability for the kingdom and helped forge a sense of national identity.

New Words and Expressions

Tudor [ˈtjuːdə] **Monarchy**	英国都铎王朝
Plantagenet [plænˈtædʒinit]	n. [英史]金雀花王朝(1154—1458)
badge [bædʒ]	n. 徽章，证章
Henry VIII	亨利八世
divorce [diˈvɔːs]	n. 离婚
frivolous [ˈfrivələs]	adj. 轻佻的，妄动的
abdicated [ˈæbdikeit]	v. 退位，放弃(职位、权力等)
dissent [diˈsent]	v. 不同意
treason [ˈtriːzn]	n. 叛逆，通敌，叛国罪
Spanish Armada [ɑːˈmɑːdə]	西班牙无敌舰队
trumped-up [ˈtrʌmptˈʌp]	adj. 捏造的，伪造的
illegitimate [ˌiliˈdʒitimit]	adj. 违法的
theology [θiˈɔlədʒi]	n. 神学
diplomatic [ˌdipləˈmætik]	adj. 外交的，老练的
charismatic [ˌkærizˈmætik]	adj. 有感召力的，有魅力的

For more information, you can check out the following link:

http://en.wikipedia.org/wiki/Tudor_dynasty

Unit 10   The Stuarts (1603—1649)

Lead-in: Listening (PPT-10)

Listen to the passage carefully, and answer the following questions:

1. Why was Charles I an unpopular king?

_____

2. From various facts, we can see that religion played an important role in politics at that time. Do you agree with this statement?

_____

Reading

The Stuart dynasty came from Scotland. In England, they faced a complicated political situation which led to six years of civil war and the downfall of a king.

1.1   James I[1], the Successor of Elizabeth I

Queen Elizabeth I, the last Tudor monarch of England, died in 1603 without an **heir**. James VI of Scotland, son of Mary Queen of Scots, succeeded her as James I of England. James was descended from Henry VIII's sister and Elizabeth's aunt Margaret Tudor, who had married the Scottish king, James IV, in 1503. His family, the Stuarts, had ruled Scotland for over 200 years.

England and Scotland now had the same king, but they still remained separate countries. James dreamed of uniting them but many English and Scottish people opposed this. He tried to make peace between Catholics, Anglicans and Puritans. The Puritans were extreme Protestants who wished to abolish church ceremony and music, bishops, church **hierarchies** and other "**popish**" traditions. James angered them by refusing to go as far as they wanted. But he ordered a new translation of the Bible, the **King James Bible**[2], to try to bring Christians together.

1.2   James the Spender

James made peace with Catholic Spain to try and ease tensions between European Catholics and Protestants, and Britain was at peace for 20 years. But in 1624 James was drawn into the Thirty Years War in Germany on the Protestant side, in support of his son-in-law, Frederick, a German prince. James got deeply into debt. The costs of running the country were growing and James himself was a **lavish** spender. He believed Parliament should obey him and grant whatever he asked for. But the Parliament and the kings' ministers had grown stronger in Tudor times, and he fell out with them when his demands for money were refused.

1.3   Charles I, Unpopular King

James I tried to please everyone. He was unpopular in England because he made mistakes, and because he was Scottish and his **Danish wife**, Anne, was **Catholic**. His belief in the rights of the king was also disliked. When he died in 1625, his son Charles became king and **inherited his unpopularity**.

Charles I also disliked parliamentary interference, and handled some situations badly. People started to take sides, and supported either the king or Parliament. This became a battle between traditional and modern ideas. When, in 1629, Parliament refused to give Charles more money and rule in his own way, he sent the parliamentarians home and tried to govern without them.

Charles ruled without Parliament for eleven years, but his court and ministers were divided over many important questions. Charles also angered Scots, who thought he had become too English, and lost their support. Parliament, called back in 1640, then united against him. It tried to limit his powers and suppress his supporters. In 1642, Charles tried to arrest five parliamentary leaders, but Parliament, including the nobility, totally opposed him.

Charles left London and raised an army. He was finally defeated and handed power to Parliament. He escaped and continued the Civil War, but was recaptured, held prisoner and executed in 1649. For 12 years, during the English Revolution and Civil War, England had no king.

New Words and Expressions

Stuart [ˈstjuət]   *n.* 英国斯图亚特王室

heir [ɛə]   *n.* 继承人，后嗣

hierarchy [ˈhaiərɑːki]	*n.* 层次，层级	
popish [ˈpəupiʃ]	*adj.* <贬>天主教的，教皇制度的	
lavish [ˈlæviʃ]	*adj.* 浪费的，滥用的	
inherit [inˈherit]	*vt.* 继承	
unpopularity [ˈʌnˌpɔpjuˈlæriti]	*n.* 不受欢迎，不受拥戴	

Notes

[1] King James：詹姆士是苏格兰女王玛丽·斯图亚特与她的第二任丈夫达恩利勋爵亨利·斯图亚特(Henry Stuart)所生的唯一儿子。1583 年，詹姆士六世亲政。1587 年，其母玛丽因卷入暗杀英格兰女王伊莉莎白一世的阴谋而被处死。1603 年，英国女王伊莉莎白一世指定詹姆士为其继承人后驾崩。于是詹姆士兼任英格兰国王，称詹姆士一世。

[2] King James Bible：钦定版《圣经》。1604 年 1 月，英国国王詹姆斯一世主持了一个宗教会议。为了调解各个教派之间的矛盾，会议做出了一个重大决定：用国王的名义出版钦定版《圣经》，并且必须保证文字不仅易读，而且好听。正是因为这个特点，钦定版后来名扬整个英语世界。

For more information, you can check out the following links:

http://www.baidu.com/ King+James+Bible

http://en.wikipedia.org/wiki/Mary,_Queen_of_Scots

Unit 11   English Civil War (1642—1660)

Lead-in: Listening (PPT-11)

Listen to the movie clip *English Civil War* carefully, and answer the following questions:

1. What are the reasons of the English Civil War?

_____

2. What are the two sides of the war? What's the result of the war?

_____

Reading

The English Civil War was fought between supporters of King Charles I and supporters of Parliament. For five years the country was run by a **dictator**, **Oliver Cromwell**.

1.1   Conflicts between the King, Charles I and the Parliament

Like his father, James I, Charles believed in "**divine right**", claiming that his right to rule came directly from God. This belief put Charles at odds with Parliament.

Charles became king in 1625 and immediately began to quarrel with Parliament over his right to imprison people who opposed him, religion and taxes. In 1629, he **dissolved Parliament**, and, for 11 years, tried to rule alone.

In 1637, Charles attempted to impose the Anglican form of public worship on the Scots. The **Presbyterian** Scots rebelled, raising an army that, in 1640, occupied part of Northern England. Charles recalled Parliament to ask for money to put down the rebellion by the Scots, but Parliament demanded reforms. Civil War broke out after Charles tried to arrest his five leading parliamentary opponents. In 1642, fighting broke out all over the country between **Royalists** (supporters of the king), known as **Cavaliers**, and supporters of Parliament, known as **Roundheads**.

1.2　The King Surrendered in 1646

The king made Oxford his capital and his forces at first held the advantage. However, Parliament secured the support of the Scottish army, and in the long run, proved superior, for it had the money to maintain a professional army. This new model army led by Sir Thomas Fairfax decisively defeated Charles' forces at Naseby in 1645. The king surrendered in 1646 after Oxford fell to the Roundheads.

1.3　The Execution of Charles I

Charles was imprisoned on the Isle of Wight, where he plotted to begin the war again with Scottish help. A second phase of fighting broke out, with Royalist risings and an attempted invasion by the Scots, but it failed. In 1648, parliamentarians who still respected the king were removed from Parliament by Oliver Cromwell. The remaining **Rump Parliament**[1], as it was called, found Charles guilty of treason and executed him in 1649.

However, at his trial and execution, he behaved with great **dignity** and this won him some sympathy. At his execution, Charles put on an extra shirt so that people would not think that, when she shivered from the cold, he was shivering with fear. His body was secretly buried by his supporters at **Windsor Castle**.

1.4　Oliver Cromwell

After Charles' execution, Parliament abolished the Monarchy and England became a Common Wealth. Parliament governed the country but it quarreled with the army, and its members argued. In 1653, Oliver Cromwell emerged as a strong leader and ruled the country as **Lord Protector**. Cromwell clashed with some parliamentarians and was forced to govern with the help of army generals. He fought a war with the Dutch over trade and control of the seas, took control of Ireland and planned colonial expansion.

His dictatorship was not universally popular because of his use of force and of high taxes charged. But he introduced education reforms and gave more equality to the English people. In 1658, Cromwell and was succeeded by his son Richard. He was not an effective ruler and the army removed him. The English people wanted a king again, and in 1660, the son of Charles I took the throne as Charles II.

1.5   King Charles II Dug out Cromwell's Remains to Avenge His Father

Crowell died in 1658 and his son succeeded him as Lord Protector, but complicated contradictions and power struggle soon forced his son to abdicate. This led to the formation of a new parliament composed of both Houses. The new parliament soon started negotiations with the son of Charles I. Subsequently, the son of Charles I mounted the throne and became known as Charles II, putting an end to the Commonwealth. Though Charles II dug out Crowell's remains to avenge his father, he was on the whole a man of shrewdness. He was in favor of cooperation with Parliament because he knew that he owed his crown to Parliament. He supported religious tolerance instead of persecution. His practical attitude enabled England to experience another period of peace and develop.

1.6   The Glorious Revolution

Upon the death of Charles II, his younger brother James succeeded the throne and became known as James II. He was unpopular, the Parliament decided to dethrone the king. They negotiated with James II's daughter Mary and son-in-law William to be joint sovereigns, with William known as William III. This was the so-called Glorious Revolution of 1688. It

THE BATTLE OF THE BOYNE
This decisive battle took place near Drogheda in 1690. The army of the recently deposed James II, last of the Stuart kings, was outnumbered by the Protestant army of William III. When William's troops crossed the Boyne River, James's troops fled. James went into exile in France, while William's rule in England was strengthened by the victory.

became caught up in the Irish question, and the English, under William III, had to defeat James.

was also known as the White Revolution because it caused no bloodshed.

New Words and Expressions

dictator [dik'teitə]	*n.* 独裁者，独裁政权执政者
Oliver ['ɔlivə] **Cromwell** ['krɔmwəl]	奥利弗·克伦威尔
divine right	神授的权力，君权神授
dissolve Parliament	解散国会
Presbyterian [ˌprezbi'tiəriən]	*adj.* 长老会的
	n. 长老教会员
royalist ['rɔialist]	*n.* 保皇主义者，保皇党人
	adj. 保皇主义者的，保皇党人的

Cavalier [ˌkævəˈliə]	*n.* 骑士堂
Roundhead [ˈraundhed]	*n.* 圆颅党(英国 1642—1652 年内战期间的议会派分子，与保皇党相对)
dignity [ˈdigniti]	*n.* 尊严，高贵
Windsor [ˈwinzə] **Castle**	温莎公爵城堡
Lord Protector	护国公
avenge [əˈvendʒ]	*vt.* 为……报复，报仇
dethrone [diˈθrəun]	*vt.* 废黜，废位赶出
joint sovereigns	共同执政
Glorious Revolution	光荣革命
White Revolution	白色革命

Note

[1] Rump Parliament *n.* (英国)尾闾议会。1) 长期议会的一部分，1648 年大整肃后仍存在，1653 年被克伦威尔解散；2) 1659 年复开，1660 年被解散。——《21 世纪大英汉词典》

For more information, you can check out the following links:

http://en.wikipedia.org/wiki/English_Civil_War

http://www.conservapedia.com/English_Civil_War

http://www.newworldencyclopedia.org/entry/English_Civil_War

Unit 12 Trade with China

Lead-in: Listening (PPT-12)

Listen to the passage carefully, and answer the following questions:

1. Why was China a rich and powerful empire? How about Chinese silk and porcelain production in Qing Dynasty?

_____

2. What were the foreign policies of Qing government?

_____

Reading

1.1   A Rich and Powerful Empire of China

At first China **prospered** under the Qing. The empire grew and trade increased particularly with Europe. Chinese silk and **porcelain** were the finest in the world and their cotton goods were cheap and of high quality. Huge quantities of Chinese tea were sold abroad when tea-drinking became fashionable in Europe during the 18th century.

The empire became so rich and powerful that its rulers were able to treat the rest of the world with contempt. Under Emperor Kangxi (1661—1722), foreign merchants were forced to kneel whenever his commands were read out. The **Manchus** also forced several nations into vassal status, including Tibet, Annam (now Vietnam), Burma, Mongolia and Turkestan, making the Chinese empire the world's largest at the time. They made a deal with the Russians over land and trade.

1.2   Trade with China

Trade with China was profitable, yet the government there didn't want "**barbarian**" influences introduced. European merchants looked for other ways to trade.

Throughout the 18th century, Chinese silk, cottons, tea, **lacquer-ware** and porcelain were highly prized in Europe, but they were expensive and in short supply. Merchants from **Portugal**, Britain, Italy and the Netherland tried to expand the China trade. But the powerful Chinese emperors, who controlled all contact between their people and foreigners, were simply not interested. Qianlong, emperor for 60 years, was a scholar and traditionalist who had no time for "barbarians". The problem for the Europeans was that they had to pay for everything in silver, as Chinese traders were not allowed to exchange foreign for Chinese goods. Also the Europeans were permitted to trade only in Guangzhou (Canton), where they were penned up in "factories" (fortified warehouses), and traded through Chinese intermediaries. European traders were very competitive, and they fought to get the best Chinese goods and to sail them home to Europe as quickly as possible to fetch the highest prices.

In 1793, The British **diplomat** Lord McCartney visited the Chinese Emperor to encourage trade relations. Such relations were rejected, so people resorted to illegal deals. Both China and Britain had little respect for each other.

1.3   The Englishman Robert Fortune[1] Stole Several Tea Plants

When, in 1839, the Chinese tried to stop the illegal opium trade, the British went to war. Even China's control of the world supply of tea was almost at an end. During the 1830s, the Englishman **Robert Fortune stole several tea plants** while travelling in China. He **took them to India and set up rival plantations** there.

1.3.1 Robert Fortune, a British Botanist

Robert Fortune (1812—1880) was a Scottish **botanist** and traveller best known for introducing tea plants from China to India.

Fortune was born in Kelloe, **Berwickshire**. He was employed in the **Royal Botanic Garden Edinburgh**, and later in the **Horticultural Society of London's Garden** at Chiswick, and following the Treaty of Nanjing in 1842 was sent out by the Society to collect plants in China.

His travels resulted in the introduction to Europe of many new, exotic and beautiful flowers. His most famous accomplishment was successfully transportation of tea from China to India in 1848 on behalf of the British East India Company.

1.3.2 Fortune Disguised himself as a Chinese merchant in Transporting Tea Plants

Similar to other European travellers of the period, such as Walter Medhurst, Fortune **disguised** himself as a Chinese merchant (see picture 1.3.2 with Fortune in the middle) during several, but not all, of his journeys beyond the newly established treaty port areas. Not only was Fortune's purchase of tea plants forbidden by the Chinese government of the time, but his travels were also

beyond the allowable day's journey from the European treaty ports. Fortune travelled to some areas of China that had seldom been visited by Europeans, including remote areas of Fujian, Guangdong, and Jiangsu provinces.

Fortune employed many different means to transport tea plants, **seedlings,** and other botanical discoveries, but he is most well known for his use of Nathaniel Bagshaw Ward's portable Wardian cases to sustain the plants. Using these small greenhouses, Fortune introduced 20,000 tea plants and seedlings to the **Darjeeling** region of India. He also brought with him a group of trained Chinese tea workers who would facilitate the production of tea leaves. With the exception of a few plants which survived in established Indian gardens, most of Chinese tea plants Fortune introduced to India **perished**. The technology and knowledge that was brought over from China, however, may have been instrumental in the later **flourishing** of the Indian tea industry.

Apart from his many contributions to botanical history, Fortune was the first European to discover that so-called black tea and green tea were actually from the same plant.

New Words and Expressions

prosper [ˈprɔspə]	v. 成功，兴隆，昌盛
porcelain [ˈpɔːslin; -lein]	n. 瓷器，瓷
Manchus [ˈmæntʃuː]	n. 满人
	adj. 满族的
barbarian [bɑːˈbɛəriən]	n. 野蛮人
lacquer-ware [ˈlækəwɛə]	n. [总称]漆器
Portugal [ˈpɔːtjugəl]	n. 葡萄牙
diplomat [ˈdipləmæt]	n. 外交官
botanist [ˈbɔtənist]	n. 植物学家
Berwickshire	n. 贝里克郡[英国苏格兰原郡名]
Royal Botanic Garden	皇家园艺会
Horticultural Society of London's Garden	伦敦园艺会
seedling [ˈsiːdliŋ]	n. 秧苗，树苗
Darjeeling [dɑːˈdʒiːliŋ]	大吉岭(印度东北部之避暑胜地)；大吉岭茶
perish [ˈperiʃ]	vi. 毁灭，死亡；腐烂，枯萎
flourishing [ˈflʌriʃiŋ]	adj. 繁茂的，繁荣的，欣欣向荣的

Note

[1] Robert Fortune："茶叶"间谍罗伯特·福钧，英国著名植物学家。

由于中国红茶的俏销，导致英国白银外流，英国政府指示东印度公司派遣间谍。1842

年《南京条约》后"罗伯特·福钧"在武夷山进行物种资源的窃取。他在武夷山时入住乡村，与当地茶农交流，研究做茶工艺。在离开武夷山之际带走了大批的茶叶种植资源及做茶、制罐师傅；并在英国的殖民地印度大肆进行茶叶的种植和加工红茶。在中国的三年采集行程，他窃取了2万株茶树至印度的大吉岭。由于他的窃取行为，在印度及锡兰引进的茶工业，结束了一直为中国茶垄断的茶市场。

早在19世纪，英国人派了他伴装中国人潜入乡间探访茶叶的秘密。见1.3.2图所示，他穿中国人的服饰，按照中国人的方式理了发，加上了一条长辫子，打扮得让乡下的农民认不出他是欧洲人（农民也没有见过欧洲人）。福钧对中国比较了解，因为1842—1845年间，他曾作为伦敦园艺会领导人在中国待过一段时间。在旅居中国过程中，他学习中文和远东的风俗习惯，熟练掌握了使用筷子的技巧，并在回国时带回了100多种西方人没有见过的植物，其中包括小巧的盆景植物。

福钧的任务充满风险。他是继葡萄牙人后第一个渗入中国内地的外国人，如果被清王朝的卫士发现，他必死无疑。此外，他还必须小心提防无处不在的强盗匪徒，对付急流险滩，靠葡萄牙人绘制的错误百出的地图寻找道路，应付随时可能患病的危险。但这些风险不但没有吓倒福钧，反而使他感到十分兴奋和刺激。正像佩雷尔施泰因所说的那样，福钧是"一个杰出的植物学家，同时也是一个冒险家"。

For more information, you can check out the following links:

http://en.wikipedia.org/wiki/Robert_Fortune

http://www.guardian.co.uk/politics/2008/jan/18/foreignpolicy.uk

http://www.ukcatia.co.uk/

Unit 13   Exploration in Oceania (1642—1820)

Lead-in: Listening (PPT-13)

Listen to the movie clip *Australia* carefully, and answer the following questions:

1. Who were the native people of Australia?

2. What was the original life style? What about the English influence on the native people?

Reading

The exploration of Oceania developed quite late compared with other parts of the world. It was pioneered by Tasman, Cook and other explorers.

1.1   Exploration of Oceania

During the 17th century, Dutch seamen explored the southern Pacific and India Oceans. By the 1620s they had found the northern and western coast of Australia, naming it "New Holland".

In 1642, the Dutchman **Abel Tasman** (1603—1659) discovered the island of Tasmania. They had sailed from **Mauritius** and travelled so far south that he did not sight Australia. Farther to the east, Tasman later reached the south island of New Zealand. After a fight with its **Maori** inhabitants he returned to Batavia in the Dutch East Indies, discovering **Tonga** and **Fiji** on the way. The next year, he sailed along the northern coast of Australia.

In 1688 and 1699, the English **navigator** William Dampier explored the western and northwestern coastline of Australia. These explorers proved that Australia was an island, but they did not settle there. The Pacific remained largely unknown as it was too distant and too poor to attract trading interest from the Europeans.

1.2   The Voyages of Captain Cook[1]

The first scientific exploration of these southern lands was undertaken by Captain James Cook, who made three voyages. The first voyage (1768—1771) took him around New Zealand. Then he landed at Botany Bay in Australia, claiming it for Britain. On his second voyage (1772—1775), he explored many Pacific islands and Antarctica. On his last voyage, begun in 1776, he visited New Zealand, Tonga, **Tahiti** and finally **Hawaii**, where he was killed in a quarrel with the islanders.

1.3　Native Peoples

The "new" lands explored by Cook had been inhabited for hundreds of years. The Maoris lived in New Zealand, and the Aborigines lived in Australia. Both peoples lived according to ancient traditions. Understandably they **were wary of** Cook and his men—the first Europeans that they had ever seen.

Aborigines had lived in Australia for thousands of years, spread over a vast continent. They lived by foraging and hunting, and using their advanced knowledge of nature. They were so different from Europeans that there was such a **clash of culture** that **aboriginal** culture was later almost wiped out.

1.3.1　The Conflicts between the Maoris and the Europeans

The Maoris, it is thought, had sailed to Aotearoa (New Zealand) from **Polynesia** around 750 AD, and were farmers, warriors and village-dwellers. As the Europeans moved into their land, **they resisted**.

In 1779, while on his third voyage to the Pacific, Captain Cook was killed in a skirmish with Hawaiians over the theft of a boat. Initially, the British had been welcome, but after this event, his crews had to sail home without their captain. (See picture 1.3.1)

In 1779, while on his third voyage to the Pacific, Captain Cook was killed in a skirmish with Hawaiians over the theft of a boat. Initially, the British had been welcome, but after this event, his crews had to sail home without their captain.

The first settlers in Australia arrived in 1788. They were **convicts** who had been transported there from Britain as a punishment for their crimes. Free settlers started to arrive in 1793. In New Zealand, whalers, hunters and traders were soon followed by **missionaries**. Many of the early settlers came from Scotland, Ireland and Wales. The settlers introduced diseases which often killed the local peoples who had no resistance to them.

1.3.2　The Maoris Were Skilled Sailors and Craft-workers

The Maoris were skilled sailors and **craft-workers** who decorated their canoes with elaborate religious carvings. When Cook arrived, there were about 100,000 Maoris in New

Zealand. Many were killed in later wars against British settlers and troops.

New Words and Expressions

Abel Tasman	亚伯·塔斯曼(一航海家名字)
Mauritius [məˈriʃəs]	n. 毛里求斯(非洲岛国)
Maori [ˈmɑːri, ˈmauri]	n. (新西兰、澳大利亚的)毛利人；毛利语
Tonga [ˈtɔŋgə]	n. 汤加
Fiji [fiːˈdʒiː, ˈfiːdʒiː]	n. 斐济
navigator [ˈnævigeitə]	n. 航海家
Tahiti [tɑːˈhiːti]	n. 塔希提岛(位于南太平洋，法属波利西亚的经济活动中心)
Hawaii [hɑːˈwaiiː]	n. 夏威夷，夏威夷岛
be wary of	提防
clash of culture	文化冲突
aboriginal [ˌæbəˈridʒənəl]	adj. 土著的
	n. 土著居民
Polynesia [ˌpɔliˈniːziə]	n. 玻利尼西亚(中太平洋群岛，意为"多岛群岛"，包括夏威夷群岛、萨摩亚群岛、汤加群岛核社会群岛等)
convict [ˈkɔnvikt]	n. 罪犯
missionary [ˈmiʃənəri]	n. 传教士
craft-worker [ˌkrɑːftˈwəːkə]	n. 工匠

Note

[1] Captain Cook：詹姆斯·库克(1728—1779)，英国著名探险家、航海家和制图学家。英法战争爆发时，他作为一名强壮的水手应征到皇家海军服役。不到一个月他被提升为大副，四年后升为船长。1759 年，他授权指挥一艘舰船参加了圣·劳伦斯河上的战斗。战后，库克作为纵帆船"格伦维尔"号的船长承担了新西兰、拉布拉多和新斯科舍沿岸的调查工作。在四年多的时间里他取得了许多重要成果。这些成果后来由英国政府予以发表。

For more information, you can check out the following links:

http://en.wikipedia.org/wiki/James_Cook

http://www.answers.com/topic/james-cook

Unit 14   The British Empire in India, Africa and Latin America

Lead-in: Listening (PPT-14)

Listen to the song "River Babylon" carefully, and answer the following questions:

1. How were the black slaves of Africa captured and taken to America to work on the plantations?

2. What sad feelings can you imagine from listening to the song?

Reading

The British Empire is the name given to United Kingdom of Great Britain and Northern Ireland and the former dominions, colonies, and other territories throughout the world from the late 1500s to the middle of the 20th century. At its height in the early 1900s, the British Empire was the largest empire in human history, "**on which the sun never set.**" It was an empire of 33 million square kilometers, taking up one fifth of the world's total dry land. The territory was about 135 times as large as Great Britain.

1.1   The British East India Company

The hold on India by the British East India Company gradually grew stronger. The British came to dominate India society, becoming its ruling **caste**.

By 1750, the British East India Company controlled the very profitable trade between Britain, India and the Far East. Its officials were skilful businessmen who had built up knowledge of Indian affairs, especially through Indians they employed. They made friends with many Indian princes, and struck bargains with both the friends and enemies of the declining Moghul rulers. Many British people in India lived rather like princes themselves. By working for the East India Company many of them became extremely rich.

1.2 Queen Victoria Was Crowned the Empress of India

The end of the Company was precipitated by a mutiny of sepoys against their British commanders, due in part to the tensions caused by British attempts to Westernise India. The Indian Rebellion took six months to suppress, with heavy loss of life on both sides. Afterwards the British government assumed direct control over India, ushering in the period known as the British Raj, where an appointed governor-general administered India and Queen Victoria was crowned the Empress of India. The East India Company was dissolved the following year, in 1858.

An 1876 political cartoon of Benjamin Disraeli (1804—1881) making Queen Victoria Empress of India. The caption was "New crowns for old ones!"

1.3 The British Government Took a "Soft Approach" towards India

By 1780, the East India Company controlled many of the more prosperous parts of India, but in 1784 the British government stopped further expansion. The company's bosses thought otherwise. When Indian states fought each other, the company often simply moved in. Around 1800, Napoleon's ambition to build an empire in India scared the British, and the government changed its policy. From 1803 to 1815, the company fought the Marathas, who ruled central India, breaking their power. In many cases they took a "soft approach", using trade to favor certain Indian states and stationing troops there "for their protection".

1.4 The British in Africa

There were two chief centers of British advance in Africa: (1) **Cape of Good Hope** at the Southern tip of the continent. (2) Egypt in North Africa.

By the beginning of the twentieth century, about one-third of Africa was controlled by Britain. Britain occupied Egypt and controlled the 163-kilometer-long **Suez Canal** in the mid 1800s.

1.5 The British in Latin America

In Latin America, the British also controlled a number of places, including some islands in central America, such as **Guiana** and **Dominica**. In addition, many islands in the Pacific and Atlantic Oceans were also controlled or claimed by the British.

New Words and Expressions

caste [kɑ:st]	*n.* 印度的世袭阶级，(具有严格等级的)社会地位，社会等级制度
Cape of Good Hope	好望角
Suez Canal	苏伊士运河(埃及东北部)
Guiana [gaiˈænə, giˈænə]	*n.* 圭亚那地区
Dominica [ˌdɔmiˈni:kə]	*n.* 多米尼加(西印度群岛岛国)

For more information, you can check out the following links:

http://en.wikipedia.org/wiki/British_Raj

http://en.wikipedia.org/wiki/British_Empire

http://www.conservapedia.com/British_Empire

Unit 15 Australia, Britain's Colony for Expelling Their Criminals

Lead-in: Listening (PPT-15)

Listen to the passage carefully, and answer the following questions:

1. When was the Commonwealth of Australia proclaimed?

_____

2. The city of Canberra was chosen as the federal capital, and what was the emblem of Australia?

_____

Reading

The original inhabitants of Australia, the **Aborigines**, faced a growing threat to their way of life as white settlers **encroached** ever further into their territories.

1.1 Aboriginal People

Australia's first inhabitants, the Aboriginal people, arrived 50,000 years ago **from Southeast Asia**. They lived in **nomadic** groups, travelling along their territories, hunting with spears and **boomerangs**, fishing from **canoes** and gathering fruits and vegetables. They had no written language but passed on valuable knowledge by word of mouth and in song.

1.2 Convicts Were Shipped from Britain to Australia as Punishment of Banishment

During the 19th century, the new nation of Australia was created. More than 174,000 convicts had been shipped from Britain to Australia, mainly to Sydney, to pass their sentence in work gangs, for periods varying from a few years to life. Transportation to the colonies had begun during the reign of Elizabeth I, was an extension of the older punishment of banishment, and it did not end until 1868.

For many convicts, Britain held only bitter memories and so it was that many of them settled in Australia after their **release**. Early settlements were founded along the coast but explorers gradually opened up the **interior**. These early farmers gradually spread into the interior, acquiring land as they went, but eventually coming into conflict with the native Australians, the Aborigines.

1.3　A List of Australian Prime Minister Kevin Rudd's Criminal Ancestors[1]

At a meeting at Kirribilli House in Sydney in 2008, Mr. Rudd was presented with two leather-bound volumes containing his family history, produced by the Church of Jesus Christ of Latter-day Saints.

Church elder Terry Vinson said Mr. Rudd had a "**true Aussie pedigree**", including free settlers and convicts.

Mr. Rudd's paternal fifth great-grandmother Mary Wade (see picture 1.3) was a London street **urchin** who made a **pittance** by sweeping streets and begging. In 1788, aged 12, she and an older girl named Jane Whiting robbed an eight-year-old girl of her dress and underwear. They were tried at London's Old Bailey in January 1789. Mary's death sentence was **commuted** to transportation to the colony of NSW.

Another relative, Catherine Lahey, was convicted in 1789 for **forging** coins because she could not pay her rent. She arrived in Sydney in 1800.

The Prime Minister's **paternal** fourth great-grandfather, Thomas Rudd, was transported to Australia in 1801 to serve a seven-year sentence for "unlawfully acquiring a bag of sugar".

He went on to become one of the founders of Campbell town and two streets in the Sydney suburb are named after him: Thomas Street and Rudd Road.

Other ancestors came to Australia as free settlers, living in Parramatta, Wagga and Queensland.

Mr. Vinson said there was great value in Australians seeking out their ancestry. "A study of our personal history helps us to respect the struggles that our ancestors **endured**—in a far different world than the one we live in today—to give us the prosperity we now enjoy," he said. The research took more than a year to complete and will be presented to the National Library next month as part of National Family History Week. "We regard today's presentation as our gift to the nation," said Mr. Vinson.

1.4　Independence and Its National Flag[2]

Britain had granted self-government to all her colonies by the 1890s, and the leaders of the colonies had come to realize that some form of union was needed.

None of the Australian colonies were willing to give up

their individual independence, so in **1890**, after fierce arguments, the colonies agreed to unite in a **federation**. **The Commonwealth of Australia** was **proclaimed** on the first day of **1901** and the city of **Canberra** was chosen as the federal capital.

1.5   Emblem of Australia[3]

Australia is the national emblem on the left side of a kangaroo, an **emu** is on the right side, both of which are animals unique to Australia, is a national symbol, a symbol of the nation, in the middle is a shield, the shield surface of the six groups Patterns were a symbol of the country's six states. St. George's red cross (the cross of a lion, four stars), a symbol of New South Wales; crown under the Southern cross the State of Victoria on behalf of the **constellation**; blue cross of Malta on behalf of the State of Queensland; **shrike** on behalf of South Australia State; black swan a symbol of Western Australia; red lion symbol of Tasmania. Top coat for a symbol of the Commonwealth countries of the seven stars angle. Around the Australian national flower decorated with Acacia, the ribbon at the bottom of the English word "Australia."

New Words and Expressions

expel [iks'pel]	v. 驱逐，开除
criminal ['kriminl]	n. 罪犯，犯罪者
aborigines [ˌæbə'ridʒiniːz]	n. 土著，原居民；(Aborigines)澳大利亚土著居民，土生动物(或植物)群
encroach [in'krəutʃ]	vi. (逐步或暗中)侵占，蚕食
nomadic [nəu'mædik]	adj. 游牧的
boomerang ['buːməˌræŋ]	n. 回飞棒，飞去来器
canoe [kə'nuː]	n. 独木舟，轻舟
banishment ['bæniʃmənt]	n. 放逐，驱逐
release [ri'liːs]	n. 释放，豁免
interior [in'tiəriə]	adj. 内部的
	n. 内部
true Aussie pedigree	纯正的澳大利亚血统，纯种澳大利亚人
urchin ['əːtʃin]	n. 顽童，小孩
pittance ['pitəns]	n. 少量；微薄的薪俸
commute [kə'mjuːt]	v. 交换；抵偿，减刑
forge [fɔːdʒ]	v. 稳步前进；铸造，伪造

paternal [pə'tə:nl]　　　　　　*adj.* 父亲的，像父亲的

endure [in'djuə]　　　　　　*v.* 耐久，忍耐

federation [ˌfedə'reiʃən]　　　*n.* 同盟，联邦；联合，联盟

the Commonwealth of Australia　澳大利亚联邦

proclaim [kleim]　　　　　　*vt.* (根据权利)要求，认领，声称，主张

Canberra ['kænbərə]　　　　　*n.* 堪培拉(澳大利亚首都)

emu ['i:mju:]　　　　　　　　*n.* 鸸鹋(产于澳洲的一种体型大而不会飞的鸟)

constellation [kɔnstə'leiʃne]　*n.* [天]星群，星座；灿烂的一群

shrike [ʃraik]　　　　　　　　*n.* [鸟]伯劳鸟

Notes

[1] A List of Australian Prime Minister Kevin Rudd's Criminal Ancestors：澳大利亚总理凯文·拉德(Kevin Rudd)的中文名是陆克文。他是一位中国通。总理原来有 6 名祖先曾经犯罪，当地一间教会更以两卷书刊整理 6 人的"丰功伟绩"，于 2008 年 7 月 31 日将两册内容作为陆克文族谱的书籍赠送给他。众所周知，许多澳大利亚人都是英国流放罪犯的后代，这些囚犯对这块蛮荒之地的开拓和发展发挥了重要的角色，到了今天，他们的犯人身份不仅未被后人唾弃，反而是加以赞颂。

[2] National Flag：澳大利亚国旗为深蓝色，左上角为英国国旗图案，表明澳大利亚与英国的传统关系，一颗最大的七角星象征组成澳的六个州和联邦区(北部地区和首都直辖区)，五颗白星代表南十字星座。

[3] Emblem of Australia：澳大利亚国徽左边是一只袋鼠，右边是一只鸸鹋，这两种动物均为澳大利亚所特有，是国家的标志，民族的象征，中间是一个盾，盾面上有六组图案分别象征这个国家的六个州。

For more information, you can check out the following links:

http://www.britishempire.co.uk/maproom/westernaustralia.htm

http://www.eurekacouncil.com.au/Australia-History/History-Pages/1066-british_empire.htm

Unit 16   Industrial Revolution and Chartist Movement in Britain

Lead-in: Listening (PPT-16)

Listen to the video *Industrial Revolution* carefully, and answer the following questions:

1. When did the Industrial Revolution happen?

2. How was women's position changed?

Reading

The Industrial Revolution is the name given to a period when great changes took place in Britain, and people began to use steam power to make goods in factories.

1.1   More Revolutionary New Machines Were Invented

During the 18th century, many people in Britain worked at home, usually producing goods by hand. There were also many farmers and farm laborers who worked on the land to grow crops to feed their families. **By the middle of the 19th century**, all this had changed. Many British people now lived in towns and worked in enormous factories, or in shops, offices, offices, railways and other businesses designed to serve the inhabitants of these industrial centres. Leading the world, British inventors continued to develop revolutionary new machines which performed traditional tasks such as spinning and weaving much faster than they could be done by hand. Machines were also used to make iron and steel. These metals were in turn used to make more machines, weapons and tools.

1.2   Many Women Gained Independence

Jobs in factories, such as **textile mills**, often required skill rather than strength. Women were as good as men for such work and many single women gained independence by earning a wage for themselves.

1.3 Chartism

In some countries, people were demanding the right to vote. This was one of the reforms that the Chartist Movement in Britain wanted. The "People's Charter" was first published there in May 1838. A petition said to have 1,200,000 signatures on it was handed in to Parliament in June 1839 but was **rejected** a month later. By February 1848, and following the revolution in France, a final petition was formed. When it was complete, it was said to have over three million names on it. On April 10, 1848 a mass march travelled across London to the Houses of Parliament to present the **petition**. Again, the petition was rejected and Chartism became a spent force.

1.4 Democratic Reforms

Recent changes had made rebellion easier. More people were able to read and newspapers told them what was happening in other countries. Few police forces existed, so troops had to be used against rioters. Most of the revolts of 1848 failed in their immediate demands, but over the next few years, nationalist feeling grew stronger and many governments began to see that democratic reforms would soon be necessary.

In Belgium, *Communist Manifesto*, written by Karl Marx and Friedrich Engels, was published.

New Words and Expressions

textile mills	纺织厂
reject [ri'dʒekt]	vt. 拒绝，抵制；否决，驳回
petition [pi'tiʃən]	n. 请愿；请愿书，诉状
democratic [ˌdemə'krætik]	adj. 民主的，民主政体的

For more information, you can check out the following links:

http://en.wikipedia.org/wiki/Industrial_Revolution

http://www.kosmix.com/topic/Industrial_Revolution

http://current.com/green/92445956_factory-town-blues.htm

Unit 17   The British Empire (1815—1913) Reached Its Height

Lead-in: Listening (PPT-17)

Listen to the passage carefully, and answer the following questions:

1. Why was the British Empire known as "the empire on which the sun never sets"?

_____

2. What kinds of reforms and achievements had been made during the Victorian Reign?

_____

Reading

During the 19th century, the British extended and **consolidated** their empire. Britain had taken over more land than any other nation in history.

1.1   Queen Victoria (1837—1901) and Polite Society

1.1.1   The Height of the British Empire

When William IV died in 1837, the English crown passed to his niece, Victoria, who was just 18 years old. When Victoria died in 1901, her reign had lasted 63 years, the longest in British history.

At its height, during the reign of Queen Victoria, the British empire included a quarter of the world's land and people. From the end of the Napoleonic Wars in 1815 to the start of World War I in 1914, Britain acquired so many new colonies that the empire stretched around the world. Britain was able to control this vast empire by its **domination** of the seas and world trade routes. Throughout the 19th century, British naval strength was unbeatable and its boats constantly patrolled countries belonging to the empire.

Because the empire covered both **hemispheres** it was known as "**the empire on which the**

sun never sets". Colonies in the Caribbean, Africa, Asia, Australia and the Pacific were ruled from London and were all united under the British monarch. Strategic harbors such as Gibraltar, Hong Kong, Singapore and **Aden** came to British hands, and vital trading routes such as the Cape route to India, or the Suez Canal (via Egypt) to the **spice** and rubber plantations of southeast Asia were also controlled by Britain.

Britain completed its conquest of India in 1819, and Queen Victoria became Empress of India in 1877.

In 1897, Victoria celebrated her **Diamond Jubilee**. The guests of honor included Indian Princes, African chiefs, Pacific Islanders and Chinese from Hong Kong.

1.1.2 A Series of Reforms and Achievements

The Victorian Age was characterized by a series of reforms. Before Victoria's time, the government had always regarded trade unions with suspicion, fearing they might become centers of revolution, but the **Trade Union Act** of 1871 legalized the trade unions and gave them financial security, allowing them to collect money in support of strike action. Compulsory education was adopted, and universities started to **enroll** women students.

1.2 East Indian Company

India was an example of a country where the British had come to trade and stayed to rule. It was the most prized colony in the empire. In 1850, India remained under the rule of the British East India Company. After the rebellion of 1857, India was placed under the rule of the British government, and its policies were more cautious. British officials left control of local affairs to the princes.

1.3 Colonial Expansion under Queen Victoria

British influence extended into mainland settlements in Central and South America and into China where it has trading outposts. Queen Victoria, herself empress of India since 1876, was a keen supporter of a foreign policy that pursued colonial expansion and upheld the empire. As more British people **emigrated** to countries within the empire, so these lands were given more freedom to govern themselves. Many colonies, notably Canada, Australia and South Africa became dominions rather than colonies and were allowed self-government.

The British taking of **Quebec** in 1759 meant the beginning of the end of New France. The battle took place in the fields outside the city. The British and French generals, James Wolfe and the Marquis de Montcalm, both died during the fighting.

With the death of General Montcalm near Quebec in 1759, the French lost their military leadership, and thus **lost control of Canada**.

1.4 End of the Empire

Towards the end of the 19th century, some colonies began to break away from British rule. Home rule was granted to Canada in 1867, and independence to Australia in 1901. Both countries became dominions, although they remained part of the British empire. The gradual loosening of ties with the British empire reflected the fact that Britain had ceased to be the leading industrial nation in the world. Germany and the United States had overtaken it, with France and Russia close behind.

New Words and Expressions

consolidate [kənˈsɔlideit]	v. 巩固
domination [dɔmiˈneiʃən]	n. 控制，统治，支配
patrol [pəˈtrəul]	v. 出巡，巡逻
hemisphere [ˈhemisfiə]	n. 半球
Aden [ˈeidn]	n. 亚丁(也门人民共和国首都，临亚丁湾)
spice [spais]	n. 香料；调味品
Diamond Jubilee	第 60 或第 75 周年纪念
Trade Union Act	工会法案
enroll [inˈrəul]	v. 登记，招收；使入伍(或入会、入学等)；参加，成为成员
emigrate [ˈemigreit]	vi. 永久(使)移居
	vt. (使)移民
Quebec [kwiˈbek]	魁北克(加拿大省名)

For more information, you can check out the following links:

http://en.wikipedia.org/wiki/Victoria_of_the_United_Kingdom

http://www.encyclomedia.com/queen_victoria.html

Unit 18 Britain Withdrew from Palestine[1] (1948—1949)

Lead-in: Listening (PPT-18)

Listen to the passage carefully, and answer the following questions:

1. Why did Britain have to withdraw from Palestine?

2. In which year did the United Nations negotiate a **ceasefire**, but conflicts between Israel and its Arab neighbors continue to this day?

Reading

Growing demands for a separate Jewish state and the flood of **refugees** from Europe forced the British to withdraw from Palestine. **Israel** became a reality.

1.1 Jewish Terrorists to Attack both the Arabs and the British

Until the end of World War I, Palestine was part of the **Ottoman Empire**. It was inhabited by Arabs and a growing number of Jews who wanted to settle in a Jewish homeland. When the Ottoman Empire **collapsed**, Palestine was ruled by Britain under **a League of Nations' mandate**. In 1917, Britain had promised its support to establish a Jewish homeland in Palestine. However, more Jews began arriving during the 1930s as problems grew in Europe.

Between 1922 and 1939, the Jewish population in Palestine had risen from 83,000 to 445,000 and **Tel Aviv** had become a Jewish city with a population of 150,000. The Arabs **resented** this and fighting often broke out between the two groups. After World War II, more Jewish people wanted to move to Palestine. Under pressure from the Arabs, Britain **restricted** the number of new settlers allowed. This led Jewish terrorists to attack both the Arabs and the British.

A secret Jewish army called Haganah (self-defence) was formed in 1920. More extremist groups were later formed, notably Irgun and the Stern Gang. Both groups thought that Britain had **betrayed** the **Zionist** cause—to establish a Jewish state in Palestine—and took part in a violent terrorist campaign against the Arabs and the British. Jewish leaders such as Chaim Weizmann and David Ben-Gurion took a more peaceful approach.

By June 1945, an enormous number of Jewish refugees, displaced by the war in Europe, were **clamoring** to live in Palestine. Despite British efforts to stop them, the number of refugees entering the country continued to increase. Pressure was brought to bear on Britain by the United States to allow the admission of 100,000 refugees, but Britain refused. It soon found itself involved in a full-scale war with Jewish terrorist organizations.

1.2 The New State of Israel

Unwilling to be caught up in another bloody and costly war, Britain took the matter to the United Nations. In 1947, the UN voted to divide Palestine into two states. One would be Jewish and the other one Arab. **Jerusalem**, which was **sacred** to Jews, Muslims and Christians, would be international. The Jews agreed to this, but the Arabs did not.

On May 14, 1948, Britain gave up its mandate to rule Palestine and withdrew its troops. On the same day the Jews, led by the **Mapai Party** leader David Ben-Gurion, proclaimed the state of Israel, and its **legitimacy** was immediately recognized by the United States and the Soviet Union.

Israel was attacked by the surrounding Arab League states of **Lebanon**, Syria, Iraq, Jordan and Egypt. Israel defeated them and increased its territory by a quarter. Nearly one million Palestinian refugees, afraid of Jewish rule, fled to neighboring Arab countries. The United Nations negotiated a **ceasefire** in 1949, but conflicts between Israel and its Arab neighbors continue to this day.

New Words and Expressions

Palestine [ˈpælistain]	n. 巴勒斯坦(西南亚一地区)
refugee [ˌrefju(ː)ˈdʒiː]	n. 难民，流亡者
Ottoman [ˈɔtəmən](=Turkish) **Empire**	奥斯曼帝国
Israel [ˈizreiəl]	n. 以色列
collapse [kəˈlæps]	vi. 崩溃，瓦解；失败；倒塌
Tel Aviv [ˌteləˈviːv]	特拉维夫(以色列港市)

resent [ri'zent]	v. 愤恨，怨恨
restrict [ris'trikt]	vt. 限制，约束，限定
betray [bi'trei]	vt. 出卖，背叛；泄露(秘密)
clamor ['klæmə]	v. 喧嚷，大声地要求
Jerusalem [dʒe'ru:sələm]	n. 耶路撒冷(巴勒斯坦著名古城)
sacred ['seikrid]	adj. 神的，宗教的；庄严的，神圣的
mandate ['mændeit]	n. (前国际联盟的)委任托管权
Zionist	n. 支持或拥护犹太人复国运动者
Mapai Party [mɑ:'pai]	n. & adj. 以色列工人党(的)
legitimacy [li'dʒitiməsi]	n. 合法(性)，正统(性)，正确(性)，合理(性)
Lebanon ['lebənən]	n. 黎巴嫩(西南亚国家)
ceasefire ['si:s,faiə]	n. 停火，停战

Note

[1] Britain Withdrew from Palestine (1948—1949)：英国从巴勒斯坦撤军。

　　第一次世界大战中，英国为保护其在苏伊士运河的利益，大力扶植、利用犹太复国主义运动，以控制巴勒斯坦地区。1917 年，英国发表《贝尔福宣言》，"赞成在巴勒斯坦建立一个犹太民族之家"。1922 年 7 月，国际联盟通过了英国对巴勒斯坦的"委任统治训令"，巴勒斯坦沦为英国的"委任统治地"。在英国统治期间，大批犹太人从世界各地迁入巴勒斯坦。犹太人和巴勒斯坦阿拉伯人不断发生暴力冲突。人肉炸弹首先由犹太复国主义者发明。1947 年，英国无法控制巴勒斯坦的局势，宣布从巴勒斯坦撤军，并将这一问题提交给联合国。

For more information, you can check out the following links:

http://en.wikipedia.org/wiki/British_Mandate_of_Palestine

http://original.antiwar.com/eland/2009/11/03/knocking-our-heads-against-a-wall-in-palestine/

Unit 19 British Commonwealth (1914—1949)

Lead-in: Listening (PPT-19)

Listen to the passage carefully, and answer the following questions:

1. When was the name British Commonwealth of Nations used instead of British Empire?

_____

2. What's the background of the formation of the British Commonwealth?

_____

Reading

In 1931, the countries that formed the British Empire joined together to form the Commonwealth. Over the next 60 years, they were given their independence.

1.1 Many Colonies Started to Clamor for Independence

The relationship between Britain and parts of its empire had begun to change by the beginning of the 20th century. Some of the large countries became independent as British **dominions**. They were self-governing, but they kept strong links with Britain. Dominions **retained** the British Crown (king or queen) as the symbolic head of state. Each dominion had a **lieutenant governor**, a native resident of that country. He or she represented the Crown.

In the 1920s, the dominions asked for a clear definition of their relationship with Britain. This was given **in 1931** in the Statute of Westminster when dominions were defined as "**autonomous** (self-ruling) communities within the British empire, equal in status united by a common **allegiance** to the Crown and freely associated as members of the British Commonwealth of Nations". After this statute, **the name British Commonwealth of Nations was used instead of British Empire**, and many colonies started to clamor for independence.

1.2 The Dominions Received Better Terms for Trading with Britain than Countries outside the Commonwealth

In 1932, the dominions received better terms for trading with Britain than countries outside the Commonwealth. Canada, Australia, New Zealand and South Africa have all become dominions before World War I. The Irish Free State all became a dominion in 1921. The First three to gain their independence after World War II were India (1947), Ceylon (1948) and Burma (1948). India and Ceylon (Sri Lanka) stayed in the Commonwealth, but Burma did not join, and the Republic of Ireland left in 1949.

New Words and Expressions

British Commonwealth	英联邦
dominion [dəˈminjən]	n. (英联邦的)自治领
retain [riˈtein]	vt. 保持，保留
lieutenant governor	副总督，副州长
autonomous [ɔːˈtɔnəməs]	adj. 自治的
allegiance [əˈliːdʒəns]	n. 忠贞，效忠

For more information, you can check out the following links:

http://en.wikipedia.org/wiki/British_Empire

http://www.wikinfo.org/index.php/British_Commonwealth

Unit 20   British Government and Politics

Lead-in: Listening (PPT-20)

Listen to the passage carefully, and answer the following questions:

1. What is U.K. made up of?

2. What are the official residences of the Monarch and the Prime Minister?

Reading

The United Kingdom of Great Britain and Northern Ireland (U.K.) is made up of Great Britain and, Northern Island, and a number of smaller islands around them. **Great Britain** is traditionally divided into three countries, or political regions: England in the south, Scotland in the north, and Wales in the southwest.

1.1   The British Government

The British system of government is known as a **constitutional monarchy**. In this system, the head of state is a monarch, king or queen, but the monarch's power is limited by a basic law known as the Constitution. Britain is regarded as a democracy because the real power of government is invested with Parliament. Britain was the first country to institute the parliamentary system in the thirteenth century. Parliament, meaning a place for argument and debate, is the nation's supreme **legislative** organ.

1.2   Political Parties

Under the British law, people are free to set up political parties, and a number of political parties exist in the United Kingdom. The law grants equal treatment to all political parties; however, only two of them are most important and they are known as the **major parties**. Consequently, politics in Britain is based on a two-party system instead of a multi-party system. The two major parties are respectively called the **Conservative Party** and the **Labor Party**.

1.3　No. 10 Downing Street

The seat of the government is the Building of Parliament, and the official residence of the British prime minister is located at No. 10 Downing Street, which is often used in the **press** to mean the prime minister.

To the present day 51 men and one woman have passed through the doors of Number 10 Downing Street as British Prime Minister. During this time an extraordinary range of characters have been handed the keys to one of the most famous front doors in the world.

1.4　The Buckingham Palace

Buckingham Palace is the official London residence of the British monarch. Located in the City of Westminster, the palace is a setting for state occasions and royal hospitality. It has been a rallying point for the British people at times of national rejoicing and crisis.

New Words and Expressions

constitutional monarchy	君主立宪政体
legislative ['ledʒisˌleitiv]	*adj.* 立法机关的
Conservative Party	保守党
Labor Party	(英国的)工党
No. 10 Downing Street	*n.* 唐宁街10号(英国首相官邸及若干政府主要部门的所在地)
press [pres]	*n.* 新闻
the Buckingham Palace	白金汉宫(英国王宫)

For more information, you can check out the following links:

http://en.wikipedia.org/wiki/Buckingham_Palace

http://en.wikipedia.org/wiki/Politics_of_the_United_Kingdom

Examination on Chapter One

Name _____   No. _____

I. Multiple choice: 30%

1. Ireland was an independent kingdom before the Anglo-Norman invaders came. _____ (1491—1547) was the first English king to conquer Ireland and force English law on the Irish people.

   A. King Henry VII   B. King Henry VIII   C. Queen Elizabeth I   D. Queen Mary

2. The Irish Republic Army, composed of radical Roman Catholics, is a military organization fighting for the independence of Northern Ireland. It often resorts to terrorist campaigns of bombing, murdering, and arson. The political wing of IRA is called _____.

   A. Sinn Fein   B. Liberal Party   C. Conservative Party   D. Labor Party

3. Britain has a _____ climate and changeable weather. Even the most reliable English weather experts find it hard to give a correct and reliable weather forecast.

   A. tropical   B. maritime   C. mild   D. chilly

4. About half of the people living in Northern Ireland reside in _____ and along the coast.

   A. Belfast   B. Edinburgh   C. Glasgow   D. Liverpool

5. The middle English period began soon after the Normans conquered England _____. For nearly three hundred years after the Norman Conquest, there were two languages in England because the Normans brought their French language and continued to speak it.

   A. in 1066   B. in 1707   B. in 1381   D. in 1603

6. The British system of government is known as a _____. In this system, the head of state is a monarch, king or queen, but the monarch's power is limited by a basic law known as the constitution.

   A. Republic   B. socialist democracy

   C. constitutional monarchy   D. bourgeoisie

7. The British Parliament consists of three branches: the monarch (queen or king), the House of _____, and the house of commons.

   A. nobles   B. gentry   C. aristocracy   D. Lords

8. The term of Parliament lasts _____ years unless the prime minister asks the monarch to dissolve Parliament.

   A. three   B. four   C. two   D. five

9. There are _____ seats in the House of Commons, representing the whole nation. To distribute the seats fairly, the United kingdom is divided into electoral districts, also known as constituencies, of nearly equal populations. Each constituency is to elect one Member of Parliament.

   A. 413   B. 166   C. 355   D. 659

10. The policemen outside London are all local forces. They are employed and paid by the county government. The famous _____ was once the headquarters of the Criminal Investigation

Department of the police force of London and as such it frequently appears in English detective stories.

A. London Police Station   B. London Office

C. Scotland Yard   D. London Investigation

11. To the west of Downing Street stands _____ which is the monarch's permanent residence in London. A few minutes' walk from the palace will take visitors to the famous Hyde Park. The northeast corner of the park is known as Speakers' Corner, which came into being in the 1860s.

A. Westminster Palace   B. Winsor Palace

C. Whitehall   D. Buckingham Palace

12. The British marriage has always been based on monogamy without exception ever since _____.

A. 11th century   B. 12th century

C. 13th century   D. the beginning of written history

13. There were some legendary heroes, such as _____, who fought to unify the kingdoms.

A. Harold   B. Canute   C. King Arthur   D. King Alfred

14. The greatest Anglo-Saxon hero who fought against the invasion of the Vikings was _____. To prevent the new invaders from landing, he built Britain's first naval force, and because of this, he later became known as "the father of the British Navy".

A. King Arthur   B. King Alfred   C. Henry VII   D. Elizabeth I

15. To strengthen his military control, William the conqueror built _____ as a military fortress. Further more, he put the administration of justice under his own control. He replaced the Witan with the Great Council that was composed of his tenants-in-chiefs.

A. the Tower of London   B. London Bridge

C. Westminster Abbey   C. Buckingham Palace

16. King _____ was said to have been the worst of English kings. Within six years of his reign, he lost all his continental territory except a tiny spot in France.

A. Henry II   B. Henry III   C. Edward IV   D. John

17. On June 15, _____, King John signed and swore to observe the charter the nobles had prepared. The charter, known as the Great Charter, or the Magna Carta, is as important to the English people as the Declaration of Independence is important to the Americans.

A. 1215   B. 1066   C.1337   D. 1453

18. Henry III was succeeded by his son Edward I. Under the rule of Edward I, England conquered Wales. The Statute of Wales in 1284 placed Wales under English law, and Edward I gave his new-born son the title _____, a title held by the heir to the throne ever since.

A. Prince of Wales   B. King of Wales   C. Prince of Britain   D. Prince of England

19. The Hundred Years' War refers to the war between _____ from 1337 to 1453.

A. Scotland and England   B. Ireland and England

C. Spain and England   D. France and England

20. To fund the war, the government in _____ started to collect a flat rate poll tax of one shilling a head. Most of the peasants had no money to pay the tax and therefore rebelled. Watt Tyler was the most important military leader of the uprising.

    A. 1381   B. 1455   C. 1485   D. 1533

21. Two years after the ending of the Hundred Years' War, England was thrown into another series of _____, generally known as the Wars of the Roses.

    A. civil wars   B. foreign expansion

    C. Bourgeoisie Revolution   D. foreign aggression

22. The Tudor Monarchy was founded by Henry VII with the ending of the Wars of Roses. There were _____ Tudor Monarchs in all who ruled England and Wales for just over 100 years.

    A. four   B. five   C. six   D. seven

23. Elizabeth avoided open hostility with Spain but secretly encouraged English _____ to plunder Spanish ships. She prevented England from getting involved in major European conflicts.

    A. Fleet   B. navy   C. ships   D. seadogs

24. _____ of 1688 was also known as the White Revolutionary because it caused no bloodshed. As a matter of fact, it was a palace coup d'etat. It marked the real beginning of constitutional monarchy.

    A. The Glorious Revolution   B. The Bourgeoisie Revolution

    C. Great Revolution   D. Parliamentary Revolution

25. With the development of economic globalization, the Labor Party openly declared to give up socialism in Britain _____, and the struggle over economic policies between the two parties came to an end.

    A. in 1995   B. 1920s   C. 1930s   D. 1940s

26. Of all the light industry, the textile industry used to be the most important. Britain was the world's largest textile industry with more than half of the total spindles of the world in the _____.

    A. 16th century   B. 17th century   C.18th century   D. 19th century

27. The British government and companies all launch _____ training programs to help workers learn new skills.

    A. vocational   B. advanced   C. common   D. free

28. The Act of Union of _____, with untied Scotland with England. The unification of the two countries gave birth to a new name—Great Britain—which has been used to mean the whole island ever since.

    A. 1707   B. 1603   C. 1558   D. 1066

29. _____ kept a diary in which he wrote what he saw and experienced in England. His diary marked the beginning of English recorded history.

A. King Alfred   B. Edward the confessor   C. Julius Caesar   D. Ben Johnson

30. After the Norman Conquest, the English language finally completed the process of changing from "Old English" into _____.

A. new English   B. advanced English   C. Middle English   D. Norman English

II. Select the letter of the answer that best matches each term at left: 10%

(   ) 1. Prince of Wales   a. famous car-maker

(   ) 2. Witan   b. author of the *Wealth of Nations*

(   ) 3. Rolls Royce   c. Scottish textile product

(   ) 4. Adam Smith   d. king or queen

(   ) 5. tweed   e. local tax

(   ) 6. denationalization   f. heir to the English throne

(   ) 7. monarch   g. Chairman of the Upper House

(   ) 8. Thread-needle Street   h. wise men

(   ) 9. Lord Chancellor   i. privatization

(   ) 10. council tax   j. center of financial business

III. Match English version with their Chinese equivalence: 10%

(   ) 1. *Origin of Species*   a. 长期议会

(   ) 2. gunpowder plot   b. 圆头党

(   ) 3. long Parliament   c. 卖官鬻爵

(   ) 4. popular sovereignty   d. 自然选择

(   ) 5. Roundheads   e. 火药阴谋

(   ) 6. Independents   f. 马尔萨斯主义(人口论)

(   ) 7. sale of office   g. 主权在民论，人民主权论

(   ) 8. natural selection   h. 君权神授论

(   ) 9. divine right of kings   i. 《物种起源》

(   ) 10. Malthusianism   j. 独立派(从国教中独立出来)

IV. Translate the following terms: 20%

1. King Arthur _____   2. Stonehenge _____

3. Vikings _____   4. Northern Ireland _____

5. Domesday Book _____   6. loanwords _____

7. Picts _____   8. Group Seven _____

9. Julius Caesar _____   10. invisible trade _____

11. value added tax _____   12. White Hall _____

13. major parties _____   14. general election _____

15. silence right _____

16. Scotland Yard _____

17. majority verdict _____

18. maximum penalty _____

19. independent candidate _____

20. çanvassing _____

V. True (T) or False (F): 10%

_____ 1. The Hundred Years' War continued without interruption for more than 100 years.

_____ 2. The ending of the Wars of the Roses marked the beginning of the Middle Ages.

_____ 3. The Tudor Monarchy was the transitional stage from feudalism to capitalism in English history.

_____ 4. Elizabethan drama rejected humanism and regarded life as a tragedy.

_____ 5. The Celts laid the foundations of the English state.

_____ 6. Roman missionaries held that the Pope's authority was supreme over church affairs.

_____ 7. Old English originated in Normandy.

_____ 8. The Norman cavalry defeated the Anglo-Saxon troop at Hastings.

_____ 9. The Norman Conquest strengthened the cultural connection between the Anglo-Saxons and their relatives in north Europe.

_____ 10. The bi-linguistic period in English history drew to an end by the late 18th century.

VI. Fill in the blanks: 20%

1. Great Britain is composed of three countries which are respectively called England, _____, and _____.

2. The official residence of the British Prime Minister is at _____.

3. The two chambers that make up the British parliament are known as _____ and _____.

4. The monarch summons and dissolves Parliament at the request of the _____.

5. The Norman _____ of 1066 was led by _____ the Conqueror.

6. Politics in Britain is based on a two-party system instead of a multi-party system. The two major parties are respectively called the _____ Party and the _____ Party.

7. The English Civil War between _____ and the _____ broke out in 1642.

8. To beat back the attacks of the parliamentary forces, Charles wrote a letter to the _____ king asking for troops, but the _____ forces intercepted the letter.

9. In 1763, France was forced to sign the _____ and surrendered Canada to Britain.

10. _____, an English Captain, discovered Australia and New Zealand in the 1770s and claimed them for Britain.

Examination on Chapter One (Answer Sheet)

Name_____ **No.**_____

I. Multiple choice: 30%

1	2	3	4	5	6	7	8	9	10

11	12	13	14	15	16	17	18	19	20

21	22	23	24	25	26	27	28	29	30

II. Select the letter of the answer that best matches each term at left: 10%

1	2	3	4	5	6	7	8	9	10

III. Match English version with their Chinese equivalence: 10%

1	2	3	4	5	6	7	8	9	10

IV. Translate the following terms: 20%

1. _____   2. _____
3. _____   4. _____
5. _____   6. _____
7. _____   8. _____
9. _____   10. _____
11. _____   12. _____
13. _____   14. _____
15. _____   16. _____
17. _____   18. _____
19. _____   20. _____

V. True (T) or False (F): 10%

1	2	3	4	5	6	7	8	9	10

VI. Fill in the blanks: 20%

1. _____ _____   2. _____ _____
3. _____ _____   4. _____ _____
5. _____ _____   6. _____ _____
7. _____ _____   8. _____ _____
9. _____   10. _____

CHAPTER TWO

History of America

Unit 1   Ancient Civilization of America

Lead-in: Listening (PPT-21)

Listen to the movie clip *2012 Doomsday* **carefully, and answer the following questions:**

1. What kind of splendid Indian Civilization does the film reflect: Maya Civilization, Toltec Civilization or Aztec Civilization?

2. Contemporary scientists have disputed the apocalyptic versions of Doomday 2012. Do you believe in this religious belief?

Reading

1.1   The Ancient Natives

Some **archaeologists** believe that the forefathers of the Indians were from Asia. More than 27,000 years ago, they say, some hunters crossed the **Bering Strait**, about 50 miles wide, from Asia into America. They were earliest Americans who made a living by hunting animals. Some of the animals that provided food for the early natives still exist today, including **buffalo**, **antelope**, and **jaguar**. To look for more animals, some of the early natives kept going south until they reached the southernmost part of South America about 8,000 years ago. As the large animals they depended on for food became scarce, the natives began to eat plant food and became known as gatherers who made a living by gathering wild food.

1.2　Maya Civilization, Toltec Civilization and Aztec Civilization

The Indian peoples, also known as the first Americans, had developed three great civilizations in North America before the arrival of the European colonists. The **first splendid Indian civilization**, known as the **Maya civilization**, developed both written words and mathematics. It dominated southern Mexico and Central America from the fourth to the tenth centuries. Maya civilization was replaced by **Toltec civilization** in the tenth century. The Toltec influence and culture expanded from central Mexico to the southwestern part of the present-day United States. After the Toltec civilization declined in the middle of the 12th century, the **Aztec civilization prevailed** in this region until the Aztec people were defeated by the Spanish colonists.

1.3　Doomsday 2012

2012 (MMXII) will be a leap year starting on a Sunday. In the **Gregorian calendar**, it will be the 2012th year of the Common Era, or of **Anno Domini**; the 12th year of the 3rd millennium and of the 21st century; and the 3rd of the 2010s decade.

It has been designated Alan Turing Year, commemorating the mathematician, computer pioneer, and code-breaker on the **centennial** of Turing's birth.

There are a variety of popular beliefs about the year 2012. These beliefs range from the spiritually **transformative** to the **apocalyptic**, and center upon various interpretations of the **Mesoamerican** Long Count calendar. Contemporary scientists have disputed the apocalyptic versions.

New Words and Expressions

archaeologist [ˌɑːkiˈɔlədʒist]	*n.* 考古学家
Bering Strait	白令海峡(西伯利亚和阿拉斯加间的海峡)
buffalo [ˈbʌfələu]	*n.* <美>[动]美洲野牛
antelope [ˈæntiləup]	*n.* 羚羊
jaguar [ˈdʒægwɑː]	*n.* 美洲虎；[军]("美洲虎")英、法合作研制的超音速攻击机
Maya [ˈmɑːjə] **Civilization**	玛雅文化
Toltec [ˈtɔltek] **Civilization**	托尔特克文化
Aztec [ˈæztek] **Civilization**	阿兹台克文化

prevail [pri'veil] *vi.* 流行，盛行；获胜，成功

Gregorian calendar [gri'gɔ:riən] *n.* [天文]格里历，阳历

Anno Domini ['ænəu'dɔminai] *adv.* 耶稣纪元后

centennial [sen'tenjəl; -niəl] *n.* 百年纪念

  adj. 一百年的

transformative [træns'fɔ:mətiv] *adj.* 有改革能力的；变化的，变形的

apocalyptic [əpɔkə'liptik] *adj.* 启示录的，天启的

Mesoamerican [,mesəuə'merikə; ,mez-] *n.* [考古]中亚美利加洲，中美洲

For more information, you can check out the following links:

http://archaeology.about.com/od/ancientcivilizations/tp/american_civ.htm

http://cybersleuth-kids.com/sleuth/History/Ancient_Civilizations/Mayans/

http://en.wikipedia.org/wiki/2012

Unit 2 Colonial America (1600—1700)

Lead-in: Listening (PPT-22)

Listen to the passage carefully, and answer the following questions:

1. In 1492, who sponsored Christopher Columbus to find a western route to India?

2. Who made up the majority of the earliest European settlers in North America?

Reading

Settlers were arriving on the North American continent in large numbers. These European peoples shaped the character of future life in the "New World."

1.1　Christopher Columbus

While the Portuguese sailed east, the Spanish sailed west. In 1517, the Portuguese had reached China.

In 1492, Spanish Queen Isabella **sponsored** Christopher Columbus, a navigator from Genoa in Italy, to find a western route to India. When he reached a group of islands across the Atlantic, he called them the West Indies. They were in fact the islands of the **Caribbean**. When he and his crew landed on Guanahani in the **Bahamas**, he claimed it for Spain.

1.2　Earliest European Settlers

The French and Spanish made up the majority of the earliest European settlers in North America, but they were later overtaken by the English and Germans. The majority of them were **protestants** who had suffered religious **persecution** in Europe. Within 20 years of the first Puritans arriving in America there were 20,000 English people living in **Massachusetts**. The colony grew and developed rapidly, with Boston as its capital. Some of these colonists moved to **Rhode Island**

and **Connecticut**.

1.3   Quakers Led by William Penn[1]

In 1625, at the mouth of the Hudson River, New York had begun as
a Dutch colony. When the English took over in 1664, English, German
and a variety of other nationalities settled there. It soon grew into a large
cosmopolitan city of traders and craftspeople. Further down the coast in
1681, in repayment of a debt, the English king gave **Pennsylvania** to a
group of **Quakers led by William Penn**. Penn was a religious idealist
and dreamed of a "holy experiment"—a new society. He assisted poor
people from Europe to settle in the colony. Many English, Scottish, Irish
and German settlers moved there to start a new life.

1.4   Pioneering Settlers

The New America was being built by hard-working, ordinary people rather than distant
European governments.

The experience of the early immigrants also contributed to the distinction of the American
culture. The early immigrants risked their lives to sail across the stormy Atlantic Ocean in small
and poorly-provided ships. Many of them left their families behind because they did not have
enough much money to pay for the passage. When they arrived in North America, they found half
of the landmass covered in dense forests. Everything was different from their home country, and
they had to struggle for survival in a strange wilderness. Their experience of hard labor for survival
contributed to the American **Labor ethics** the **glorified labor**.

1.5   Native People

At first, the Native Americans and European settlers both gained from mixing together—in
some cases **coexisting** peacefully with each other. But as more settlers arrived, native lands were
seized. There were several atrocities, and native distrust of and resistance to the settlers grew. Local
conflicts arose, leading to war in the 1670s. The settlers won, and native resistance declined. Some
native peoples were actively driven from their homelands. As European takeover became certain, a
gradual tide of migrations began.

New Words and Expressions

colonial [kə'ləunjəl]	*adj.*	殖民的，殖民地的
sponsor ['spɔnsə]	*vt.*	发起，主办
	v.	赞助
Caribbean [kæri'bi(:)ən]	*n.*	加勒比海
Bahamas [bə'hɑːməz]	*n.*	巴哈马群岛
protestant ['prɔtistənt]	*n.*	新教；新教徒
persecution [ˌpəːsi'kjuːʃən]	*n.*	迫害，烦扰
Massachusetts [ˌmæsə'tʃuːsits]	*n.*	马萨诸塞州
Rhode Island [rəud'ailənd]	*n.*	(美国)罗得岛州(或译作罗德艾兰州)
Connecticut [kə'netikət]	*n.*	(美国)康涅狄格州
cosmopolitan [ˌkɔzmə'pɔlitən]	*adj.*	世界性的，全球(各地)的
Pennsylvania [pensil'veinjə, -niə]	*n.*	(美国)宾夕法尼亚州
ethics ['eθiks]	*n.*	伦理，道德规范
glorified labor		劳动光荣
coexist [kəuig'zist]	*vi.*	共存

Note

[1] Quakers Led by William Penn：贵格派的一位举足轻重的人物是威廉·潘(William Penn)。他是英国海军中将之子，因为加入贵格派被父亲从家里赶出来，然后四处宣教，并跟福克斯会合。后来他父亲去世，英国王室欠他父亲很多钱，所以以一片美洲的土地来偿还。于是潘从传教士摇身一变成为了一片土地的君王，他用自己的姓氏给这片土地命名为Pennsylvania。他带领很多信徒一起来到宾夕法尼亚，施行开明的政策，在那片土地上禁止宗教迫害，推行信仰自由和平等。

For more information, you can check out the following links:

http://en.wikipedia.org/wiki/Colonial_history_of_the_United_States

http://en.citizendium.org/wiki/Colonial_America

Unit 3 The Founding of the USA (1763—1789)

Lead-in: Listening (PPT-23)

Listen to the song "Yankee Doodle[1]" carefully, and answer the following questions:

1. Who does "Yankee Doodle" refer to?

_____

2. What's the background of the song?

_____

Reading

People in the thirteen colonies in America were dissatisfied with British rule. They fought for their independence, and a new nation was born.

1.1 The Declaration of Independence

The British wanted to govern the old French territories and collect higher taxes to pay for soldiers to defend these newly won lands. They raised taxes **levied** in the thirteen colonies. Local colonial **assemblies** argued that it was unfair for Britain to tax the American colonies, since they had no say in running the British government. They said "taxation without representation is **tyranny**". The colonies banned all British imports, and on July 4, 1776, representatives from all colonies adopted **the Declaration of Independence**, claiming the right to rule themselves.

1.2 Independence

Guided by the ideas of **Thomas Jefferson**, and influenced by the **Enlightenment**, the American Declaration of Independence stated in 1776: **"We hold these truths to be self-evident, that all men are created equal, that they are endowed by their Creator with certain inalienable rights, that among these are Life, Liberty and pursuit of happiness."[2]**

In 1775, Ethan Allen and a band of 83 men attacked the British garrison at Fort Ticonderoga. This was one of the first military actions in the American Revolutionary War.

The American Revolutionary War had begun in 1775. At first the British were successful, despite the problems of fighting nearly 5,000 kilometers from home. But the Americans had an advantage because they were fighting on home territory, and they believed in their cause. Six years after the conflict began, the British army surrendered at Yorktown, Virginia in 1781, having been defeated by George Washington's troops. Britain eventually recognized American independence in the Treaty of Paris, 1783.

In 1775, Ethan Allen and a band of 83 men attacked the British garrison at Fort Ticonderoga. This was one of the first military actions in the American Revolutionary War.

1.3　The Statue of Liberty

The *Statue of Liberty* is one of the most recognized symbols of **American freedom** anywhere. Standing tall on Liberty Island in the middle the of the Hudson River in New York City Harbor, the Statue of Liberty was given to the US by the French in 1886. The French gave the Statue of Liberty, or Statue de la Liberté, to the United States as a token of friendship.

The statue depicts Lady Liberty standing tall with the torch of freedom raised with her right arm. Her left hand holds a stone tablet close to her. The tablet contains the date July 4, 1776, which acknowledges and **commemorates the American Declaration of Independence**.

The Statue of Liberty is 151 feet tall and is made from pure copper on a steel framework. Lady Liberty's **thorny** crown has seven points representing the seven seas. The torch represents a burning passion for freedom and contains a flame that is coated in gold leaf. The broken **shackles** at the base of Lady Liberty's feet represent freedom from oppression.

1.4　The US Constitution

In 1783, after signing the peace treaty with the British, the people of the new United States of America had to decide on the best way to run their country. They decided to have a president, elected every four years. He would rule with the help of a **Congress** (divided into a **House of Representatives** and a **Senate** made up of representatives from the States), and a **Supreme Court**. The draft Constitution (set of legal rules) for the new government contained three important statements about the American nation.

First, it was to be a union. The colonists who had fought against the British would stay together to govern their own country. Second, each of the states would hold their own assembly, and run a state government as they liked. Third, neither the president, the Congress, nor the

Supreme Court would ever be allowed to control the central government of America on their own. A system of checks and balances would make sure that the power was shared among these three areas of government.

These were new ideas influenced by the Enlightenment, and never tried out before. The revolutionary Constitution became law in 1789. This new nation, with its short history and its people with many bad memories from their own past, was the world's first proper democratic republic, ruled according to collectively agreed laws. Only 150 years later, it was to become the world's leading nation.

New Words and Expressions

levy ['levi]	*v.* 征收，征集，征用
assembly [ə'sembli]	*n.* 集合，集会
tyranny ['tirəni]	*n.* 暴政，苛政，专治
the Declaration of Independence	《独立宣言》
Thomas Jefferson ['dʒefəsn]	托马斯·杰斐逊(1743—1826，美国政治家，第三任总统，《独立宣言》的起草人)
Enlightenment [in'laitnmənt]	*n.* 启蒙运动
the Statue of Liberty	自由女神像
commemorate [kə'meməreit]	*vt.* 纪念
thorny ['θɔːni]	*adj.* 多刺的，痛苦的
shackle ['ʃækl]	*n.* 手铐，脚镣；桎梏，束缚物
constitution [ˌkɔnsti'tjuːʃən]	*n.* 宪法，国体，章程
Congress ['kɔŋgres]	*n.* (美国等国的)国会，议会
House of Representatives	*n.* (美国、新西兰、澳大利亚等国的)众议院
Senate ['senit]	*n.* 参议院，上院
Supreme Court	最高法院

Notes

[1] Yankee Doodle：《扬基歌》。早在美国革命以前，在这些英国殖民地上《扬基歌》的曲调和歌词的某些段落就已经很流行。甚至在 18 世纪 70 年代以前，英军就曾唱《扬基歌》来嘲笑殖民者。歌词的早期版本是嘲笑这些殖民地居民的勇气以及他们粗俗的衣着和举止。"扬基"是对新英格兰土包子的轻蔑之词，而"嘟得儿"的意思即蠢货或傻瓜。然而，在美国革命期间，美军却采用《扬基歌》作为他们自己的歌，以表明他们对自己朴素、家纺的衣着和毫不矫揉造作的举止感到自豪。多年来，这首歌一直被当作非正式的国歌，广受欢迎。

[2] "We hold these truths to be self-evident, that all men are created equal, that they are endowed by their Creator with certain inalienable rights, that among these are Life, Liberty and pursuit of happiness."

译文："我们认为下述真理是不言而喻的：人人生而平等，造物主赋予他们若干不可让与的权利，其中包括生存权、自由权和追求幸福的权利。"

For more information, you can check out the following links:

http://www.statueliberty.net/

http://www.tsl.state.tx.us/exhibits/forever/freedom/page3.html

Unit 4 The End of Slavery (1792—1888)

Lead-in: Listening (PPT-24)

Listen to the song "Old Man River" carefully, and answer the following questions:

1. What river does "Old Man River" refer to?

2. What mood can we feel from listening to the song, and what kind of sad life can you imagine about the black slaves?

Listen to "I have a dream" by Martin Luther King, and answer the following questions:

1. When was the *Emancipation Proclamation* signed?

2. Who signed this famous *Emancipation Proclamation* in order to give freedom to black slaves?

Reading

The European colonies in America depended heavily on slave labor. But in the mid-18th century many people were questioning the morality of this.

1.1 Slave Trade

Throughout the 18th century, Britain, France and Spain grew rich on taxes and profits from their colonies. Much of this wealth was created by slave labor. Denmark, Sweden, Prussia, Holland also traded in slaves. Africans were sold to Europeans by slave dealers and local rulers, who saw slave-trading as a means of punishing criminals, getting rid of enemies, disposing of captives and getting rich. Nobody knows how many slaves were sold in all, but historians have estimated that 45 million slaves were shipped from Africa between 1450 and 1870, although only 15 million survived.

1.2　Ending the Slave Trade

Between 1777 and 1804, slavery was made illegal in the northern United States. But slave **smuggling** continued. The British navy clamped down on slave-trading from 1815 onwards, but slavery itself was still legal elsewhere.

1.3　Slavery Was Banned in the USA in 1863

In the USA, northerners supported emancipation while southerners wanted to keep their slaves. In 1831 slave **revolt** in Virginia led to harsh laws to control slaves in the southern states. Slavery was finally banned in the USA in 1863, in Cuba in 1886 and in Brazil in 1888. The Arabic slave trade in Africa ended in 1873.

1.4　Lincoln's Emancipation Proclamation

In a June 1858 speech Lincoln had stated, "A house divided against itself cannot stand. I believe this government cannot endure permanently half slave and half free. I do not expect the Union to be dissolved. I do not expect the house to fall, but I do expect it will cease to be divided."

In 1865, Lincoln declared that the Civil war was over and that **Lincoln's Emancipation Proclamation** was in effect. All slaves were free.

New Words and Expressions

smuggle ['smʌgl]　　　　　　　　　*v.* 走私
revolt [ri'vəult]　　　　　　　　　*v.* 反抗，起义
Lincoln's Emancipation Proclamation　林肯的《解放黑奴宣言》

For more information, you can check out the following links:

http://www.answers.com/topic/emancipation-proclamation
http://en.wikipedia.org/wiki/Ol'_Man_River

Unit 5   American Civil War (1861—1865)

Lead-in: Listening (PPT-25)

Listen to "Abraham Lincoln's Gettysburg Address" carefully, and answer the following questions:

1. Why was the battle of Gettysburg a turning point in the Civil War?

2. When did Abraham Lincoln make the Gettysburg Address?

Reading

Around the middle of 19th century, the United States was a divided country, and the largest division was between the north and the south.

1.1   Conflicts between the North and the South

In the United States around 1850, the north had nearly all of the trade, industry, railways and cities while the south was a land of farms, especially cotton and tobacco plantations, that relied on slave labour. However, slavery was banned in the north.

Abraham Lincoln (1809—1865) was elected President of the USA in 1860. He belonged to the Republican Party, which opposed slavery, although he was not an abolitionist himself. Many southern states refused to live under such a government, and led by Jefferson Davis (1808—1889), they announced in December, 1860 that they were seceding from (leaving) the Union and forming the Confederate States of America. The United States government declared that they had no right to do this.

1.2   The Battle of Gettysburg

The battle of Gettysburg (July 1—3, 1863) was a turning point in the Civil War. The battle was the bloodiest ever fought on American soil, but was an important Union victory by General George

Meade, who stopped an invasion of the south by General Robert E Lee's confederate army. From this point onwards, the south's chances of winning the war declined.

1.3   The Gettysburg Address

In November 1863, President Abraham Lincoln was invited to make a "few appropriate remarks" at the dedication of a national ceremony at Gettysburg. His speech lasted about two minutes and is today regarded as a masterpiece. Abraham Lincoln summed up the central issue of the war-the survival of a nation dedicated to freedom.

1.4   The End of the Civil War

In 1864, in spite of Lee's skilful tactics General Grant captured Richmond, the capital of the south. General Sherman marched through Georgia and the other southern states, capturing Atlanta. He followed this victory with a "march to the sea," during which he destroyed towns and farms. Short of men, money, weapons and food, Lee surrendered on April 9, 1865, ending the civil war. More than 600,000 soldiers had died, many from diseases such as typhoid. Five days later, Abraham Lincoln was assassinated in Washington.

1.5   Ku Klux Klan and Terrorism

The people of the south resisted most of the aspects of the Reconstruction. Many ex-slaves who had fought on the Union side returned home expecting more freedom in the south. However, the **Ku Klux Klan** and other racist organizations began a campaign of murder and terrorism in 1866 with the aim of stopping black Americans gaining civil rights. Northern troops withdrew, Reconstruction ended and the Democrats took over the south.

New Words and Expressions

the Gettysburg Address	葛底斯堡演讲
Ku Klux Klan	(美国的)三 K 党

For more information, you can check out the following links:

http://www.newworldencyclopedia.org/entry/Gettysburg_Address

http://en.wikipedia.org/wiki/Ku_Klux_Klan

http://www.wwenglish.com/en/voa/spec/2005/04/200504215427.htm

Unit 6 USA: the Plains Wars (1849—1913)

Lead-in: Listening (PPT-26)

Listen to the song "Oh, Susanna"[1] carefully, and do the following exercises:

1. What's the background of the song "Oh, Susana"?

_____

2. Do you know anything more about the "American Westward Movement"?

_____

Reading

The wide-open plains of the American Midwest, that had once seemed vast and endless. In the 1800s, they became the scene of a struggle for land ownership.

1.1 Native American Way of Life Began to Change

Many groups of Native Americans lived on the **Great Plains** of the American west and had done so for thousands of years. This vast area stretched from the **Mississippi River** in the east to the **Rocky Mountains** in the west, and from Canada in the north to Texas in the south. Until the 17th century, many Plains tribes were farmers. They grew maize, beans and other foods, but they also hunted buffalo on foot using bows and arrows. Their way of life on the plains began to change during the 17th century when the **Spanish introduced the horse**.

With horses, the Native Americans could follow the buffalo with ease. The buffalo not only provided them with meat, but also with tools and weapons fashioned from the animals' bones, and tepees and clothing made with the skins. Some of the larger groups of Native Americans became known as the "Plain nations". Early white settlers forced some groups to move west from their original homelands east of the Mississippi River.

1.2 Settlers Move West

The government encouraged people to migrate westward. Under the **Homestead Act of**

1862[2], a family could have 65 hectares for a small fee, provided they did not sell the land for five years. More land was given to those who made improvements by drilling wells or planting trees. The Act encouraged farmers to move into and settle on the Great Plains.

The government also encouraged the building of railways, which carried people into unsettled regions. It gave land to the railways so generously that many lines were built simply to obtain land. By 1869, the Union Pacific Railroad was completed, joining America from coast to coast.

1.3   Struggle for Survival

The opening of the railways soon changed the face of America. They brought even more settlers to the traditional homelands of the Native Americans. The two different kinds of society came into conflict. When local Native American chiefs signed land agreements with the settlers they meant different things to the two sides. The settlers' idea of private property meant nothing to the Native Americans who thought they could still use the land for hunting. A struggle for survival began. Many Native Americans bought guns and attacked settlers' homesteads, their wagon trains, the railways and the US **cavalry**.

Starting in 1866, a series of wars took place. The US president Rutherford B. Hayes stated in 1877, "Many, if not most, of our Indian wars had their origin in broken promises and acts of injustice." Killing the buffalo, on which the Plains nations depended for food, was enough to destroy the Native Americans. There were about 15 million buffalo in 1860, but by 1885, only 2,000 were left. The survivors of the Plains nations were forced onto reservations, often with poor land on which they were expected to grow crops.

1.4   Slaughter of Native Americans

The Native Americans were used to hunting and did not want to farm. They were not allowed to become American citizens and had few civil rights. Fierce battles with soldiers resulted in the deaths of thousands of the Native American groups. The last battle was at Wounded Knee in South Dakota in 1890, when soldiers slaughtered 200 Sioux. Soon, all the groups were moved onto the reservations and the Native American way of life was finished for ever.

In the 1830s, the **Chickasaw tribe** was forced to move to a **reservation** in **Oklahoma** where they were told that the land was theirs "as long as the grass grows and the waters run." But the central and western parts were thinly populated and sought after by white settlers. In 1906, the Chickasaw rose up to stop their land from being taken, but were **suppressed** by the United States Cavalry.

New Words and Expressions

plain [pleɪn]	n. 平原，草原
Mississippi [ˌmisiˈsipi] **River**	密西西比河(发源于美国中北部湖沼区，南注墨西哥湾，是世界上最大的河流之一)
Rocky Mountains	落基山脉
cavalry [ˈkævəlri]	n. 骑兵
slaughter [ˈslɔːtə]	n. 屠宰，残杀，屠杀
Chickasaw [ˈtʃikəˌsɔː] **tribe**	契卡索人(美国马斯科吉印第安人一个部落成员，过去住在密西西比州北部和田纳西州的部分地区，现在住在俄克拉荷马州)
reservation [ˌrezəˈveiʃən]	n. (印第安人的)保留地
Oklahoma [ˌəukləˈhəumə]	n. 俄克拉荷马州
suppress [səˈpres]	vt. 镇压，抑制，查禁

Notes

[1] Oh! Susanna：由斯蒂芬·福斯特自撰歌词的《噢，苏珊娜》于 1847 年在匹兹堡的"雄鹰沙龙"上首次演出后，便逐渐风靡全美。翌年美国西部发现金矿后，大批的淘金者就是唱着这支生动、活泼的歌直奔加利福尼亚的。这支歌成了美国西部开发时期的一首代表性的具有时代特征的民歌。

[2] Homestead Act of 1862：1862 年《宅地法》体现了无偿分配西部国有土地的原则，对于加速美国西部开发，促进美国农业资本主义道路的发展，具有深远的意义。

For more information, you can check out the following links:

http://wiki.answers.com/Q/When_did_the_settlers_move_west

http://www.britannica.com/EBchecked/topic/462761/Plains-Indian/260989/The-Plains-Wars

http://wiki.jxwmw.cn/index.php?doc-view-132222

http://en.wikipedia.org/wiki/Oh!_Susanna

Unit 7   Further Immigration to America

Lead-in: Listening (PPT-27)

Listen to the passage carefully, and answer the following questions:

1. Why is the United States of America called the Melting Pot or Mosaic?

_____

2. To prevent undesirable people from immigrating into America, the US government set up a special port of entry on Ellis Island in New York harbor in 1892. Do you think it has positive influence on American history?

_____

Reading

The United States is a nation created by immigrants, and immigrants continue to affect American society significantly today.

1.1   Ellis Island

To prevent undesirable people from immigrating into America, the US government set up a special port of entry on **Ellis Island** in New York harbor in 1892, **barring** undesirable people such as prostitutes, convicts, the mentally **retarded**, beggars and revolutionaries who advocated the overthrow of government through violence. By the time the port was closed in 1954, it had received more than 20 million immigrants.

The possibility of making their fortune attracted people of many nationalities to the American gold fields. Thousands of Chinese people traveled to **California** in the 1850s and the 1870s to work as laborers.

1.2   Melting Pot or Mosaic

As a nation of immigrants, the US population was characterized by multiplicity. For many years in history, the United States was likened to a "**melting pot**." It meant that as immigrants from different regions and cultures came to live in the United States, their old ways of life melt away, and they became part of the American culture.

The traditional concept of "melting pot" was challenged after the 1960s. Today some people compare America to a **mosaic** because many new immigrants refuse to give up their cultural distinctiveness. Often groups of people from the same culture live together in their own communities, such as **Chinatowns** in a number of cities and Little Cuba in Florida. There are also areas almost exclusively populated by other ethnic groups, such as Korean immigrants and Mexican immigrants. As a result, America is compared to a picture of many distinctive colors, and these colors do not fully mix with each other.

In the photo, we can see two American children in Chinatown are in the traditional Chinese costumes with the dragon and phoenix designs.

New Words and Expressions

barring ['bɑːriŋ]	*prep.* 不包括，除非
retarded [ri'tɑːdid]	*adj.* 智力迟钝的，发展迟缓的
Melting Pot	大熔炉
mosaic	*n.* 镶嵌，镶嵌图案(这里指美国的多元文化)
Chinatown ['tʃainətaun]	*n.* <美>唐人街

Note

[1] Ellis Island: 爱丽斯岛，亦译作埃利斯岛。美国纽约湾的一个岛，在 1892 年至 1954 年的 60 多年移民潮期间，曾有超过 1 千 2 百万的移民抵达此地，在尖峰期间，每天均有 5000 人在这个移民大厅等待移民官的询问和检疫。如今，爱丽斯岛在经过整建工程之后，已成为令人注目与动容的移民博物馆。遥想当年满怀希望寻找自由与机会的移民群，一旦未通过身体健康检疫，就得面临被遣返回国的悲惨命运，使得爱丽斯岛对移民而言，是仅有一线之隔的"希望之岛"与"眼泪之岛"。

For more information, you can check out the following links:

http://en.wikipedia.org/wiki/Ellis_Island
http://en.wikipedia.org/wiki/Melting_pot

Unit 8　The Great Depression (1929—1939)

🎧 Lead-in: Listening (PPT-28)

Have you seen a classical American film *Waterloo Bridge* (《魂断蓝桥》). The film depicts the sufferings of people during the World War I and Great Depression years. "Auld Lang Syne" is the theme song of the film.

Listen to the song "Auld Lang Syne" carefully, and answer the following questions:

1. What's the song's background?

2. How do you understand the following sentence "The causes of the Great Depression can be traced back to the end of **World War I**"?

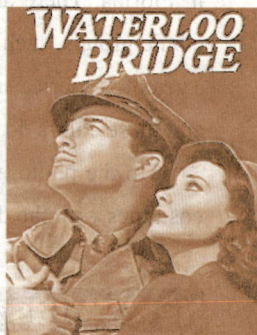

📖 Reading

After World War I, the economy of the USA saw rapid growth. The **Wall Street Crash** of 1929 brought an abrupt end to this and led to worldwide depression.

1.1　The Cause of the Great Depression

The causes of the Great Depression can be traced back to the end of **World War I**. In 1919, the treaty of Versailles forced Germany to pay huge compensation to the victorious Allies. Many Germans lost all their savings as the value of money collapsed. In Britain, France and the United States, industry struggled to adjust to peacetime trade. Millions of soldiers came home and looked for jobs. Trade unions called workers to strike against employers who demanded wage cuts. The first ever General Strike in Britain happened in 1926. Food prices fell so low that many farmers were ruined and gave up their land.

During the 1920s, the rapid growth of the American economy was partly due to the repayment of several billion dollars of war loans made by London to New York. The growth was also encouraged by the economic policies of presidents Harding and Coolidge. The price of shares in the USA had been forced up beyond their real value by reckless speculators.

1.2   The Wall Street Crash

In October 1929, people began to panic and sell their shares rapidly. On a single day, 13 million shares were sold on the New York Stock Exchange. This started an economic crisis known as the Wall Street Crash (named after New York's financial district) which soon affected the whole world.

Many people lost all their money. Banks and business closed and unemployment began to increase. By 1933, the worst year of the Depression, there were 12 million people unemployed in the USA alone. Those who were still in work saw their salaries halved and more than 85,000 business failed.

The situation in the United States was made worst by a **drought** in the agricultural centre of the country. The soil turned to dust in many places and blew away in the wind, leading to crop failure. Thousands of farmers and their families were forced to leave their land to start a new life on the west coast.

1.3   Roosevelt's New Deal

For the first two years of the Depression, the United States government and President Hoover took little direct action, believing that the economy would recover naturally. Franklin D. Roosevelt was elected President in 1932 and in 1933 he introduced the New Deal to combat the problems caused by the Depression. This was a set of laws designed mainly to ease the worst of the property, provide support for the banks and protect people's savings. Farms prices were supported, a minimum wage was introduced and huge programme of construction was begun to create employment. The New Deal helped considerably, but it was not until 1939, when the outbreak of World War II gave an enormous boost to heavy industry, that the Depression came to an end.

New Words and Expressions

the Great Depression [di'preʃən]	经济大萧条
Wall Street Crash	华尔街风暴
drought [draut]	*n.* 干旱，缺乏
Roosevelt's New Deal	罗斯福新政
President Hoover ['huːvə]	(美国)胡佛总统

For more information, you can check out the following links:

http://en.wikipedia.org/wiki/Great_Depression_in_the_United_States

http://en.wikipedia.org/wiki/New_Deal

Unit 9   The United Nations (1945—1948)

Lead-in: Listening (PPT-29)

Listen to the passage carefully, and answer the following questions:

1. When was the United Nations established?

2. What's the purpose of the United Nations?

Reading

At the end of World War II, the victorious **Allied powers** divided Germany into four zones. The United Nations was established to **keep international peace**.

1.1   Aim of the United Nations

On **April 25, 1945**, the UN organization was set up formally at a conference in San Francisco. It aimed to keep international peace and solve problems by international cooperation.

1.2   Universal Declaration of Human Rights

The term "United Nations" (UN) was first used in **January 1942** when the Atlantic Charter was signed by the Allies. In the charter, they agreed to fight the Axis countries and not to make any separate peace agreements. The UN planned to be stronger than the League of Nations had been. It had a powerful security council which would decide what should be done if disputes broke out. Members were to contribute arms and personnel to peacemaking missions organized by the UN. In 1948, the UN issued a **Universal Declaration of Human Rights** which was not binding.

1.3   UNDP (United Nations Development Programme)

New York, 19 February 2010—More than a month after the **Haiti earthquake**, Haitians are working diligently to rebuild their country and be better prepared for the hurricane season starting in June. To support them with this effort, the United Nations Development Programme (UNDP) has asked for $103.9 million under the recently-launched revised UN Humanitarian Appeal for $1.4 billion. The primary focus is to jump starting the local economy and **rehabilitate** essential social **infrastructure**. Much more money is needed to help Haitians rebuild their lives.

New Words and Expressions

allied powers	同盟国
Universal Declaration of Human Rights	1948 年联合国颁发的《世界人权宣言》
UNDP	联合国开发计划署
Haiti earthquake	海地地震
rehabilitate [ˌriː(h)əˈbiliteit]	v. 使(身体)康复，使恢复，使复原
infrastructure [ˈinfrəˈstrʌktʃə]	n. 基础设施，下部构造，基础下部组织

For more information, you can check out the following link:

http://en.wikipedia.org/wiki/United_Nations

Unit 10 The End of the Cold War (1945—1989)

Lead-in: Listening (PPT-30)

Listen to the song "The answer is blowing in the wind" carefully, and answer the following questions:

1. During the Cold War, American government started the war against Vietnam, and American people suffered greatly, how do you describe the feeling of the "Lost Generation" after the war?

2. How do you explain the theme of the song "The answer is blowing in the wind"?

Reading

At the end of World War II, **tensions** between East and West and the build-up of nuclear weapons almost brought the world to the **brink** of a third world war.

1.1 Competition between USSR and USA

The USSR and the USA fought together as allies against Germany and Japan in World War II, but in 1945, these two great countries, known as superpowers, became rivals and then enemies. This division became known as the Cold War, a war conducted in the main without fighting. The USA and USSR "fought" by making threats and by strengthening their armed forces.

Both countries built up an enormous **stockpile** of nuclear weapons. Peaceful, friendly contacts between the peoples ceased. The USSR became completely shut off from the rest of the world by Soviet troops. The British statesman **Sir Winston Churchill** memorably described the frontier between East and West as an "**iron curtain**" in a speech that he gave in Missouri, USA, on March 5, 1946.

The Cold War dominated world politics for many years. On one side, the United States became the leader of **NATO** (North Atlantic Treaty Organization), a military alliance of Western nations ranged against the communist powers. On the other side, the USSR dominated the **Warsaw Pact**, a military alliance of East European states that backed communism.

1.2   Shanghai Communiqué in 1972 and President Nixon's Foreign Policies

President Nixon[1] who succeeded Johnson as president pursued a policy known as "**Vietnamization**", which meant gradually replacing American soldiers with South Vietnamese troops. Nixon's foreign policy was based on a new doctrine known as "détente"—a policy to reduce confrontation with socialist countries. To carry out his **détente policy**, Nixon tried to improve relations with socialist countries such as China and the Soviet Union, supporters of North Vietnam. In **1972**, President Nixon made a historic trip to China and signed the **Shanghai Communiqué** with Chinese Premier **Zhou Enlai**, a step that eventually led to formal diplomatic relations. In 1973, the Nixon administration signed the peace treaty with North Vietnam. With ending of war, universities students began rejecting radical movements and became more oriented toward individual careers. This finally led to the appearance of the yuppie generation composed of successful and prosperous baby-boomers.

1.3   The Berlin Wall Finally Fell in November 1989

In 1945, the USA, France and Britain took control of West Germany and the USSR controlled the East Germany. The capital, Berlin, inside East Germany, was also divided, and in 1948, the Soviets closed all access to West Berlin. The Western Powers brought in essential supplies by air until the Russians lifted the blockade in May 1949. From 1949 to 1958, three million people escaped from East to West Berlin. In 1961, East Germany closed off this escape route by building the Berlin Wall through the centre of the city. It crossed tramlines and roads, and created an area on either side known as no man's land.

The Berlin Wall, built in 1961 to divide east and West Berlin, finally fell in November 1989.

1.4   Cuban Missile Crisis

Although the USA and USSR never actually fought, they came close to it. The world held its breath for a whole week in October 1962 when the US president, **John F. Kennedy**, received air force photographs showing that the USSR was building the missile launch sites in Cuba. From there, the nuclear missiles could reach and destroy many US cities. On October 22, the president ordered a naval blockade of Cuba. The United States made plans to invade Cuba, and the world braced itself for nuclear war. Finally, on October 28, **Nikita Khrushchev**, the Soviet leader, backed down and agreed to remove the missiles and destroy the Cuban launch sites. The crisis was over.

1.5   The End of the Cold War

In the 1980s, the friendly relationship between US president Ronald Reagan and the Soviet leader **Mikhail Gorbachev** helped to reduce Cold War tensions, and by 1897, they had agreed to abolish medium-range nuclear missiles. In 1989, Gorbachev allowed the communist countries of Eastern Europe to elect democratic governments, and in 1991, the USSR broke up into 15 republics. The Cold War was over. On March 12, 1999, Hungary, Poland and the Czech Republic joined NATO. The Joining ceremony was held at the Harry S. Truman memorial library in Independence, Missouri, in the United States.

New Words and Expressions

tension ['tenʃən]   *n.* 紧张(状态)，不安

brink [briŋk]   *n.* (峭岸、崖的)边缘

stockpile ['stɔkpail]   *n.* 积蓄，库存

iron curtain   丘吉尔的"铁幕"演讲

Warsaw Pact   《华沙条约》

Shanghai Communiqué   中美联合发表的《上海公报》

Vietnamization [ˌvjetnəmaiˈzeiʃən, ˌviːte-, viˌet-; -miˈz-]

                                                             n. (越南战争时美国政府的)战争越南化(政策)

détente policy   冷战的缓和政策

Cuban Missile Crisis   古巴导弹危机

Nikita Khrushchev [kruʃˈtʃɔːf]   赫鲁晓夫(前苏共第一书记)

Mikhail Gorbachev   戈尔巴乔夫(前苏联国家领导人)

Note

[1] President Nixon：1972 年 2 月 21 日 11 时 30 分，首次访华的美国总统尼克松还没完全走到舷梯下面，尼克松就远远地朝周恩来伸过双手，刚下飞机，就与前来迎接的周恩来握手相贺，这个跨越了最辽阔海洋的握手震撼了世界，标志着一个时代过去了，另一个新的时代开始了。尼克松访问中国 7 天，美国电视对尼克松的中国之行，作了全程的卫星

直播，全世界首次以这种方式见识了新中国。

1972 年 2 月 28 日，中美双方经过反复磋商，终于在上海发表了《联合公报》，尼克松将自己访华一周称为"改变世界的一周"，中美两大国在当时的世界格局中，各自转了一个 180 度的大弯来之不易，对于冷战中的世界是巨大的冲击，特别是前苏联直接感受到了这一冲击的力度。

For more information, you can check out the following links:

http://www.history.com/topics/cold-war

http://www.history.com/topics/cold-war/videos#10-hottest-moments-of-cold-war-10

Unit 11　Space Exploration (1957—2000)

Lead-in: Listening (PPT-31)

Listen to the national anthem of the United States "The Star-Spangled Banner" carefully, and fill in the blanks. It was a well-known American patriotic song in history, and now is the first part of the well-known national anthem.

The Star Spangled Banner

oh, say can you see, by the dawn's early ___1___,

what so proudly we hailed at the twilight's last ___2___?

whose broad stripes and bright stars, through the perilous fight,

o'er the ramparts we ___3___, were so gallantly streaming?

and the rockets' red glare, the bombs bursting in air,

gave proof through the night that our flag was still there.

o say, does that star-spangled banner yet wave o'er the land of

the ___4___ and the home of the brave?

on the shore, dimly seen through the mists of the deep, where the foe's haughty host in dread silence reposes, what is that which the ___5___, o'er the towering steep, as it fitfully blows, half conceals, half discloses?

now it catches the gleam of the morning's first beam, in full glory reflected now shines on the ___6___: 'tis the star-spangled banner! o long may it wave o'er the land of the free and the ___7___ of the brave.

Reading

Space exploration began in 1957 when the USSR launched **Sputnik I**, the first artificial satellite to orbit the Earth. In 1969, the first man walked on the moon.

1.1　Space Competition between the Two Superpowers

The development of technology during World War II helped scientists to realize that one day it might be possible for people to travel in space. Cold War **rivalry** between the USA and the USSR

triggered a space race. Both sides felt that being the first nation in space would increase their **prestige**. They also hoped that space science would help them develop new, more powerful weapons.

The Soviets achieved the first "space first" when they sent a satellite into orbit around the Earth in 1957. Soon, both sides were investing enormous amounts of time and money in space science. The Soviets achieved another space first in 1961 when Yuri Gagarin became the first man in space. Other notable achievements by both countries included **probes** being sent to the Moon and past Venus, further manned flights, spacewalks and the launch of communications satellites.

The Apollo programme of space flights enabled the USA to land men on the Moon. Between July 1969 and December 1972, the USA successfully carried out six of these missions, the last three involving the use of a Lunar Roving Vehicle.

1.2   Man on the Moon

In 1961, the United States president, John F. Kennedy, said that his scientists would send a man to the Moon by 1970. In fact, the first manned Moon landing took place on July 20, 1969 with the American Apollo 11 mission. The crew consisted of **Neil Armstrong, the first man to set foot on the Moon**, Edwin "Buzz" Aldrin, who was the second man to walk on the Moon, and Michael Collins who remained in lunar orbit in the command and service module. Armstrong described walking on the Moon as "One small step for a man, one giant leap for mankind.

1.3   Aim of an International Space Station

The ending of the Cold War and the economic crisis of the 1970s led the two superpowers to scale down their space programme. However, the Soviets gained valuable experience with long-endurance flights on permanent space stations. Cooperation between the two countries is important for the future construction of an international space station.

1.4   Space Shuttles

In the USA, the National Aeronautics and Space Administration (NASA) required a reusable space vehicle to construct and serve planned space stations. The space shuttle could take off like a rocket—with a large payload—and return to Earth like a plane. The launch of the first shuttle in 1981 marked a new phase in space exploration. Since that first flight, space shuttles have carried a variety of payloads and retrieved and repaired satellites. In 1995, the space shuttle Atlantis docked with the Russian space station Mir, marking an important step forward in international cooperation.

1.5　Exploring Deep Space

Unmanned space probes have flown by, or landed on, every planet in the solar system except Pluto. Soviet probes succeeded in landing on Venus in 1975 and sent back pictures. In 1976, two US Viking craft landed on Mars and began observations that lasted for six years. In 1977, the US launched the two Voyager missions which traveled round the solar system using the "slingshot" technique—the spacecraft being flung from planet to planet by their gravitational fields. Before they disappeared into deep space, they transmitted valuable data and color photographs of Jupiter, Saturn, Uranus and Neptune.

The Hubble space telescope, launched by the US in 1990, enabled scientists to produce high-resolution images of objects billions of light years way, and provide valuable information about the Universe.

New Words and Expressions

Sputnik ['spʌtnik] **I**	n. (苏联)人造地球卫星一号
rivalry ['raivəlri]	n. 竞争，竞赛；敌对，敌对状态
trigger ['trigə]	vt. 引发，引起，触发
prestige [pres'tiːʒ; -'tiːdʒ]	n. 声望，威望，威信
Neil Armstrong ['ɑːmstrɒŋ]	尼尔·阿姆斯特朗(美国宇航员，1969 年 7 月登陆月球，成为第一个登上月球的地球人)
NASA ['næsə]	abbr. National Aeronautics and Space Administration (美国)国家航空和航天局

For more information, you can check out the following link:

http://en.wikipedia.org/wiki/The_Star-Spangled_Banner

Unit 12   America and Wars in the Middle East

Lead-in: Listening (PPT-32)

Listen to the passage carefully, and answer the following questions:

1. When did Iraq invade Kuwait in order to improve its sea access?

_____

2. Which side won the battle at last, Iraq or the Multinational Force?

_____

Reading

1.1   Cause of the War

Rivalries within the Arab world have often been caused by the region's **oil deposits**. In 1990, **Iraq** invaded **Kuwait** in order to improve its sea access. The UN Security council passed several resolutions that demanded that Iraq immediately withdraw its troops. When **Saddam Hussein** refused, a **multinational force** led by the Americans forced him to withdraw. Kuwait City was liberated within the first five days and thousands of Iraqi soldiers were captured. Retreating Iraqi forces caused huge ecological damage because they **set fire to** most of Kuwait's oil wells.

More than 600 Kuwaiti oil wells were set on fire by the Iraqi forces causing massive environmental and economic damage to Kuwait.

Other tensions in the region are caused by religious differences. There are two main forms of Islam, Sunni and Shiite. Sunnis follow "the practice of the Prophet". Shiites follow the teachings of the Prophet Muhammad's son-in-law, Ali.

1.2   Saddam Hussein and the Multinational Force

Saddam Hussein (b.1937) is the leader of Iraq. He fought a costly war against Iran (1980—1988) and invaded Kuwait in August 1990. **US, Britain** and other Middle East forces drove him out in February 1991.

The US forces mounted a massive international military campaign to liberate their ally Kuwait when Iraq invaded in 1990. Preparation for the war was extensive but the actual fighting was fairly short-lived.

1.3 Saddam Was Hanged in on 30 Dec. 2006

"The president, the leader Saddam Hussein is a martyr and God will put him along with other martyrs. Do not be sad nor complain because he has died the death of a holy warrior," said Sheik Yahya al-Attawi, a cleric at the Saddam Big Mosque.

"I don't believe that Saddam's execution would remotely help bring peace to the country. Even politically I think it would carry more negative consequences than positive ones."

—Italian Premier Romano Prodi

New Words and Expressions

oil deposits	石油资源
Iraq [i'rɑːk]	*n.* 伊拉克共和国
Kuwait [ku'weit]	*n.* 科威特(中东国家)
Saddam Hussein	萨达姆·侯赛因
multinational force	多国部队

For more information, you can check out the following link:

http://en.wikipedia.org/wiki/Invasion_of_Kuwait

Unit 13   American Government and Politics

Lead-in: Listening (PPT-33)

Listen to the passage carefully, and answer the following questions:

1. What are the three branches of the Federal Government?

2. Which place is the official residence of the US President?

Reading

1.1   Separation of Power

Politically，the United States is considered as a democracy, which means power belongs to the people. The form of the US government is known as **Federal Republic**, which is based on constitutional **separation of power** between the **federal government** and **state governments**. It is different from the traditional system in which the central government had total power and supreme leader.

Under the principle of separation of power, the federal government is divided into three branches: the **legislative**, the **executive** and the **judicial**. They share the powers delegated to the federal government. Although these three branches are outwardly separate, they cooperate with each other for major actions that require **consensus**; therefore, no single branch can make **arbitrary** decisions by claiming to be the supreme representative of American people.

1.2   Three Branches of the Federal Government

1.2.1 The Legislative Branch

The **Congress** is the legislative branch of the federal government. The central function of Congress is to make federal laws. According to the US Constitution, "all legislative powers" granted to the federal government "shall be vested in a Congress of the United States." Composed of representatives elected by the people, Congress is empowered to collect taxes and levy duties, to pay national debts, to regulate foreign commerce, and to raise armies and pay for them.

Another important function of Congress is to make investigations. It has the implied authority to make independent investigations and oversee the executive branch.

Under the principle of separation of power, the US Congress is divided into two chambers: the **Senate** and the **House of Representatives**. The two chambers are granted equal powers for making federal laws, but the House has some exclusive powers that it does not share with the Senate. These exclusive powers include the **impeachment power** and the initiation of revenue bills. Impeachment refers to the process by which Congress can remove public officials, including the president, from office. Only the House has the power to start the process and file charges. The House, for example, impeached President Bill Clinton in 1998, but failed to remove him.

The House of Representatives is commonly known as the House. For ever since 1910, the House has had a permanent membership of 435. The seats in the House are distributed among the 50 states according to their populations. The life of a Congress is **two** years, the Representatives come up for reelection every two years; however, here is no limit on the number of terms.

The Senate is the other subdivision of the US Congress. Representation in the Senate is based on the principle of state equality. The Senate comprises **100 Senators**, two from each of the fifty states. Senators have been directly elected in state-wide elections held in even-numbered years since 1913. The term of office is **six** years, with one third of the Senate seats up for election every two years. A Senator must be at least thirty years of age and a citizen of the United States for nine years.

The presiding officer of the Senate is the Vice-President of the United States who serves as Chairman when the Senate is in session.

1.2.2 The Judicial Branch

The federal judicial branch refers to the federal law court. The US Constitution vests the federal judicial power, including the power to conduct trials, in the federal courts. Only the law court, including the judge and jury, has the authority to declare a person guilty. Neither Congress nor the president or executive branch officials can do so.

The federal judicial branch is composed of three tiers, the Supreme Court, the eleven federal courts of appeals, and the 91 federal district courts.

1.2.3 The Executive Branch

The executive branch of the federal government is officially known as the Administration. It is headed by the chief executive, the President of the United States, who is also the head of state. The president is elected by citizens of the United States for a four-year term through nation-wide general elections.

The President has a **Cabinet** to help him. Members of the Cabinet are appointed by the president with the approval of the Senate, and their salaries are fixed by Congress. The Cabinet includes the Vice President and the heads of 15 executive departments. These heads include the Secretaries of State, Treasury, Defense, Homeland Security, Commerce, etc.

There are also some staff offices to help the president with his daily work. One of them is the White House Staff. It consists of the president's most intimate personal aides, generally known as his **think-tank**. They help the president to keep in touch with Congress, heads of various departments, the press and the public.

In spite of his wide-ranging power, the action of the president is strictly limited by the Constitution. He must ask Congress for every dollar his administration plans to spend by submitting his budget proposal to Congress. His nomination of officials needs the approval of the Senate.

1.3　General Election

The United States holds a general election every **four** years to elect a president. The law provides that every natural-born American citizen of 35 years of age and older can run for the presidency, but in fact only one of the candidates nominated by the two major parties, the Republicans and the Democrats, can win the general election.

American voters attach great importance to the candidate's moral character in addition to his competence. They regard honesty as a top requirement for the presidency. Jimmy Carter's words "**I do not lie**" contributed to his success in the campaign of 1976.

Candidates criticize each other's policy proposals, but their campaign assistants sometimes resort to a method known as mud-throwing, which aims to defame the rival candidate by exposing his personal flaw. In 1988, Jesse Jackson was compelled to give up his personal campaign for nomination after newspapers revealed his improper relationship with a young woman. Politicians resort to mud-throwing because they know American want to elect a clean, noble and honest president.

The general election, held in November in each election year, is technically divided into two stages. During the first stage, states elect their presidential electors. The number of presidential electors for each state is equal to the total number of its Representatives in Congress plus two Senators. California has more than 50 presidential electors while Nevada has only four. The total number of presidential electors for the nation is 538, with 3 from Washington, D.C.

1.4　The White House Is the Official Residence of the US President

The White House is the official residence and principal workplace of the President of the United States. Located at 1600 Pennsylvania Avenue NW in Washington, D.C., it was built between 1792 and 1800 of white-painted Aquia sandstone in the late Georgian style and has been the residence of every US President since John Adams. When Thomas Jefferson moved into the home in 1801, he (with architect Benjamin Henry Latrobe) expanded the building outward, creating two colonnades which were meant to conceal stables and storage.

In 1814, during the War of 1812, the **mansion** was set **ablaze** by the British Army in the

Burning of Washington, destroying the interior and charring much of the exterior. Reconstruction began almost immediately, and President James Monroe moved into the partially reconstructed house in October 1817. Construction continued with the addition of the South Portico in 1824 and the North in 1829. Because of crowding within the executive mansion itself, President Theodore Roosevelt had nearly all work offices relocated to the newly constructed West Wing in 1901. Eight years later, President William Howard Taft expanded the West Wing and created the first Oval Office which was eventually moved as the section was expanded. The third-floor attic was converted to living quarters in 1927 by augmenting the existing hip roof with long shed dormers. A newly constructed East Wing was used as a reception area for social events; both new wings were connected by Jefferson's colonnades. East Wing alterations were completed in 1946, creating additional office space. By 1948, the house's load-bearing exterior walls and internal wood beams were found to be close to failure. Under Harry S. Truman, the interior rooms were completely dismantled and a new internal load-bearing steel frame constructed inside the walls. Once this work was completed, the interior rooms were rebuilt.

Today, the White House Complex includes the Executive Residence (in which the First Family resides), the West Wing (the location of the Oval Office, Cabinet Room, and Roosevelt Room), and the East Wing (the location of the office of the First Lady and White House Social Secretary), as well as the Old Executive Office Building, which houses the executive offices of the President and Vice President.

The White House is made up of six stories—the Ground Floor, State Floor, Second Floor, and Third Floor, as well as a two-story basement. The term White House is regularly used as a metonym for the Executive Office of the President of the United States and for the president's administration and advisors in general. The property is owned by the National Park Service and is part of the President's Park. In 2007, it was ranked second on the American Institute of Architects's list of "America's Favorite Architecture."

1.5 Capitol Hill

Capitol Hill, aside from being a **metonym** for the United States Congress, is the largest historic residential neighborhood in Washington, D.C., stretching easterly in front of the United States Capitol along wide avenues. It is one of the oldest residential communities in Washington, and with roughly 35,000 people in just under two square miles, it is also one of the most densely populated.

As a geographic feature, Capitol Hill rises in the center of the District of Columbia and extends eastward. Pierre L'Enfant, as he began to develop his plan for the new Federal City in 1791, chose to locate the "Congress House" on the crest of the hill, facing the city, a site that L'Enfant characterized as a "pedestal waiting for a monument."

The Capitol Hill neighborhood today straddles two quadrants of the city, Southeast and Northeast, and a large portion is now designated as the Capitol Hill historic district. The name Capitol Hill is often used to refer to both the historic district and to the larger neighborhood around it. To the east of Capitol Hill lies the Anacostia River, to the north is the H Street corridor, to the south are the Southeast/Southwest Freeway and the Washington Navy Yard, and to the west are the National Mall and the city's central business district.

New Words and Expressions

Federal Republic [ri'pʌblik]   n. 联邦共和国

separation of power   政权分离

legislative ['ledʒis,leitiv]   n. 立法机关

executive [ig'zekjutiv]   n. 行政机关

judicial [dʒu(:)'diʃəl]   n. 司法机关

consensus [kən'sensəs]   n. 一致同意，多数人的意见；舆论

arbitrary ['ɑ:bitrəri]   adj. 独裁的，专断的

impeachment [im'pi:tʃmənt]   n. 弹劾，指摘

Cabinet ['kæbinit]   n. (美)内阁

think-tank   n. 智囊团

candidate ['kændidit]   n. 候选人

mansion ['mænʃən]   n. 大厦，官邸

ablaze [ə'bleiz]   adj. & adv. 闪耀的(地)，发光的(地)

Capitol Hill   n. 美国国会山，美国国会

metonym ['metənim]   n. [修辞]换喻(metonymy)中所使用的词或短语

For more information, you can check out the following links:

http://en.wikipedia.org/wiki/Separation_of_powers

http://en.wikipedia.org/wiki/Capitol_Hill,_Washington,_D.C.

Unit 14 National Economy of the United States

Lead-in: Listening (PPT-34)

Listen to the passage "You've got to find what you love" by Steve Jobs carefully, and answer the following questions:

1. Do you know anything about Steve Jobs, CEO of Apple Computer and of Pixar Animation Studios? Has he ever graduated from college?

2. Why did he leave Reed College after six months' study?

3. Why was he fired by the company he started?

Reading

1.1   The Only Super Power in the World

The United States is the largest economy and the only super power in the world. With about 5% of the world population, the United States produces about 25% of the total world output. The US economy features the use of high technology. It leads the world in such fields as **information technology (IT)**, computers, space, nuclear energy, electronics and military products.

1.2   The US Dollar Is Still Used as an International Currency

The US dollar is still used as an international **currency**, and many other currencies are pegged to it. The position of US dollar as an international currency was formally established at the **Bretton Woods Conference**[1], which was held at Bretton Woods in New Hampshire in 1945 and attended by 45 nations. The conference also set up the **International Monetary Fund**, the

World Bank, and **Gatt** world trading system. According to an agreement reached at the conference, the US dollar was **convertible** into gold at a fixed price of $35 per ounce.

1.3 The United States Plays a Very Important Ecomonic Role

The United States plays a very important role in promoting the healthy development of the world economy. Some Western economists, who regard the United States as the dynamic engine of the world economy, even argue " When the United States coughs, the rest of the world catches cold."

1.4 Fiscal Year 2009 US Federal Spending and Fiscal Year 2009 US Federal Receipts

The United States public sector spending amounts to about a third of the **GDP**.

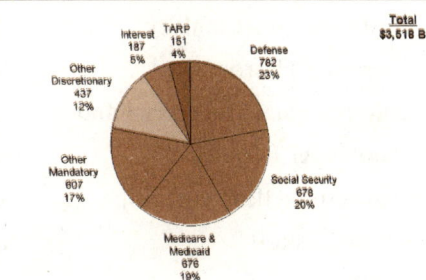

US Federal Spending – Fiscal Year 2009 ($ Billion)

Each level of government provides many direct services. The federal government, for example, is responsible for national defense, backs research that often leads to the development of new products, conducts space exploration, and runs numerous programs designed to help workers develop workplace skills and find jobs (including higher education). Government spending has a significant effect on local and regional economies—and even on the overall pace of economic activity.

State governments, meanwhile, are responsible for the construction and **maintenance** of most highways. State, county, or city governments play the leading role in financing and operating public schools. Local governments are primarily responsible for police and fire protection.

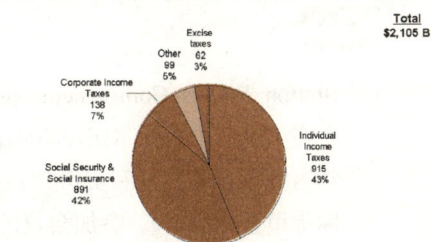

US Federal Receipts – Fiscal Year 2009 ($ Billion)

Overall, federal, state, and local spending accounted for almost 28% of gross domestic product in 1998.

As of January 20, 2009, the total US federal debt was $10.627 trillion (an increase of 85.5 percent over the previous eight years). The borrowing cap debt ceiling as of 2005 stood at $8.18 trillion. In March 2006, Congress raised that ceiling an additional $0.79 trillion to $8.97 trillion, which is approximately 68% of GDP. Congress has used this method to deal with an encroaching debt ceiling in previous years, as the federal borrowing limit was raised in 2002 and 2003. As of October 4, 2008, the "Emergency Economic **Stabilization** Act of 2008" raised the current debt ceiling to $ 11.3 trillion.

The federal government's debt rose by almost $1.4 trillion in 2009, and now stands at $12.1 trillion. While the US public debt is the world's largest in absolute size, another measure is its size relative to the nation's GDP. As of 2009 the debt was 83 percent of GDP. This debt, as a percent of GDP, is still less than the debt of Japan (192%) (the overwhelming number of owners of JGBs are

Japanese) and roughly equivalent to those of a few western European nations, including Greece. The total debt is projected to continue increasing significantly during President Obama's administration to nearly 100% of GDP, its highest level since World War II. Some projections put public debt at 200% of GDP by 2038.

Bruce Bartlett estimates that Medicare and Social Security are facing a combined unfunded liability of $106.4 trillion. Nation's total private net worth is $51.5 trillion, according to the Federal Reserve.

New Words and Expressions

information technology	信息技术
currency ['kʌrənsi]	*n.* 流通；货币，通货
International Monetary Fund	*n.* 国际货币基金会
Gatt, GATT [gæt]	*abbr.* 关贸总协定(General Agreement on Tariffs and Trade)
convertible [kən'və:təbl]	*adj.* 可自由兑换的
fiscal ['fiskəl]	*adj.* 财政的，国库岁入的
GDP	*abbr.* 国内生产总值(Gross Domestic Product)
maintenance ['meintinəns]	*n.* 维护，保持
stabilization [,steibilai'zeiʃən]	*n.* 稳定性

Note

[1] Bretton Woods Conference：布雷顿森林会议。联合国货币及金融会议的别称。1944 年 7 月在美国新罕布什尔州布雷顿森林的华盛顿山大旅社举行。45 个国家通过了将在未来 28 年内控制世界贸易和货币体系的一项综合性协定。会议通过了美国的提案，达成了《国际货币基金协定》。参加会议的国家同意建立一个国际货币制度，由新成立的国际货币基金组织及其辅助机构国际复兴开发银行来加以管理。国际货币基金组织为保持国际汇率的稳定、多边贸易和货币的可兑换性而设立。根据协定，确定了一盎司黄金等于 35 美元的官价。成员国货币的平价按一定数量的黄金和美元表示，美国承担接受各国政府或中央银行向美国兑换黄金的义务，由此建立起美元与其他成员国货币间的固定比价，确立了以美元为中心的固定汇率制体系。

For more information, you can check out the following links:

http://en.wikipedia.org/wiki/Economy_of_the_United_States

http://news.stanford.edu/news/2005/june15/jobs-061505.html

Examination on Chapter Two

Name _____   No. _____

题　型	一、填空	二、翻译	三、配对	四、判断	五、阅读	六、短文	总　分
分　值	25	20	15	15	20	5%	100
得　分							
阅卷人							

I. Fill in the blanks: 25%

1. The first splendid Indian civilization, known as the M_____ c_____, developed both written words and mathematics. It dominated southern Mexico and Central America from the fourth to the tenth centuries.

2. In 1492, S_____ Q_____ Isabella sponsored Christopher Columbus, a navigator from Genoa in Italy, to find a western route to India. When he reached a group of islands across the Atlantic, he called them the West Indies. They were in fact the islands of the Caribbean.

3. Some archaeologists believe that the forefathers of the Indians were from A_____. More than 27,000 years ago, they say, some hunters crossed the B_____ Strait, about 50 miles wide.

4. The F_____ and S_____ made up the majority of the earliest European settlers in North America, but they were later overtaken by the English and Germans. The majority of them were protestants who had suffered religious persecution in Europe.

5. The experience of the early immigrants also contributed to the distinction of the American culture. The early immigrants risked their lives to sail across the stormy Atlantic Ocean in small and poorly-provided ships. Their experience of hard labor for survival contributed to the American Labor ethics the g_____ l_____.

6. Local colonial assemblies argued that it was unfair for Britain to tax the American colonies, since they had no say in running the British government. They said "taxation without representation is tyranny". The colonies banned all British imports, and on July 4, 1776, representatives from all colonies adopted the D_____ of I_____, claiming the right to rule themselves.

7. Guided by the ideas of Thomas Jefferson, and influenced by the E_____, the American Declaration of Independence stated in 1776: "We hold these truths to be self-evident, that all men are created equal, that they are endowed by their Creator with certain inalienable rights, that among these are Life, L_____ and pursuit of happiness."

8. In 1783, after signing the peace treaty with the British, the people of the new United States of America had to decide on the best way to run their country. They decided to have a president, elected every f_____ years. He would rule with the help of a C_____ (divided into a

House of Representatives and a Senate made up of representatives from the States), and a Supreme Court. The draft Constitution (set of legal rules) for the new government contained three important statements about the American nation.

9. Many groups of Native Americans lived on the Great Plains of the American west and had done so for thousands of years. This vast area stretched from the Mississippi River in the east to the Rocky mountains in the west, and from Canada in the north to Texas in the south. Until the 17th century, many Plains tribes were farmers. They grew maize, beans and other foods, but they also hunted b_____ on foot using bows and arrows. Their way of life on the plains began to change during the 17th century when the S_____ introduced the horse.

10. To prevent undesirable people from immigrating into America, the US government set up a special port of entry on E_____ Island in New York h_____ in 1892, barring undesirable people such as prostitutes, convicts, the mentally retarded, beggars and revolutionaries who advocated the overthrow of government through violence. By the time the port was closed in 1954, it had received more than 20 million immigrants.

11. As a nation of immigrants, the US population was characterized by multiplicity. For many years in history, the United States was likened to a "m_____ p_____". It meant that as immigrants from different regions and cultures came to live in the United States, their old ways of life melt away, and they became part of the American culture.

12. The traditional concept of "melting pot" was challenged after the 1960s. Today some people compare America to a m_____ because many new immigrants refuse to give up their cultural distinctiveness. Often groups of people from the same culture live together in their own communities, such as C_____ in a number of cities and Little Cuba in Florida. There are also areas almost exclusively populated by other ethnic groups, such as Korean immigrants and Mexican immigrants. As a result, America is compared to a picture of many distinctive colors, and these colors do not fully mix with each other.

13. After World War I, the economy of the USA saw rapid growth. The Wall Street C_____ of 1929 brought an abrupt end to this and led to worldwide d_____. In October 1929, people began to panic and sell their shares rapidly. On a single day, 13 million shares were sold on the New York Stock Exchange. This started an economic crisis which soon affected the whole world.

14. At the end of World War II, the victorious Allied powers divided Germany into four zones. The United Nations was established to keep international p_____. On April 25, _____, the UN organization was set up formally at a conference in San Francisco. It aimed to keep international peace and solve problems by international cooperation.

15. Both countries built up an enormous stockpile of nuclear weapons. Peaceful, friendly contacts between the peoples ceased. The USSR became completely shut off from the rest of the world by Soviet troops. The British statesman Sir Winston Churchill memorably described the frontier

between East and West as an "i_____ c_____" in a speech that he gave in Missouri, USA, on March 5, 1946.

16. In 1972, President Nixon made a historic trip to China and signed the S_____ C_____ with Chinese Premier Zhou Enlai, a step that eventually led to formal diplomatic relations. In 1973, the Nixon administration signed the peace treaty with North Vietnam. With ending of war, universities students began rejecting radical movements and became more oriented toward individual careers. This finally led to the appearance of the yuppie generation composed of successful and prosperous baby-boomers.

17. Rivalries within the Arab world have often been caused by the region's o_____ deposits. In 1990, Iraq invaded Kuwait in order to improve its sea access. The UN Security council passed several resolutions that demanded that Iraq immediately withdraw its troops. When S_____ Hussein refused, a m_____ force led by the A_____ forced him to withdraw. Kuwait City was liberated within the first five days and thousands of Iraqi soldiers were captured. Retreating Iraqi forces caused huge ecological damage because they set fire to most of Kuwait's oil wells.

18. Under the principle of s_____ of power, the federal government is divided into three branches: the l_____, the e_____ and the j_____. They share the powers delegated to the federal government. Although these three branches are outwardly separate, they cooperate with each other for major actions that require consensus; therefore, no single branch can make arbitrary decisions by claiming to be the supreme representative of American people.

19. The House of Representatives is commonly known as the House. For ever since 1910, the House has had a permanent membership of _____. The seats in the House are distributed among the 50 states according to their populations. The life of a Congress is _____ years, the Representatives come up for reelection every two years; however, here is no limit on the number of terms.

20. The Senate is the other subdivision of the US Congress. Representation in the Senate is based on the principle of state equality. The Senate comprises _____ Senators, two from each of the fifty states. Senators have been directly elected in state-wide elections held in even-numbered years since 1913. The term of office is _____ years, with one third of the Senate seats up for election every two years. A Senator must be at least thirty years of age and a citizen of the United States for nine years.

21. The presiding officer of the Senate is the V_____ of the United States who serves as C_____ when the Senate is in session.

22. The United States holds a general election every f_____ years to elect a president. The law provides that every natural-born American citizen of _____ years of age and older can run for the presidency, but in fact only one of the candidates nominated by the two major

parties, the Republicans and the Democrats, can win the general election.

23. American voters attach great importance to the candidate's m_____ c_____ in addition to his competence. They regard honesty as a top requirement for the presidency. Jimmy Carter's words "I do not lie" contributed to his success in the campaign of 1976.

II. Translate the following phrases into Chinese: 20%

1. the Gettysburg Address _____

2. Ku Klux Klan _____

3. Ellis Island _____

4. North Atlantic Treaty Organization _____

5. Separation of Power _____

6. democracy _____

7. Federal Republic _____

8. Congress _____

9. federal law _____

10. Senate _____

11. House of Representatives _____

12. impeachment power _____

13. the Judicial Branch _____

14. Cabinet _____

15. Secretary of State _____

16. the White House _____

17. Capitol Hill _____

18. the United Nations _____

19. Rocky mountains _____

20. protestant _____

III. Select the letter of the answer that best matches each term at left: 15%

(   ) 1. tornado   a. black slaves

(   ) 2. Old Man River   b. typhoon

(   ) 3. juvenile delinquents   c. *Life on the Mississippi*

(   ) 4. unwilling immigrants   d. America's national bird

(   ) 5. hurricanes   e. ice box

(   ) 6. bald eagle   f. trade deficit

(   ) 7. Alaska   g. Penn's wood

(   ) 8. Mark Twain   h. teenage offenders

(   ) 9. trade imbalance   i. strong rotating wind

( ) 10. Pennsylvania   j. Mississippi

( ) 11. separation of power   k. division of power

( ) 12 oversight   l. watchful care

( ) 13. hearing   m. opportunity of being heard

( ) 14. popular sovereignty   n. judicial process

( ) 15. judicial proceedings   o. supremacy of the people

IV. True (T) or False (F): 15%

____ 1. The central part of the United States is composed of big mountains.

____ 2. The US government has to station a large number of troops along its border.

____ 3. American family houses are mostly built of bricks and cement.

____ 4. The Niagara Falls is situated on the Mississippi River.

____ 5. The US population was characterized by the lack of multiplicity.

____ 6. The mosaic concept is totally accepted by all Americans.

____ 7. American families with low income have to live in the suburbs.

____ 8. The traditional dividing line between the South and the North is the Potomac River.

____ 9. The United States is divided into eleven appeals regions known as "circuits".

____ 10. Both the US Congress and the president can declare a person guilty.

____ 11. The US Congress can override the president's veto by a two-thirds majority.

____ 12. Integrated education requires white and black children to attend the same school.

____ 13. In federal criminal trials, a majority verdict is acceptable.

____ 14. The jury is composed of judges.

____ 15. Members of the US Senate are called Senators.

V. Reading comprehension: 20%

Passage One

Elizabeth I became queen of England and Ireland in 1558. She ruled for 45 years and, due to her active involvement in government, England went through a period of stability, and cultural and economic expansion.

Elizabeth aided European Protestants and sent out English pirates against Spanish ships and colonies. She made a settlement between English Catholics and Protestants, and fought a war with Spain, defeating the Spanish Armada. England began to develop overseas ventures, and at home its industries and economy grew. This was Shakespeare's time, when English culture and society flowered, preparing the ground for an English period of imperial greatness.

Encouraged by the pope, Catholic Spain, led by Philip II, launched their fleet of 130 ships, the Invincible Armada, in an attempt to defeat Protestant England.

Mistakenly, the planned land reinforcement did not arrive in time. The exposed fleet was driven to the north and hit by vicious storms.

The Spanish fleet had to retreat via Ireland's west coast. During this withdrawal, most ships and their crews were lost.

In all, 63 Spanish ships were lost, only 4 in battle.

1. During Queen Elizabeth's reign, the economic situation of England is generally _____.

    A. prosperous   B. backwards   C. stable   D. underdeveloped

2. England fought a war with Spain, defeating the Spanish Armada, here "Armada" means _____.

    A. invincible fleet   B. inevitable fleet

    C. merchant ships   D. well-equipped fleet

3. The Spanish Armada was defeated mainly due to _____.

    A. vicious storms   B. laziness of Spanish soldiers

    C. Spanish ships were not well-equipped   D. most of the soldiers got ill

Passage Two

At first China prospered under the Qing. The empire grew and trade increased particularly with Europe. Chinese silk and porcelain were the finest in the world and their cotton goods were cheap and of high quality. Huge quantities of Chinese tea were sold abroad when tea-drinking became fashionable in Europe during the 18th century.

The empire became so rich and powerful that its rulers were able to treat the rest of the world with contempt. Under Emperor Kangxi (1661—1722), foreign merchants were forced to kneel whenever his commands were read out. The Manchus also forced several nations into vassal status, including Tibet, Annam (now Vietnam), Burma, Mongolia and Turkestan, making the Chinese empire the world's largest at the time. They made a deal with the Russians over land and trade.

Trade with China was profitable, yet the government there didn't want "barbarian" influences introduced. European merchants looked for other ways to trade.

Throughout the 18th century, Chinese silk, cottons, tea, lacquerware and porcelain were highly prized in Europe, but they were expensive and in short supply. Merchants from Portugal, Britain, Italy and the Netherland tried to expand the China trade. But the powerful Chinese emperors, who controlled all contact between their people and foreigners, were simply not interested. Qianlong, emperor for 60 years, was a scholar and traditionalist who had no time for "barbarians". The problem for the Europeans was that they had to pay for everything in silver, as Chinese traders were not allowed to exchange foreign for Chinese goods. Also the Europeans were permitted to trade only in Guangzhou (Canton), where they were penned up in "factories" (fortified warehouses), and traded through Chinese intermediaries. European traders were very competitive, and they fought to get the best Chinese goods and to sail them home to Europe as quickly as possible to fetch the highest prices.

In 1793, The British diplomat Lord Macartney visited the Chinese Emperor to encourage trade relations. Such relations were rejected, so people resorted to illegal deals. Both China and Britain had little respect for each other.

When, in 1839, the Chinese tried to stop the illegal opium trade, the British went to war. Even China's control of the world supply of tea was almost at an end. During the 1830s, the Englishman Robert Fortune stole several tea plants while travelling in China. He took them to India and set up rival plantations there.

4. Chinese _____ were the finest in the world.

   A. cotton and silk   B. silk and tea

   C. silk and porcelain   D. gold and porcelain

5. Throughout the _____ century, the Chinese silk, cottons, tea, lacquerware and porcelain were highly prized in Europe.

   A. 17th   B. 18th   C. 19th   D. 20th

6. The foreign businessmen were regarded as "barbarians" in Qing Dynasty. The problem for the Europeans was that they had to pay for everything in _____.

   A. paper money/note   B. gold

   C. silver   D. currency

7. The Europeans traded through Chinese intermediaries, here "intermediaries" means _____.

   A. middlemen or merchants   B. journalists

   C. clerks in the press   D. government leaders

Passage Three

In 1931, the countries that formed the British empire joined together to form the Commonwealth. Over the next 60 years, they were given their independence.

The relationship between Britain and parts of its empire had begun to change by the beginning of the 20th century. Some of the large countries became independent as British dominions. They were self-governing, but they kept strong links with Britain. Dominions retained the British Crown (king or queen) as the symbolic head of state. Each dominion had a lieutenant governor, a native resident of that country. He or she represented the Crown.

In the 1920s, the dominions asked for a clear definition of their relationship with Britain. This was given in 1931 in the Statute of Westminster when dominions were defined as "autonomous (self-ruling) communities within the British empire, equal in status… united by a common allegiance to the Crown and freely associated as members of the British Commonwealth of Nations". After this statute, the name British Commonwealth of Nations was used instead of British empire, and many colonies started to clamor for independence.

In 1932, the dominions received better terms for trading with Britain than countries outside the Commonwealth. Canada, Australia, New Zealand and South Africa has all become dominions before World War I. The Irish Free State all became a dominion in 1921. The First three to gain their independence after World War II were India (1947), Ceylon (1948) and Burma (1948). India and Ceylon (Sri Lanka) stayed in the Commonwealth, but Burma did not join, and the Republic of Ireland left in 1949.

8. Which of the following statements is true?

    A. Countries in the British Commonwealth gained their independence in 1932.

    B. The Commonwealth was organized by Britain and Ireland.

    C. The British Commonwealth was formed in 1931.

    D. The British Commonwealth means the British Empire.

9. Each dominion had a lieutenant governor, _____.

    A. he or she should be a native resident

    B. he or she should be a government leader for more than 5 years

    C. whether he is a native or a foreigner

    D. he or she is directly appointed by the British Crown

10. Which of the following statements is true?

    A. The Irish Free State all became a dominion in 1921.

    B. The Republic of Ireland left the British Commonwealth 40 years later.

    C. The first three to gain their independence after World War II were Canada, India, Ceylon.

    D. Burma left the Commonwealth in 1949.

VI. Paragraph translation: 5%

Guided by the ideas of Thomas Jefferson, and influenced by the Enlightenment, the American Declaration of Independence stated in 1776: "We hold these truths to be self-evident, that all men are created equal, that they are endowed by their Creator with certain inalienable rights, that among these are Life, Liberty and pursuit of happiness."

The American Revolutionary War had begun in 1775. At first the British were successful, despite the problems of fighting nearly 5,000 kilometers from home. But the Americans had an advantage because they were fighting on home territory, and they believed in their cause. Six years after the conflict began, the British army surrendered at Yorktown, Virginia in 1781, having been defeated by George Washington's troops. Britain eventually recognized American independence in the Treaty of Paris, 1783.

Examination on Chapter Two (Answer Sheet)

Name _____ **No.** _____

题　型	一、填空	二、翻译	三、配对	四、判断	五、阅读	六、短文	总　分
分　值	25	20	15	15	20	5	100
得　分							
阅卷人							

I. Fill in the blanks: 25%

1. _____, _____   2. _____, _____
3. _____, _____   4. _____, _____
5. _____, _____   6. _____, _____
7. _____, _____   8. _____, _____
9. _____, _____   10. _____, _____
11. _____, _____   12. _____, _____
13. _____, _____   14. _____, _____
15. _____, _____   16. _____, _____
17. _____, _____, _____, _____
18. _____, _____, _____, _____
19. _____, _____   20. _____, _____
21. _____, _____, _____, _____
22. _____, _____   23. _____, _____

II. Translate the following phrases into Chinese: 20%

1. _____ 2. _____ 3. _____ 4. _____ 5. _____
6. _____ 7. _____ 8. _____ 9. _____ 10. _____
11. _____ 12. _____ 13. _____ 14. _____ 15. _____
16. _____ 17. _____ 18. _____ 19. _____ 20. _____

III. Select the letter of the answer that best matches each term at left: 15%

1	2	3	4	5	6	7	8	9	10	11	12	13	14	15

IV. True (T) or False (F): 15%

1	2	3	4	5	6	7	8	9	10	11	12	13	14	15

V. Reading comprehension: 20%

1	2	3	4	5	6	7	8	9	10

VI. Paragraph translation: 5%

CHAPTER THREE

A Brief Introduction to Intercultural Business Communication

Unit 1   The European Union (EU) and Its Emblem

Lead-in: Listening (PPT-35)

Listen to the passage carefully, and answer the following questions:

1. What do EU and COE refer to? How many stars does it consist of on a blue background?

2. The number of stars on the flag is fixed at 12. Is it related to the number of member states of the EU?

Reading

1.1   The Flag of Europe

The Flag of Europe is the flag and **emblem** of the European Union (EU) and Council of Europe (COE) (it is also used to indicate the euro or eurozone countries). It consists of a circle of 12 golden (yellow) stars on a blue background. The blue represents the west, the number of stars represents completeness while their position in a circle represents unity. The stars do not vary according to the members of either organisation as they are intended to represent all the peoples of Europe, even those outside European **integration**.

The flag was designed by Arsène Heitz and Paul Lévy in 1955 for the COE as its symbol, and the COE urged it to be adopted by other organisations. In 1985 the EU, which was then the European

Economic Community (EEC), adopted it as its own flag (having had no flag of its own before) at the initiative of the European Parliament. The flag is not mentioned in the EU's treaties, its incorporation being dropped along with the European Constitution, but it is formally adopted in law.

1.2 Symbol of the Flag

The number of stars on the flag is fixed at 12, and is not related to the number of member states of the EU. This is because it originally was the flag of the Council of Europe, and does not have a relationship with the EU. In 1953, the Council of Europe had 15 members; it was proposed that the future flag should have one star for each member, and would not change based on future members. West Germany objected to this as one of the members was the disputed area of Saarland, and to have its own star would imply sovereignty for the region. Twelve was eventually adopted as a number with no political **connotations** and as a symbol of perfection and completeness because of the **ubiquity** of the number for groups in European cultures and traditions such as:

- 12 stars crowning the head of the **Virgin Mary**[1] in the book of *Revelation*, Chapter 12
- 12 hours on a clock
- 12 sons of Jacob
- 12 tribes of Israel
- 12 **Biblical** minor **prophets**
- 12 **ounces** in a **troy pound**
- 12 semitones in an octave
- 12 days of Christmas
- 12 Caesars chronicled by Suetonius
- 12 **Olympian Gods**
- 12 labours of Hercules
- 12 tables of Roman Law
- 12 books of *Paradise Lost* and the *Aeneid*
- 12 hues in the colour wheel, star or sphere (western art)

1.3 Monetary Union

Sixteen EU countries have introduced the **euro** as their sole currency. The creation of a European single currency became an official objective of the EU in 1969. However, it was only with the advent of the Maastricht Treaty in 1993 that member states were legally bound to start the monetary union no later than 1 January, 1999. On this date the euro was duly launched by eleven of the fifteen member states of the EU. It remained an accounting currency until 1 January, 2002, when euro notes and coins were issued and national currencies began to phase out in the Eurozone, which by then consisted of twelve member states. The Eurozone has since grown to sixteen countries, the most recent being Slovakia which joined on 1 January, 2009.

New Words and Expressions

emblem ['embləm]	*n.*	象征，徽章
integration [,inti'greiʃən]	*n.*	综合，共同体
connotation [,kɔnəu'teiʃən]	*n.*	内涵
ubiquity [juː'bikwəti]	*n.*	(同时的)普遍存在
Biblical ['biblikəl]	*adj.*	圣经的
prophet ['prɔfit]	*n.*	先知，预言者；提倡者
ounce [auns]	*n.*	盎司；少量
troy pound		金衡磅
Olympian [əu'limpiən] **Gods**		奥林山神
euro	*n.*	欧元

Note

[1] Virgin Mary：圣母玛利亚(耶稣基督之母)。

For more information, you can check out the following links:

http://en.wikipedia.org/wiki/European_Union

http://www.daylife.com/topic/European_Union

Unit 2　Trade Relationship between China and Western Countries in 2010 Shanghai Exposition

Lead-in: Listening (PPT-36)

Listen to the passage carefully, and answer the following questions:

1. "The construction scheme for the China Pavilion contains rich elements of Chinese culture and could well display Chinese wisdom." What's the name of the red architecture?

   _____

   _____

2. What hall will provide provinces, municipalities, autonomous regions and other areas a platform to display their urban achievements?

   _____

   _____

Reading

1.1　2010 Shanghai Expo

Expo 2010 (simplified Chinese: 2010 上海世界博览会) will be held in Shanghai, China and is a scheduled **World Expo** in the tradition of international fairs and expositions. The theme of the exposition will be *"Better City—Better Life"* and signifies Shanghai's new status in the 21st century as a major economic and cultural center. It is expected to generate the largest number of visitors in the history of the world's fairs in terms of gross numbers. The Expo logo features the Chinese character 世 ("world") modified to represent three people together with the 2010 date. The Expo will take place from **May 1—October 31, 2010**. The Shanghai 2010 Expo will feature a highly **sophisticated** online version called Expo Shanghai Online operated by Tencent Holdings Ltd.

1.2　China Pavilion

With an estimated cost of 1.5 billion yuan, its design features a traditional style red architecture called "**oriental** crown". Organizers said the project is a significant **milestone** in the countdown to the 2010 event, signaling the beginning of full-scale construction of the Expo's core projects.

"The construction scheme for the China Pavilion contains rich elements of Chinese culture and could well display Chinese wisdom."

Located at the crossing of two horizontal and vertical axes in the Pudong part of Expo garden, the China Pavilion comprises of three parts. The first is the national hall, which is 20,000-sq-m, 30,000-sq-m for provinces and regions, and 3,000-sq-m shared between Hong Kong, Macao and Taiwan.

The oriental crown, standing 63 meters in height, uses traditional dougong brackets and features wooden brackets fixed layer upon layer between the top of a column and a crossbeam.

As a permanent landmark in the inner part of Pudong New Area, the structure will adopt **ecological** sound technologies and energy-saving measures. These include the sun-shading design, **exterior** of the domestic pavilion is a **buffer** zone for heat or cold, as well as ecological landscaping on the roof could lower energy demands effectively.

During the Expo, the main structure will be used for an exhibition based on the theme of "Chinese wisdom in urban development" by explaining the values of harmony, nature and spirit. The domestic hall will provide provinces, **municipalities**, **autonomous regions** and other areas a platform to display their urban achievements, designers said.

1.3　Trade Relationship between China and Western Countries

On the economic side, the EU has become a major trading partner for China (it ranks second for Chinese imports, third for Chinese exports). The EU is also a major foreign investor in China.

In welcoming China as a new member of the WTO, the organization expands its membership by 1.2 billion people, that is to say by a quarter. It is the WTO's greatest leap in the history of the organization. Congratulations are in first place due to China. This has been a long and **arduous** negotiation, one that took a full fifteen years to complete. In retrospect, the history of the last fifteen years of negotiations has also been the history of China's own reform process, its gradual opening-up, and its **integration** into the world economy. The phenomenal 7% compound average annual growth rates, which are expected to continue in the future, testify to the success of the government economic policies. People in China are on average four times as wealthy today as they were in 1978, when the open door policy was started. That is a unique achievement for a country of its size. So even if at times the WTO negotiations have been difficult for Chinese and WTO negotiators alike, today the organization can pride itself on the results achieved and rejoice in having made new friends in the process.

New Words and Expressions

sophisticated [sə'fistikeitid]	*adj.* 富有经验的；久经世故的
oriental [,ɔ(:)ri'entl]	*n.* 东方人
	adj. 东方诸国的，亚洲的，东方的；(珍珠等)最优质的
milestone ['mailstəun]	*n.* 里程碑，里程标，重要事件，转折点
ecological [,ekə'lɔdʒikəl]	*adj.* 生态学的，社会生态学的
exterior [eks'tiəriə]	*adj.* 外部的，外在的
buffer ['bʌfə]	*n.* 缓冲器
municipality [mju:,nisi'pæliti]	*n.* 市政当局，自治市
autonomous region	自治区

For more information, you can check out the following links:

http://news.yahoo.com/s/nm/20100522/pl_nm/us_china_usa_1

http://news.yahoo.com/video/world-15749633/19494312#video=19964778 Oil spill impacts
Louisiana beach

Unit 3　Trade Relationship between China and the United States

Lead-in: Listening (PPT-37)

Listen to the video "**Remarks by President Barack Obama at Town Hall meeting with future Chinese leaders, Shanghai, China**"[1] carefully, and answer the following questions:

1. What did Obama see in Shanghai that caught the attention of the world?

2. What conclusion did he make by saying "It was here, 37 years ago, that the Shanghai Communiqué opened the door to a new chapter of engagement between our governments and among our people?"

Reading

1.1　USA Pavilion Theme[2]

The theme of the USA Pavilion is "Rising to the Challenge." This powerful theme will be woven throughout the **dynamic**, emotional story about the American spirit of perseverance, **innovation**, and community building that the Pavilion will present in a series of multi-dimensional, hi-tech presentations. The Pavilion presents America as a place of opportunity and **diversity** where people come together to create positive changes. The Pavilion theme encompasses many core values central to the American spirit: **Sustainability**, Teamwork, Health, Technology, and Innovation. These values create a foundation for the American people where dreams are limitless and opportunities are within reach.

The shape of the USA Pavilion shadows that of an eagle, a creature that is uninhibited by boundaries. It also serves as the national emblem for America, a country that offers limitless opportunities. Beyond the expression of opportunity, the eagle has been designed with its wings opened as a gesture to welcome guests into the USA Pavilion.

1.2　USA Pavilion Design

Positioned at the West Expo Gate in the Americas zone, the USA Pavilion will cover a span of 6,000 square meters (60,000 square feet) and will be one of the largest Pavilions at the Expo. Scheduled for completion in March 2010, the Pavilion is expected to be one of the most visited pavilions with up to 60 million Chinese visitors plus 10 million international visitors over a period of six months.

In accordance with US legal requirements, the USA Pavilion is being funded and operated through a non-profit organization Shanghai Expo 2010, Inc. Ms. Ellen Eliasoph and Mr. Nick Winslow are Co-Founders of the organization and it has been **sanctioned** by the US Department of State to raise the funds necessary to build and operate the official US Pavilion at World Expo Shanghai 2010. The US Department of State appointed Jose Villarreal as the US Commissioner General of Section of the United States Exhibition to Shanghai 2010 World Expo. Organizers welcome the opportunity to share the American story with visitors and demonstrate America's commitment to strengthening US-China relations and engagement in Asia. Not only does the pavilion provide corporate sponsors an unsurpassed marketing platform but all participants are able to show support for the environmental theme of the Exposition.

The USA Pavilion will consist of two levels with 20 percent of that space for commercial use and the remaining 80 percent for general public use. The main level will house the exterior queue area, Act I theater, Act II theatre, Act III area, VIP entry, retail facilities, and food services. The second level will house the urban farm, VIP facilities and administration offices. Equipped with sophisticated technology, the Pavilion will showcase a wide spectrum of events, performances and exhibits. In fact, the USA Pavilion is a show in three acts. Act I, "The American Spirit," is a call to collaboration, and a celebration of freedom, diversity, innovation, and opportunity. Act II, "The Garden," illustrates the power of an individual to inspire and transform a community. Last, Act III, "Opportunities and Innovation," is a themed area that highlights the use of technology and innovation to achieve more sustainable communities

In line with the Expo theme of "Better City, Better Life," this urban structure was designed by Clive Grout, an architect with World Expo experience. He has used state of the art technical features to ensure energy efficiency while highlighting the sustainability message of the Expo. In fact, the USA Pavilion will introduce nature to its urban structure through a central greenery cascade and a waterfall that uses recycled water. It will also feature a forested entry and an urban farm that is modeled after Michelle Obama's garden at the White House and represents the rural in the city sub-theme of the Exposition.

Sponsors provided the funds (USD61 million) to build what amounts to an **unquantifiable** and "**unprecedented** opportunity for US companies and organizations to hoist their flags in one of the most important centers of world commerce and cultural exchange." (Hilary Clinton) This sum covers all costs incurred in the construction, staffing, operations, showcase and post-Expo building demolition and materials removal.

1.3   USA Is Mainland China's Top Export Destination[3]

USA is China's top export destination in 2008, with a year-on-year increase of about 8.4% from 2007, according to **China's Bureau of Statistics**. The total volume of export from Mainland China to USA amounts to $252.3 billion, followed by Hong Kong (China) and Japan. The other important export markets to China are: Germany, Netherland, UK, Russia, Singapore and India. The trade relationship between China and USA has been a central topic between top leaders of both nations for all the time.

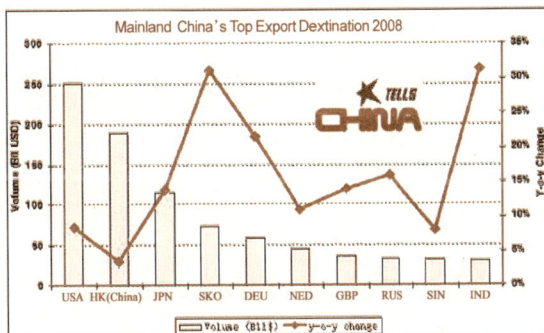

Mainland China's Top Export Dextination 2008

New Words and Expressions

dynamic [dai'næmik]	*adj.* 动力的，动力学的；动态的
innovation [ˌinəu'veiʃən]	*n.* 改革，创新
diversity [dai'və:siti]	*n.* 差异，多样性
sustainability [ˌsteinə'biləti]	*n.* (细胞的)可染性
sanction ['sæŋkʃən]	*v.* 批准，同意；支持，鼓励
unquantifiable [ʌnkwɔnti'faiəbl]	*adj.* 不可测量的，难以计算的
unprecedented [ʌn'presidəntid]	*adj.* 空前的
China's Bureau of Statistics	中国统计局

Notes

[1] Remarks by President Barack Obama at Town Hall meeting with future Chinese leaders, Shanghai, China：奥巴马于 2009 年 11 月 20 日在上海会见青年学生的演讲。

[2] USA Pavilion Theme：美国馆的主题为"拥抱挑战(Rising to the Challenge)"。美国馆的外观宛如翱翔不羁、展翅欲飞的雄鹰，它也是美国的国徽，象征着美国给人们提供了无限良机。此外，展翅的雄鹰犹如张开的双臂，欢迎各方来宾入馆参观。

[3] USA Is Mainland China's Top Export Destination：美国是中国大陆最大的出口市场。根据中国统计局公布的数据，中国在 2008 年向美国出口了价值 2 千 5 百亿美元的商品。

For more information, you can check out the following links:

http://en.expo2010.cn/c/en_gj_tpl_38.htm

http://www.gulfoodusapavilion.com/

http://www.cuyoo.com/html/guoji/2009/1117/12385.html

http://seoul.usembassy.gov/ea_111609a.html

Unit 4   Trade Relationship between China and Canada

Lead-in: Listening (PPT-38)

Listen to the Canadian national anthem carefully, and answer the following questions:

1. Why does the Canadian national anthem have two versions: The one on the left is in English, the other on the right is in French?

2. Please translate the Canadian national anthem into Chinese.

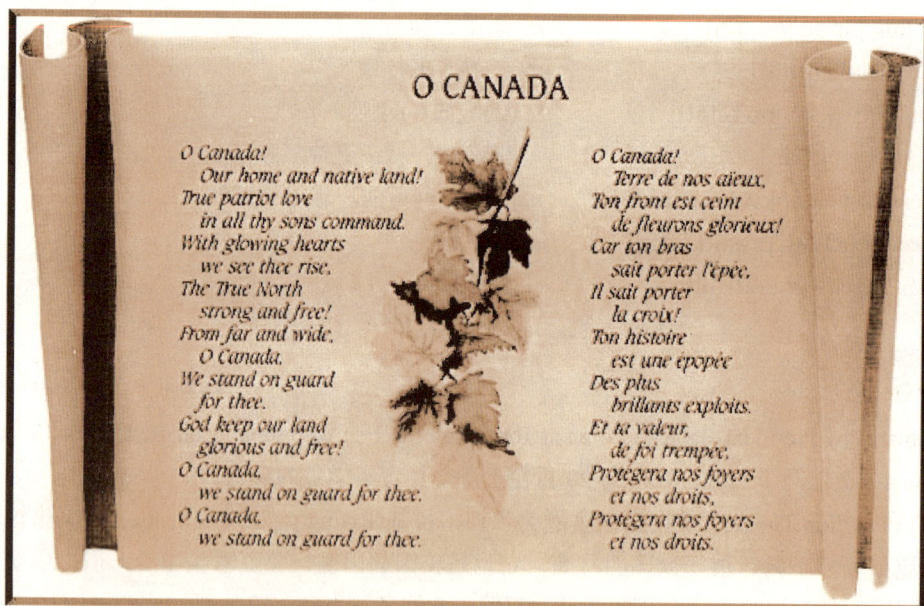

O CANADA

O Canada!
  Our home and native land!
True patriot love
  in all thy sons command.
With glowing hearts
  we see thee rise.
The True North
  strong and free!
From far and wide,
  O Canada,
We stand on guard
  for thee.
God keep our land
  glorious and free!
O Canada,
  we stand on guard for thee.
O Canada,
  we stand on guard for thee.

O Canada!
  Terre de nos aïeux,
Ton front est ceint
  de fleurons glorieux!
Car ton bras
  sait porter l'épée,
Il sait porter
  la croix!
Ton histoire
  est une épopée
Des plus
  brillants exploits.
Et ta valeur,
  de foi trempée,
Protégera nos foyers
  et nos droits.
Protégera nos foyers
  et nos droits.

Reading

1.1 Canada Pavilion

This design was completed by Canada Government in **collaboration** with the world famous, Cirque du Soleil. The Canada Pavilion is themed as "The Living City, **Inclusive**, Sustainable, and Creative".

Canada Pavilion is located in Zone C of Pudong area according to the layout of Expo site and has a planned area of 6,000 square meters. The pavilion is comprised of three large **geometric** structures and anchored by an open public area where the visitors can access to the pavilion or enjoy various cultural and artic performances.

Based on the design, Canada Pavilion is expected to attract up to 5.5 million visitors. In order to represent the recycling technology, the exterior wall of Canada Pavilion will be covered by a special kind of greenery and the rainwater will be recycled by a drainage system for use inside the pavilion. Large exhibits and articles are prohibited in the pavilion to maximize the exhibition space and secure the **ventilation** within exhibition area and open eye shot.

1.2 Trade Relationship between China and Canada

Canada's relationship with China has certainly flowered during the 2000s. **China is now Canada's second-largest trading partner**, trailing only to the US. In the first Canada-China Business Forum, held in 2005 during a visit by President Hu Jintao to Canada, the two governments set a target to increase bilateral trade to USD30 billion by 2010. That goal was met in 2007, when trade between the two countries climbed to USD30.38 billion.

According to statistics from the General Administration of Customs of the People's Republic of China, the volume of bilateral trade between China and Canada reached USD34.52 billion in 2008, a year-over-year increase of 13.8 percent. Canada's exports to China reached USD12.73 billion, a 16 percent increase over 2007, while Canada's imports from China stood at USD21.79 billion USD, a 12.6 percent increase over 2007.

According to a recent Fraser Institute study of the economic relationship between China and Canada, "There are unexploited opportunities for further gains from trade that can enrich both countries." That statement is **applicable** as well to India, which is becoming increasingly open to international investment and is home to a younger population.

While **most of Canada's imports from China are manufactured goods, direct Canadian exports to China are primarily resources**: Almost 35 percent of exports comprise **pulp**, organic chemicals and **non-ferrous metals**.

The prospects for **resource-focused economies** such as Canada's are strong in the long term because of the enormous potential demand from an emerging Chinese middle class. For example, Su Shulin, the chairman of China Petroleum & Chemical Corp, China's biggest oil refiner, said domestic oil demand has shown signs of recovery. Daily fuel sales have risen to about 310,000 metric tons, compared with a record low of 280,000 barrels in December.

And the Chinese government plans to tap its USD1.95 **trillion** currency reserves to secure resources. Chinese state-run companies have been told to acquire resources abroad as prices of commodities, led by energy and industrial metals, decline.

1.3 Dr. Norman Bethune[1] and Anti-Japanese War

Despite the tragic result that Dr. Bethune dead from blood poisoning, the **keystone** is that he **sacrificed** both body and soul to help Chinese in Anti-Japanese War. Leading a medical team, Norman Bethune, a Canadian doctor, arrived Yan'an with some **critical** medical facilities in March, 1938. He contacted Chairman Mao, then immediately initiated to construct a field hospital. Someone suggested he should keep a distance about 40 km from the battlefront. But he said, "The longer distance there is between hospital and front line, the more wounded will die in the road. So he built the hospital in the range of enemy's fire." For saving the soldier, he paid no attention to his safety. **Transferring** is necessary during the war. But wherever the war fired, there was Bethune. Withal wherever there was Bethune, there was a field hospital.

Bethune devoted all his energy in **surgery**. Once he had 71 operations in two days. Bethune totally focused on caring patients. When he had no surgery, he would check the wounded and invented some equipment for them. During his check, if he found some nurses fell asleep as tiredness, he would be pretty angry and stern criticized them. But as the saying is "Teaching him fishing is better than giving him a fish", thus Bethune not only cured the patient but also taught Chinese colleagues and medical students curing.

New Words and Expressions

collaboration [kəˌlæbəˈreiʃən]	n. 协作，通敌
inclusive [inˈkluːsiv]	adj. 包含的，包括的
geometric [dʒiəˈmetrik]	adj. 几何的，几何学的
ventilation [ventiˈleiʃən]	n. 通风，流通空气
applicable [ˈæplikəbl]	adj. 可适用的，可应用的
pulp [pʌlp]	n. (水果的)果肉；纸浆
non-ferrous metals	有色的、非铁或钢的金属
trillion [ˈtriljən]	num. 万亿
keystone [ˈkiːstəun]	n. 重点，要旨，基本原理
sacrifice [ˈsækrifais]	n. & v. 牺牲，献出；献祭，供奉
critical [ˈkritikəl]	adj. 危急的；关键的
transfer [trænsˈfəː]	n. & vt. 转移，调转；调任；传递；转让，改变
surgery [ˈsəːdʒəri]	n. 外科，外科学；手术室，诊疗室

Note

[1] Dr. Norman Bethune：诺尔曼·白求恩，著名的国际主义战士。抗日战争时期，白求恩放弃了国内待遇优厚的工作条件和优越舒适的生活环境，不远万里来到中国，支援中国的抗日战争。

For more information, you can check out the following links:

http://en.wikipedia.org/wiki/Expo_67_(pavilions)

http://en.wikipedia.org/wiki/Canada_(Epcot)

http://baike.baidu.com/view/1395927.htm?fromenter=O+Canada&fr=ala0_2#3

Unit 5 Trade Relationship between China and Central-South America

Lead-in: Listening (PPT-39)

Listen to the song "La Isla Bonita" carefully, and answer the following questions:

1. Why are there some Spanish words in the song?

_____

2. What does "La Isla Bonita" mean in English?

_____

Listen again, and fill in the blanks:

La Isla Bonita

Last night I ___1___ of San Pedro

Just like I'd never gone, I knew the song

A young girl with eyes like the desert

It all seems like yesterday, not far away Chorus

Tropical the island ___2___

All of nature, wild and free

This is where I long to be

La isla bonita

And when the samba ___3___

The sun would set so high

Ring through my ears and sting my eyes

You Spanish lullaby

I fell in love with San Pedro

Warm wind carried on the sea, he called to me

Te dijo te amo

I prayed taht the days would last

They went so fast

Tropical the island breeze

All of nature, wild and free

This is where I long to be

La isla bonita

And when the samba played

The sun would set so high

Ring through my ears and sting my eyes

You ___4___ lullaby

I want to be where the sun ___5___ the sky

When it's time for siesta you can watch them go by

Beautiful faces, no ___6___ in this world

Where a girl loves a boy

And a boy loves a girl

Reading

1.1 Central and South American Joint Pavilion Is Built from Old Industrial Site

Mentioning Central and South America, **samba**, **tango**, **rumba** and many other kinds of dances in the remote continents **dazzle** people's minds. Fortunately in 2010, people will be able to enjoy the wonderful Latin American songs and dances without leaving the country at a spacious square in front of the **Central and South American Joint Pavilion**.

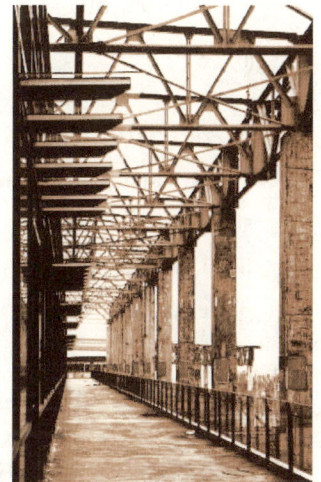

1.2 The Charming Local Folk Customs and the Tremendous Social and Economic Achievements Made by the Latin American Countries Will Be Showcased

Most Central and South American countries choose to participate in the Shanghai World Expo either at rented pavilions or joint pavilions provided by the expo organizer.

Except Brazil and Argentina that will use rented pavilions, quite a number of other Central and South American countries will gather together before May 1, 2010 at the Central and South American Joint Pavilion, which covers an area of over 10,000 square meters and will vividly **showcase** the

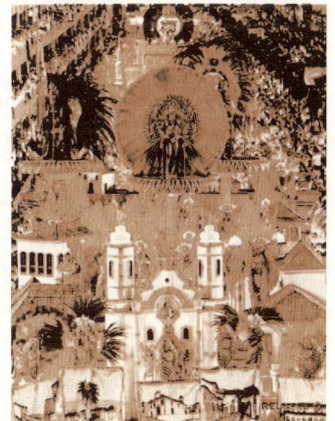

charming **local folk customs** and the tremendous social and economic achievements made by the Latin American countries.

Exhibitors who enter the pavilion may not know that the spacious area was originally a thick **plate** shop of the Shanghai No. 3 Steel Works, a typical industrial building constructed at the end of the last century. In the sun, the dark reddish brown and gray high pillars line up all neatly. Although it seems dull, the reporter is unwilling to leave every time and wonders how **spectacular** it was when **crimson steel plates** were rolled in and where the former workers are now. Raise your head and look at the blue and silent sky for a long period, then look at the words of "Central and South American Joint Pavilion" on the door. The old green steel frames still look very vigorous.

New Words and Expressions

samba ['sæmbə]   n. 桑巴舞(一种源自非洲的巴西舞)

tango ['tæŋgəu]   n. 探戈

rumba ['ruːmbə]   n. 伦巴舞(由古巴黑人民间舞蹈发展而成的一
                                                 种交际舞)

dazzle ['dæzl]   v. (使)眼花，眩耀

Central and South American Joint Pavilion   中美洲和南美洲联合展示馆

showcase ['ʃəukeis]   n. 展示

local folk customs   当地习俗

plate [pleit]   n. 盘子，金属板，图版；金银餐具

                                                 vt. 给……装钢板

spectacular [spek'tækjulə]   adj. 引人入胜的，壮观的

For more information, you can check out the following links:

http://events.ubm.com/event?eid=518

http://www.bostonharborwalk.com/placestogo/location.php?nid=6&sid=36

Unit 6   Chilean President Cuts Ribbon for Chile's Pavilion in Shanghai

Lead-in: Listening (PPT-40)

Listen to the passage carefully, and answer the following questions:

1. Do you know what kind of corporation was "Dole Chile Fresh Fruit International"?

2. Have you ever seen Dole fresh fruit at your local supermarkets?

Reading

1.1   Chile Was the First Latin American Country to Sign a Free Trade Agreement

SHANGHAI, China-Chilean President Michelle Bachelet on Thursday attended the **ribbon-cutting ceremony** here to put the finishing touch on Chile's pavilion for the 2010 Universal Exposition, which Santiago considers to be the main event for **propelling** bilateral relations with the Asian giant.

Chile signed its 2010 World Expo participation contract with China in Shanghai, becoming the first Latin American country to officially sign on.

The signing came as a Chilean government delegation, led by Chilean President Michelle Bachelet, visited Shanghai for two days as part of an ongoing Chilean Week in Shanghai.

Shanghai Mayor Han Zheng met Bachelet and her delegation before the two sides witnessed Chile's Expo contract signing ceremony.

"We highly appreciate Chile's full support and

active participation in the Shanghai Expo and wish Shanghai has a closer trade and economic partnership with Chile and Chilean entrepreneurs," Han said.

Bachelet, the first-ever woman Chilean president who is on her first visit to China after becoming president in 2006, arrived in the city on Monday evening and attended an entrepreneurs **seminar** in the city.

She delivered a speech at the seminar entitled "Chile, a Strategic Partner in Latin America," which focused on Chile's strategic partnership with China

"Chile attaches great importance to developing bilateral ties with China, and we will also exert our advantages to serve as a platform for Chinese companies to enter Latin America," she said when talking with Han.

Chile was the first Latin American country to sign a free trade agreement and is **the second-largest trading partner with China in the region**.

As China's major port city, Shanghai's economic and trade volume accounts for about a third of the two countries' total. The city's trade volume with Chile increased by more than 100 percent last year, Han said.

Bachelet said in her speech that Chile needed to further expand its position in developing cooperation with China.

1.2　Dole Chile Fresh Fruit International[1]

The Self-sustaining Cellular Reefer Vessel (Banana Ship) Dole Chile and her sister vessel, the Dole Columbia, marked a new departure in **reefer** ship technology. Prior to their delivery, AP Moller's large containerships were the world's largest reefer ships with the ability to carry up to 700 refrigerated TEU.

The two Dole self-sustaining fully cellular vessels combine a hatch coverless configuration, with a record-breaking concentration of **perishable cargo carrying capacity**. Dole Chile has a capacity of 1,000 40ft containers or 2,000 TEUs. This equates to approximately 2m cbf, making the Dole sisters the largest cold storage vessels in the world.

Dole Chile was built by Howaldtswerke-Deutsche Werft (HDW) in Kiel for Dole Fresh Fruit International, and delivered in 1999.

New Words and Expressions

ribbon-cutting ceremony　　　　　剪彩典礼

propel [prəˈpel]	*vt.* 推进，驱使
seminar [ˈseminɑː]	*n.* 研究会，讨论发表会
reefer [ˈriːfə(r)]	*n.* <美俚>冷藏车，冰箱
perishable [ˈperiʃəbl]	*adj.* 容易腐烂的
cargo carrying capacity	载货容积，载物能力

Note

[1] Dole Chile Fresh Fruit International：智利是拉美水果出口大国，占南半球新鲜水果出口量的 50%。最近 15 年以来，智利水果种植面积增长 30%，由 17 万公顷增加到 22 万公顷。最大的出口企业为多乐国际公司。

For more information, you can check out the following links:

http://gcaptain.com/maritime/blog/interesting-ship-dole-chile/

http://www.expo2010chile.cl/en

Unit 7　China, Britain Develop Stronger Relations

Lead-in: Listening (PPT-41)

Listen to the video "China-Britain Relationship" carefully, and answer the following questions:

1. What level of relationship has China and Britain established?

2. In what fields has China and Britain cooperated with each other?

Reading

1.1　Britain Plans to Embed Its World Expo Pavilion

The United Kingdom will **embed** more than 60,000 seeds, which can be planted after the World Expo 2010, into the structure of its pavilion to urge people to protect natural species from extinction.

The UK Expo team has signed a contract with the Expo organizer to participate in Expo Online. The country also updated its Expo pavilion design, which will be an open gift box "from Britain to the Chinese people".

The seeds will be put inside 60,000 needle-like **protrusions** covering the surface of the 6,000-square-meter pavilion. The seeds will be well-protected and will not grow during the 184-day event, Carma Elliot, British consul general in Shanghai, was quoted as saying by Thursday's *Shanghai Daily*.

The seeds demonstrate the concept of **sustainability**, the diversity of nature and urge people to protect the environment for future generations, Elliot said.

The idea promotes the **Millennium** Seed Bank Project, an international conservation project launched by the country's Royal Botanic Gardens in 2000. It is designed to provide an insurance policy against the **extinction** of plants

in the wild by storing seeds for future use. The project aims to collect seeds from 24,000 **species** of plants by 2010.

The UK team is choosing seeds for the pavilion from a seed bank in Kunming, Yunnan Province, which is the Chinese branch of the project, Elliot said, adding they are still considering how to use the seeds after the Expo ends.

The UK Pavilion—"A Pavilion of Ideas"—will look like a huge "light box" with thousands of needle-like protrusions tipped with tiny colored lights to display images. Construction on the pavilion began in March.

1.2   China, Britain Develop Stronger Relations—Premier Wen's "Trip of Confidence" to Europe

Chinese Premier Wen Jiabao shakes hands with British Prime Minister Gordon Brown during the dinner Brown hosts for him at the British prime minister's **official residence** on the **outskirts** of London Jan. 31, 2009. Chinese Premier Wen Jiabao arrived in London on Jan. 31 for a three-day visit to Britain.

BEIJING, Feb. 2—Relations between China and Britain have come a long way in the past 30 years. Partnerships have deepened, and both sides are seeking to work closer together in these tough economic times.

Since establishments of bilateral ties at the **ambassador-level** in March 1972, Sino-British relations has overcome a variety of challenges and achieved steady progress.

From the **return of Hong Kong to China** to the forging of a strategic partnership in 2004. After assuming office in 2007, Prime Minister Gordon Brown said relations with China are important to Britain, especially on economic issues.

British Prime Minister Gordon Brown said, "Relationship between China and Britain are very strong. The trade between China and Britain is growing very fast indeed. It is not just one-way, it is two-way."

Trade volume in 2008 was worth over 40 billion US dollars. Britain has accumulated investment in China of more than 15 billion US dollars.

Britain was one of the earliest west-European countries to tap into the Chinese market, and the two countries have long-established cooperative partnership. **Economic ties are particularly strong in the fields of energy, chemicals and the environment**.

In January 2008, Chinese premier Wen Jiabao met with Gordon Brown in Beijing. The two sides signed 800-million-US dollars worth of contracts on education, energy and the environment. The two sides hoped to boost bilateral trade volume to 60 billion US dollars.

Chinese premier Wen Jiabao said, "We have established a very good work and personal relationship. We had a frank exchange of views on a wide range of issues. Through our joint efforts, the Sino-British relationship has entered a new stage of comprehensive development."

"Comprehensive" means focusing not just on economic issues. Culture exchanges have also **bonded** the two nations.

London will succeed Beijing as the host city of the Olympics, so it's naturally sharing China's experiences in hosting the Summer Games. But it's also forging stronger links with China to weather the economic downturn together.

New Words and Expressions

embed [im'bed]	vt.	使插入，使嵌入，深留
protrusion [prə'tru:ʒən]	n.	伸出，突出
sustainability [ˌsteinə'biləti]	n.	(细胞的)可染性
millennium [mi'lenjəm]	n.	太平盛世；一千年
extinction [iks'tiŋkʃən]	n.	消失，消灭，废止
species ['spi:ʃiz]	n.	种类
official residence		官邸
outskirts ['autskə:ts]	n.	边界，(尤指)市郊
ambassador-level		大使级
bond [bɔnd]	v.	结合

For more information, you can check out the following links:

http://www.cctv.com/english/20090202/101124.shtml

http://news.xinhuanet.com/english/2009-02/02/content_10751023.htm

Unit 8   China Has Become the Main Export Market for French Wine

Lead-in: Listening (PPT-42)

Listen to the passage carefully, and answer the following questions:

1. What's the theme of the French Pavilion?

2. According to a recent Vinexpo study, by 2012, China will have become the 7th largest consumer of wine. What's the reason?

Reading

1.1   France Pavilion in 2010 Shanghai Expo

The France Pavilion is unique in terms of both form and technologies. It will present France's contribution in the sustainable urban development for one of the biggest economic **metropolises** in the planet.

1.2   National Flag of France

The national flag of France is a tricolour featuring three vertical bands coloured royal blue (hoist side), white, and red. It is known to English speakers as the **French tricolour** or simply the **tricolour**.

Blue and red are the traditional colors of Paris, used on the city's coat of arms. Blue is identified with Saint Martin, red with Saint Denis. At the storming of the Bastille in 1789, the Paris militia wore blue and red cockades on their hats. White had long featured prominently on French flags and is described as the "ancient French colour" by Lafayette. White was added to the "revolutionary" colors of the militia cockade to "nationalize" the design, thus creating the tricolor cockade. Although Lafayette identified the white stripe with the nation, other accounts identify it with the monarchy.

1.3　China Overtakes UK as Top Castel Export Destination

February 12, 2010 *By James Lawrence*

China has overtaken the UK to become the main export market by volume for French global wine firm Castel.

The company saw their sales to China **soar** by more than 243% by the end of May 2009.

In total, Castel exported almost 14m bottles to China last year, and expects sales will reach close to 20m bottles in 2010.

A representative from Castel said, "We experienced an exceptionally strong **decline** in our exports to the UK, volumes falling from 14m to 10m bottles, largely due to the weakness of **sterling** against the euro, the increase in duties on **alcohol** and the general **economic downturn**."

"We expect to recover some of the markets we lost last year in UK in 2010, but China is perhaps set to **stretch** its lead."

According to a recent Vinexpo study, by 2012, China will have become the 7th largest consumer of wine.

1.4　Jean-François Millet[1]

The son of a small peasant farmer of Gréville in Normandy, Millet (1814—1875) showed a precocious interest in drawing, and arrived in Paris in 1838 to become a pupil of Paul Delaroche. He had to fight against great odds, living for long a life of extreme **penury**.

His memories of rural life, and his intermittent contacts with Normandy, however, impelled him to that concern with peasant life that was to be characteristic of the rest of his artistic career. His paintings on rural themes attracted growing acclaim and between 1858 and 1859 he painted the famous **Angélus** (Musée d'Orsay), which 40 years later was to be sold for the sensational price of 553,000 francs.

Commissioned by a wealthy American, Thomas G. Appleton, and completed during the summer of 1857, Millet added a **steeple** and changed the initial title of the work, Prayer for the Potato Crop to The Angelus when the purchaser failed to take possession in 1859. Displayed to the public for the first time in 1865, the painting changed hands several times, increasing only modestly in value, since some considered the artist's political sympathies suspect. Upon Millet's death a decade later, a bidding war between the US and France ensued, ending some years later with a price tag of 800,000 gold francs.

The **disparity** between the apparent value of the painting and the poor estate of Millet's surviving family was a major impetus in the invention of the droit de suite, intended to compensate artists or their heirs when works are resold.

New Words and Expressions

metropolis [mi'trɔpəlis]	n. 首都，主要都市，都会，大城市
tricolour ['traikələ]	n. 三色旗 adj. 三色的
soar [sɔː]	v. 高飞；剧增
	n. 高飞范围，高涨程度
decline [di'klain]	vi. 下降
sterling ['stəːliŋ]	n. 英国货币，标准纯银
	adj. 英币的，纯银制的，纯正的
alcohol ['ælkəhɔl]	n. 酒精，酒
downturn ['dauntəːn]	n. 低迷时期
stretch [stretʃ]	v. 伸展，伸长 n. 一段时间，一段路程，伸展
penury ['penjuri; -juəri]	n. 贫困，贫穷
steeple ['stiːpl]	n. 尖塔
disparity [dis'pæriti]	n. 不一致

Note

[1] Jean-François Millet：让·弗朗索瓦·米勒。创作了许多法国人民乃至全世界家喻户晓的名画作品《播种者》、《牧羊女》、《拾穗者》、《晚钟》、《扶锄的男子》、《喂食》、《春》等。在19世纪60年代之前，人们并不认可他的作品。直到1867年，米勒的作品在巴黎博览会上获得了社会的第一次承认，并在法国画坛引起了极大的反响，人们逐渐认识了米勒艺术的真正价值。他的一生，物质生活极为不幸，有时甚至几幅作品仅换得一双小孩子的鞋。而他死后，法国为购回《晚钟》一画，竟花了80多万法郎。天才和不幸在人的命运中往往结伴而行。1875年12月22日，画家在巴比松逝世。

For more information, you can check out the following links:

http://english.eastday.com/e/expo/u1a5110610.html

http://www.wines-info.com/en/item.aspx?col=189

http://en.wikipedia.org/wiki/Flag_of_France

Unit 9   Friendship between China and Italy since Qing Dynasty

Lead-in: Listening (PPT-43)

Listen to the passage carefully, and answer the following questions:

1. Please give a brief introduction to Giuseppe Castiglione, Italian-Chinese Painter Lang Shining.

2. What's the style of his painting?

Reading

1.1   Giuseppe Castiglione, Italian-Chinese Painter Lang Shining[1]

Giuseppe Castiglione, born in Milan, Italy, entered the Jesuit order at the age of 19, came to China in 1715, and was appointed court painter at the Imperial Palace in Beijing. He served in this position under three emperors (Kang Xi, Yong Zheng and Qian Long), painting under the Chinese name Lang Shining. He became a key figure in the artistic revival of the time, introducing Chinese painters to perspective, **three-dimensionality** and other western techniques. Combining typical Chinese material with western technique, he was particularly known for portraits and animals, especially horses. Very popular with the postal services, Castiglione's paintings are on almost 40 stamps, and one stamp is dedicated to the Old Summer Palace at Beijing which he also designed.

Castiglione painted in European style, but featured many Chinese themes. During his time in China, he designed the Western-Style Palaces in the imperial gardens of the Old Summer Palace. He stayed in Beijing until his death in 1766; he was buried in the European Missionary Graveyard in Beijing.

1.2   ICE: Bright Outlook for the Trade Development between China and Italy

Although the global financial crisis has forced many institutions to cut the expenses and reduce investment, the enthusiasm of ICE[2] keeps on. Maurizio Forte, the chief representative of ICE in Shanghai has expressed recently that ICE will continue to participate in CIFIT[3] this year, and it is the fifth time for ICE to attend CIFIT.

"Although the global economy and the overall trade are in depression, the economic relationship between China and Italy maintains good momentum of development. Both Chinese market share in Italy and Italian market share in China show the sign of increase," said Maurizio Forte yesterday.

Data from Chinese Customs and MOFCOM also verified Maurizio Forte's view. According to the statistics of Chinese General Administration of Customs, **Italy ranked the third exported country for China in EU**, following Germany and France, and the export volume reached 11.66 billion dollars with an increase of 14%. Meanwhile, Italy was the fourth biggest imported country for China in EU. Last year the import turnover of Italy from China increased by 25.64%, and that was 26.6 billion dollars. Also the statistics from MOFCOM showed that in 2008 Italian FDI to China reached 0.493 billion dollars with an increase of 41.77%.

However, Maurizio Forte also admitted that as the global economy was still in recovery in the first half of 2009, trade between China and Italy was affected. Data of the this period showed that while the total Chinese imported turnover was decreased by 25%, the exported volume of Italy to China still remains at 5.25 billion dollars with only a small decrease of 9.8%. The imported turnover of Italy to China in the first half of 2009 was 9.5 billion dollars with a fall of 23.8% comparing with last year. "This situation means that China is an attractive market for Italy to develop trade."

Maurizio Forte said, "I hope the outlook concerning trade between China and Italy in 2009 will be as promising as that in 2008, or at least the decrease in both imported turnover and exported volume in the second half of 2009 can be **alleviated**."

He expressed that Italy was going to promote investment opportunities in fields like logistics and life science, especially biological medical technology, information and communication technology, renewable energy resources and tourism.

New Words and Expressions

three-dimensionality	三维
alleviate [ə'liːvieit]	*vt.* 减轻

Notes

[1] Guiseppe Castiglione (1688—1766)：原名朱塞佩·伽斯底里奥内，中文名为郎世宁，中国清代宫廷画家兼建筑师、天主教耶稣会修士。1688 年生于意大利米兰，清康熙帝五十四年(1715)作为天主教耶稣会的修道士来中国传教，随即入宫进入如意馆，成为宫廷画家，曾参加圆明园西洋楼的设计工作，任职康、雍、乾三朝，在中国从事绘画达 50 多年。由于带来了西洋绘画技法，向皇帝和其他宫廷画家展示了欧洲明暗画法的魅力，郎世宁先后受到了康熙帝、雍正帝、乾隆帝的重用。

[2] ICE：全球展览业协会。

[3] CIFIT：中国国际投资贸易洽谈会。

For more information, you can check out the following links:

http://www.manresa-sj.org/stamps/3_Castiglione.htm

http://www.arthistoryarchive.com/arthistory/asian/Giuseppe-Castiglione.html

http://baike.baidu.com/view/31621.htm

http://www.chinafair.org.cn/china/News/258690.html

Unit 10   Siemens Confident of Maglev Train Deal with China

Lead-in: Listening (PPT-44)

Listen to the passage carefully, and answer the following questions:

1. What will German Pavilion showcase?

2. How about the Maglev Train of China with Siemens?

Reading

1.1   German Pavilion

It will showcase German urban life and how the country's design and products can help solve urbanization problems.

2010-03-19—As the countdown to the Shanghai World Expo gets closer today we take a look at the German Pavilion. One of the main attractions at the pavilion is its "Balancity" exhibition, which encourages visitors to use teamwork and their imagination.

The German Pavilion coined the term "Balancity" to signify a city in balance. The 6,000 square meter pavilion is composed of three floating spaces and one cone-shaped structure. Visitors to the pavilion are encouraged to let their imagination run wild. The heart of the Balancity is the "Energy Source". The huge sphere weights one ton and has a three meter-diameter. Its surface is **adorned** with thousands of LEDs, with images, colors and shapes. The sphere swings back and forth to the rhythm of visitors' cheers. The louder they shout, the greater the sphere swings. And the greater the swinging motion the more vivid the colors become. The design demonstrates the idea that much can be achieved when people work together. In the Design Factory, hundreds of "Made in Germany" products will fly overhead.

Marion Conrady, press officer of German Pavilion said, "We always try to…I think it will become very interesting because everything will be design in the notion." "Balancity" is expected to attract 50-thousand visitors daily, meaning more than 9 million people could visit the pavilion during the whole Expo. Organizers at the German Pavilion are adding the finishing touches to its decoration with the entire project expected to be completed next month.

1.2 Siemens Confident of Maglev Train Deal with China[1]

The Shanghai **Maglev** Train connects the Pudong international airport to the Shanghai **subway**. The 30 km (18-mile) trip takes just over seven minutes. Trains can travel at speeds of up to 430 kph (268 mph). Germany's Siemens and ThyssenKrupp co-developed the technology.

April 3, 2010, *China Daily* — German industrial giant Siemens A.G. said on Thursday it was confident a deal could be reached with China to extend a high-speed magnetic rail line, but it did not say when an agreement would be signed.

"I am very confident that we will come to a (positive) conclusion," Richard Hausmann, chief executive of Siemens' operations in China, told Reuters in an interview.

"We are negotiating very intensively, but I can not say when a deal would be reached," said Hausmann.

Siemens and German steel firm ThyssenKrupp A. G. are leading a consortium that wants to extend a **magnetic levitation train track** at Shanghai by 160 km (100 miles) to Hangzhou.

Earlier this month, German media reported that the project could be scrapped. Many believe the snags hinge on technology transfer agreements that the Chinese are insisting on.

Hausmann said the Chinese government needed to make a decision soon if it wanted to have the rail link running in time for the 2010 World Expo in Shanghai.

The current 30 km track links Shanghai's airport and the city centre. In 2003, China became the first country in the world to get such a train, which travels up to 430 km an hour.

The German company also expects trials for a Chinese standard for third generation (3G) wireless telecommunications network to be completed by July, after which, if successful, licences could be issued.

Siemens has formed a joint venture with China's largest telecommunications gear maker, Huawei Technologies Co. [HWT.UL], to develop TD-SCDMA technology.

Telecoms companies like Motorola and Nokia could be in line for large pieces of an estimated $12 billion in orders for network gear when the licenses are issued, which many expect to be in the second half of this year.

Nokia and Siemens just days ago formed the world's fourth-biggest telecoms infrastructure company in a tie-up worth up to some 30 billion euros ($38 billion). (US$=8.00 yuan)

New Words and Expressions

adorn [ə'dɔːn]   *v.* 装饰

maglev ['mæglev]   *n. & adj.* 磁力悬浮火车(的)

levitation [ˌlevi'teiʃən]   *n.* 轻轻浮起，升在空中

Note

[1] Siemens Confident of Maglev Train Deal with China：中国政府以四万亿元人民币刺激经济的计划使一推再推的上海磁悬浮列车线路延长问题再次提上了日程。蒂森克虏伯集团负责磁悬浮技术，慕尼黑的西门子集团则为全段线路提供电力供应和全套传导和安全保障技术。

For more information, you can check out the following links:

http://en.expo2010.cn/c/en_gj_tpl_43.htm

http://www.chinadaily.com.cn/bizchina/2006-06/22/content_623668.htm

Unit 11   China, Austria Seek Stronger Ties with Five Deals

Lead-in: Listening (PPT-45)

Listen to the passage carefully, and answer the following questions:

1. What forms an important part of Austria's economy, accounting for almost 9% of the Austrian gross domestic product?

2. Which city in Austria receives about a fifth of tourist overnight stays compared to Vienna, which ranks it 2nd in the summer season?

Reading

1.1   Austria Pavilion

Austria began construction of its pavilion on May 1, 2009. The structure, also about 2,000 square meters in size, will take visitors on a journey through **snow-capped** mountains, forests, flowing rivers and urban landscapes. It will display Austria's natural scenery and landmark buildings such as Vienna City Hall under the theme "Feel the Harmony."

The pavilion will take a **porcelain** outer skin in red and white colors, which represent the colors of the Austria national flag. **The red color also takes on Chinese meaning of the color of good luck**.[1]

1.2   China, Austria Seek Stronger Ties with Five Deals

Presidents of China and Austria on Wednesday witnessed the signing of a package of deals and **vowed** to **uplift bilateral relationship**. "China would like to work with Austria to bring relationship to a new high," Chinese President Hu Jintao told visiting Austrian President Heinz Fischer.

1.3   Tourism in Austria

Tourism forms an important part of Austria's economy, accounting for almost 9% of the Austrian gross domestic product.

Vienna attracts a major part of tourists, both in summer and winter. **Salzburg** receives about a fifth of tourist overnight stays compared to Vienna, which ranks it 2nd in the summer season. In the winter season, a number of winter sport resorts in western Austria overtake Salzburg in the number of tourist overnight stays: Sölden, Saalbach-Hinterglemm, Ischgl, Sankt Anton am Arlberg, and Obertauern.

Visits to Austria mostly include trips to Vienna with its Cathedral, its "Heurigen" (wine pubs) and romantic Waltz music events.

Of great touristic importance are the Austrian skiing, hiking and mountaineering resorts in the Alps as well as family-friendly recreation areas. The same applies to the numerous Austrian lakes.

New Words and Expressions

snow-capped	*adj.* 积雪盖顶的(山)
porcelain [ˈpɔːslin; -lein]	*n.* 瓷器，瓷
	adj. 瓷制的，精美的；脆的
vow [vau]	*n.* 誓约
	v. 宣誓，立誓，发誓
uplift [ʌpˈlift]	*v.* 促进，提高
Salzburg [ˈsæltsbəːg]	萨尔茨堡(奥地利城市)

Note

[1] The red color also takes on Chinese meaning of the color of good luck：奥地利馆不但有《蓝色多瑙河》优美的曲调、森林里清新的空气，甚至还有白雪皑皑的阿尔卑斯山。奥地利馆红白双色的设计不仅将奥地利国旗的色彩蕴含其中，也突出了具有中国传统特色的幸运色彩"红色"。

For more information, you can check out the following links:

http://www.china.org.cn/video/2010-02/22/content_19452658.htm

http://en.wikipedia.org/wiki/Flag_of_Austria

http://en.wikipedia.org/wiki/Tourism_in_Austria

Unit 12 Trade Relationship between China and Holland

Lead-in: Listening (PPT-46)

Listen to the passage carefully, and answer the following questions:

1. Who was the Dutch post-Impressionist painter whose work had a far-reaching influence on 20th century art for its vivid colors and emotional impact?

2. Why are some 1,600 paper-made pandas on display at a square in Amsterdam, capital city of the Netherlands, October 30, 2008?

Reading

1.1 Dutch Pavilion

Dutch Pavilion shows the Commercial **orientation** of the government and the people. In terms of commerce as well as on other levels, the Dutch enjoy collaborating with others. They have been internationally orientated for centuries and value openness and **accessibility**. **Amsterdam** is home to more nationalities than any other city in the world and Dutch **dredging companies** and **dike** builders operate on a global scale.

When people think of the Netherlands, a low lying country with numerous dams, **tulips** and clogs come to mind. At the upcoming World Expo in Shanghai, the country will demonstrate that it has far more to offer.

The Dutch pavilion is called "Happy Street," which is mainly composed of a **pedestrian** strip shaped like the number "8," a lucky number in China that suggests fortune. The entire street is **in the shape of the number eight**[1]—an **auspicious** number in Chinese culture. Twenty-six small houses will be elevated along the 400-meter long main pedestrian strip. The houses will present exhibitions exploring themes such as energy, water, city space and many other urban issues.

Construction of the "Happy Street" will be completed by February, 2010. In the meantime, the

Dutch port city of **Rotterdam** will be represented at the Urban Best Practices Area, with a focus on water and delta technology. The Netherlands is world famous for building on pile foundations.

Around 40 percent of the country lies below sea level. The country hopes visitors can get a personal experience of what its like living below sea level. It also wants to share its experience in the management of water resources.

1.2 Vincent Willem van Gogh

Vincent Willem van Gogh (30 March 1853—29 July 1890) was a Dutch **post-Impressionist** painter whose work had a far-reaching influence on 20th century art for its vivid colors and emotional impact. He suffered from anxiety and increasingly frequent bouts of mental illness throughout his life, and died largely unknown, at the age of 37, from a self-inflicted gunshot wound.

Little appreciated during his lifetime, his fame grew in the years after his death. Today, he is widely regarded as one of history's greatest painters and an important contributor to the foundations of modern art. Van Gogh did not begin painting until his late twenties, and most of his best-known works were produced during his final two years. He produced more than 2,000 artworks, consisting of around 900 paintings and 1,100 drawings and sketches. Although he was little known during his lifetime, his work was a strong influence on the Modernist art that followed. Today many of his pieces— including his numerous self-portraits, landscapes, portraits and sunflowers—are among the world's most recognizable and expensive works of art.

1.3 Holland Is China's Second Largest Trade and Investment Partner

The 14th China-Holland Joint Economic and Trade Committee Meeting was held in Beijing on December 8, 2008.

Heemskerk said the Dutch government attaches great importance to the economic and trade cooperation between Holland and China and this Joint Economic and Trade Committee Meeting was a great success. **Holland is China's second largest trade and investment partner** in all the member States of the EU, and over 100 Chinese enterprises have found their development opportunities in Holland. Both sides should enhance cooperation, and especially prevent the appearance of trade protectionism with the financial crisis as a backdrop.

1.4　Paper-made Pandas on Display in Amsterdam[2]

Some 1,600 paper-made pandas are on display at a square in Amsterdam, capital city of the Netherlands, October 30, 2008. Initiated by the World Wildlife Fund (WWF), this display is to call on a worldwide concern over the remaining 1,600 pandas remaining in the wild.

New Words and Expressions

orientation [ˌɔ(ː)rienˈteiʃən]	*n.*	方向，方位，定位；倾向性；向东方
accessibility [ˌækəsesiˈbiliti]	*n.*	易接近，可到达
Amsterdam [ˈæmstəˈdæm]	*n.*	阿姆斯特丹(荷兰首都)
dredging [ˈdredʒiŋ]	*n.*	挖泥，捕捞
dike [daik]	*n.*	堤防
	vt.	筑堤提防
tulip [ˈtjuːlip]	*n.*	[植]郁金香；郁金香花；郁金香球茎
pedestrian [peˈdestriən]	*n.*	步行者
	adj.	徒步的
auspicious [ɔːsˈpiʃəs]	*n.*	吉兆的，幸运的
Rotterdam [ˈrɔtədæm]	*n.*	鹿特丹[荷兰西南部港市]
post-Impressionist [ˌpəustimˈpreʃənist]	*n.*	后期印象派的画家
	adj.	后期印象派的
self-inflicted [ˈselfinˈfliktid]	*adj.*	自己造成的

Notes

[1] in the shape of number eight：在许多中国人的印象中，荷兰无非是飞利浦、范巴斯滕、郁金香和木屐的故乡。在今年的上海世博会上，荷兰馆却颠覆"展馆"的概念，用一条名为"快乐街"的街道来展示荷兰别样的风貌。一条长约 400 米的"8"字形街道，26 个独立的小型展馆沿街分布，充满奇思妙想的荷兰馆，外观酷似一个游乐园，这就是荷兰馆将在上海世博会上展现的独特创意。

[2] Paper-made pandas on display in Amsterdam：为了引起人们对世界上仅存的 1600 只野生熊猫的关注，世界野生动物基金会在荷兰阿姆斯特丹一广场举办了 1600 只纸质熊猫的展示会。

For more information, you can check out the following links:

http://www.meet-in-shanghai.net/expo_pavilions_dutch.php

http://en.wikipedia.org/wiki/Vincent_van_Gogh

Unit 13 Luxemburg, Green Heart of Europe

Lead-in: Listening (PPT-47)

Listen to the passage carefully, and answer the following questions:

1. When did China and Luxembourg establish their formal diplomatic relations?

2. How many **investment projects** does Luxembourg have in China at the end of last year?

Reading

1.1   Luxemburg Pavilion[1]

The idea "**forest and fortress**" comes from the **literal** meaning of the Chinese term for Luxembourg. The EXPO pavilion, built from steel, wood and glass, will be an open fortress around with greenery. The 15-meter-high main structure will resemble an ancient castle with large openings surrounded by medieval towers.

1.2   From the Architects

The motto of the EXPO is: "Better city, better life." It was this motto, the international nature of the event and the location China that provided the intellectual starting point for the design. The pavilion, a monolithic sculptural form, reflects little Luxembourg, its **permeability** mirrors global exchange and communication. But the meaning of the word "Luxembourg" in Chinese—lùsên bâo means woods and castle—is also taken up and translated into architecture. The pavilion is conceived as an open castle in green surroundings.

At the center of the complex: a tower (20 meters tall), with a **silhouette** with a very abstract, clearly "exaggerated" form that can be traced back to the traditional type of the Luxembourg single-family house—this tower is contained in a rectangle formed by a kind of castle wall with many large openings to allow the unimpeded flow of visitors. The area between the tower and the wall is intensively planted (Luxembourg: "the green heart of Europe").

"All the materials are **recyclable**," said the architect of the pavilion, Francois Valentiny. Also, the outside walls will be translucent, on which Chinese characters will be shown. The exhibition area of the pavilion is about 1,300 square meters. The downstairs hall will stage a satellite video show displaying live scenes from the country. "Visitors will be able to talk with Luxembourg people through satellite. And we will bring live programs of Luxembourg events here," said Jeannot Krecke, the country's Minister of the Economy and Foreign Trade.

The country unveiled its plan at a ceremony to mark the signing of the participation contract with EXPO organizers. Luxembourg is the fourth country to sign the contract, after Ukraine, Hungary and Switzerland. The design plan is very unique, and not only presents Luxemburg's reputation as the "green heart of Europe," but also embodies the theme of the Shanghai EXPO. "Better city, better life," said Hong Hao, director of the Bureau of Shanghai World EXPO Coordination.

"The objective of the project is to demonstrate the concept of sustainable development through the structure and the content of the pavilion," said Robert Goebbels, the commission general of Luxembourg.

1.3   China-Luxembourg Relationship

The relationship between China and Luxembourg can be **traced back to 1972** when these two countries established their formal diplomatic relations. Luxembourg and China have a close relationship and exchanges between the two governments are very frequent. The Prime Minister of the Grand Duchy of Luxembourg has visited China many times in the last few years, and he has set up a good relationship with Chinese leaders. The relationship between these two countries has greatly developed in the political, economic, cultural aspects since then.

In economic aspect, at the time when China and Luxembourg established diplomatic relations, the volume of trade between these two countries was 90,000 US dollars. By 2002, the bilateral trade volume exceeded 100 million US dollars. The total trade between the two countries in 2006 reached nearly 20 billion US dollars from which we can notice the **momentum** of trade growth.

The most exports from China to Luxembourg do not consider Luxembourg as the final market, but through which they can transport to regions around. Luxembourg's investment in China is not tremendous, Luxembourg has, at the end of last year, **115 investment projects** in China, and the negotiated amount reached 740 million US dollars and the actual investment amounted to 310 million US dollars. However Luxembourg has only 45 million population, these figures are still quite **substantial**.

New Words and Expressions

fortress [ˈfɔ:tris]	*n.* 堡垒，要塞	
literal [ˈlitərəl]	*adj.* 文字的，照字面上的；无夸张的	
permeability [ˌpə:miəˈbiliti]	*n.* 渗透性	
silhouette [ˌsilu(:)ˈet]	*n.* 侧面影象，轮廓	
investment project	投资方案/计划	
momentum [məuˈmentəm]	*n.* 动力，要素	
substantial [səbˈstænʃəl]	*adj.* 坚固的，实质的；真实的，充实的	

Note

[1] Luxemburg Pavilion：卢森堡国家馆的主题是"小也是美"，突出了卢森堡"欧洲绿色心脏"的国家的特殊身份。展馆的设计者设想出了一种几乎只用独块巨石的雕刻方法，这实际上受到了中文传统译名"卢森堡"的影响。中文"卢森堡"的意思是"森林和堡垒"，所以卢森堡展馆自喻为一个周围绿树环绕的开放堡垒。展馆的建筑结构就像有很多大出口的壁垒，面向邻近的空间，由中世纪的塔楼包围在里面。为了强调展馆对外部的开放性，围墙上嵌有各种半透明的平面，上面用汉字表达很多信息。

For more information, you can check out the following link:

http://www.archicentral.com/luxembourg-pavilion-for-shanghai-expo-2010-by-francois-valentiny-24905/

Unit 14 China-Denmark Trade Grows Fast

Lead-in: Listening (PPT-48)

Listen to the passage carefully, and answer the following questions:

1. What has been the symbol of Copenhagen and Denmark for almost 100 years?

2. To mark the mutually beneficial relations, what kind of partnership did the two sides agree to launch?

Reading

1.1 Denmark Pavilion

The whole building is a **loop**, and you get to ride it on one of 1,500 fucking city bicycles they brought over from the DK. You know what else they are bringing? A "little mermaid" statue that has been a symbol of **Copenhagen** and Denmark for almost 100 years.

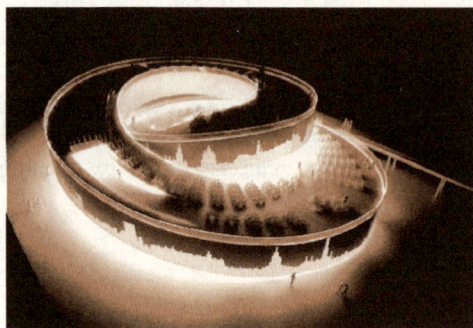

1.2 China-Denmark Trade Grows Fast

According to **statistics** of Denmark, trade with China has been growing faster than with any of its other major trading partners. Trade in the service industry has become an important part of the bilateral trade.

In 2007 China became the fourth largest importer of Danish products and services. According to statistics of China's customs, trade between China and Denmark reached 6.4 billion USD in 2007. By the end of 2007, Denmark had 504 companies in China, with contracts of 2.2 billion USD and the actual investment of 1 billion USD. The actual investment in 2007 was 124 times that of 1982 when Danish companies began to invest in China.

1.3   Joint Statement between China and Denmark

Following is the full text of Joint Statement between China and Denmark on the Establishment of a Comprehensive Strategic Partnership[1].

Joint Statement

Between the Government of the People's Republic of China

and the Government of the Kingdom of Denmark

on the Establishment of a Comprehensive Strategic Partnership

At the invitation of H.E., Wen Jiabao, Premier of the State Council of the People's Republic of China, H.E. Anders Fogh Rasmussen, Prime Minister of the Kingdom of Denmark, came to China to attend the 7th Asia-Europe Meeting and to pay an official visit on 20th—25th October 2008. During the official visit, President Hu Jintao and Premier Wen Jiabao held talks with Prime Minister Rasmussen.

The leaders reviewed the considerable progress of the bilateral relations and the fruitful cooperation in the political, economic, cultural, educational, scientific and technological fields since the establishment of diplomatic relations in 1950. Bilateral relations have been steadily enhanced with greater political mutual trust and respect and expanded economic cooperation and trade.

The two sides agreed that they shared a common interest in working together on bilateral, **multilateral** and global issues. To mark the mutually beneficial relations, the two sides agreed to launch a Comprehensive Strategic Partnership, which would encompass all areas of bilateral relations, and to strengthen their bilateral and multilateral cooperation.

New Words and Expressions

loop [luːp]   n. 环，线(绳)圈
Copenhagen [ˌkəupən'heigən]   n. 哥本哈根
statistic [stə'tistik]   n. 统计量
                                          adj. 统计的，统计学的
multilateral ['mʌlti'lætərəl]   adj. 多边的，多国的

Note

[1] Joint Statement between China and Denmark on Establishment of Comprehensive Strategic Partnership：中国和丹麦之间关于建立全面战略伙伴关系的联合声明。

For more information, you can check out the following link:

http://www.gov.cn/english/2010-04/27/content_1594029.htm

Unit 15　Trade Relationship between China and Sweden since 1730s

Lead-in: Listening (PPT-49)

Listen to the passage carefully, and answer the following questions:

1. What are the construction and layout of the Swedish Pavilion designed to showcase?

2. Who was the Swedish chemist, engineer, innovator, armaments manufacturer and the inventor of dynamite?

Reading

1.1　Swedish Pavilion

The Swedish Pavilion at the Shanghai World Expo 2010 is comprised of four large cubic structures, and the first cube at the pavilion's entrance will be made of **spruces** which grow abundantly in Sweden. Jan Soderlind, who is charge of the Swedish Forest Industries Federation, participated in the construction of the Sweden Pavilion, and told *Oriental Morning Post* that both the construction and layout of the Swedish Pavilion are designed to showcase a perfect balance between Swedish cities and forests, as well as its timber industry that has been developing in a **sustainable** way.

1.2　Alfred Nobel, Inventor of Dynamite and Institutor of the Nobel Prize

Alfred Bernhard Nobel (Stockholm, Sweden, 21 October 1833—Sanremo, Italy, 10 December 1896) was a Swedish chemist, engineer, innovator, armaments manufacturer and the inventor of **dynamite**. He owned Bofors, a major armaments manufacturer, which he had redirected from its previous role as

an iron and steel mill. Nobel held 355 different **patents**, dynamite being the most famous. In his last will, he used his enormous fortune to institute the Nobel Prizes. The synthetic element nobelium was named after him.

1.3 Trade Relationship between China and Sweden since 1730s

A **replica** of the 18th century wooden **merchant ship** *Gotheborg*[1], which reached the southern Chinese city of **Canton** several times in the late 1730s and early 1740s, is an important symbol for the friendly exchanges between China and Sweden.

The 2006 return of the reconstructed *Gotheborg* to Canton and Shanghai has enhanced the friendship between the Chinese and Swedish peoples and thus helped a lot in promoting the growth of the bilateral relationship.

New Words and Expressions

spruce [spruːs]	*n.* 云杉
sustainable [səˈsteinəbl]	*adj.* 可持续发展的
dynamite [ˈdainəmait]	*n.* 炸药
patent [ˈpeitənt, ˈpætənt]	*n.* 专利权，专利品
replica [ˈreplikə, riˈpliːkə]	*n.* 复制品
Canton [ˈkænˈtɔn]	*n.* 广州(旧称)

Note

[1] merchant ship *Gotheborg*："哥德堡号"——瑞典仿古船。1745 年 9 月 12 日，瑞典商船 "哥德堡号"满载着中国的商品，经过整整 30 个月的航行，驶回自己的家乡之港哥德堡。2006 年 08 月 29 日，上海举行 "哥德堡号"访沪欢迎仪式。它完美再现了历史上的 "海上丝绸之路"。

For more information, you can check out the following links:

http://en.wikipedia.org/wiki/Alfred_Nobel

http://www.cctv.com/english/special/news/20091229/102828.shtml

http://www.fmprc.gov.cn/eng/wjb/zzjg/xos/gjlb/3361/3363/t330161.htm

http://www.china.org.cn/english/culture/213558.htm

Unit 16 Switzerland Pavilion

Lead-in: Listening (PPT-50)

Listen to the passage carefully, and answer the following questions:

1. What is this country famous for?

_____

2. Where is the Palace of Nations, the European headquarters of the United Nations?

_____

Reading

1.1 Switzerland Pavilion

The country, famous for its **chocolate**, **watch and natural scenery**, revealed its detail plan after signing the participation contract with the Bureau of Shanghai World Expo Coordination.

The design, chosen out of the 104 candidates through a world-wide competition, focuses on the sustainable development as well as harmony and balance, which coincide with the Chinese philosophy of Yin and Yang.

The most distinguished feature of the pavilion is the outside curtain, made from degradable soybeans and dye-sensitized solar cells that are capable of generating electricity, introduces Salchli.

The curtain will present an image of forest, which will remind people of the nature, said Salchli. And the fiber of the curtain could be degraded after being disposed in the soil in two weeks.

1.2 The Reversed Swiss Flag Became the Symbol of the Red Cross Movement

Switzerland is a landlocked country whose territory is geographically divided between the Alps, the Central Plateau and the Jura.

The Swiss **Confederation** has a long history of **neutrality**—it has not been in a state of war internationally since 1815—and did not join the United Nations until 2002. Switzerland is home to many international organizations, including the World Economic Forum, the International Olympic

Committee, the Red Cross, the World Trade Organization, **FIFA**, and the second largest UN office. On the European level it was a founder of the European Free Trade Association.

Switzerland comprises three main linguistic and cultural regions: German, French, and Italian, to which the Romansh-speaking valleys are added. The Swiss therefore do not form a nation in the sense of a common ethnic or linguistic identity. The strong sense of belonging to the country is founded on the common historical background, shared values (federalism, direct democracy, neutrality) and Alpine symbolism. The establishment of the Swiss Confederation is traditionally dated to 1 August 1291; Swiss National Day is celebrated on the anniversary.

1.3   The Palace of Nations, the European Headquarters of the United Nations in Geneva

An unusual number of international institutions have their seats in Switzerland, in part because of its policy of neutrality. Geneva is the birth place of the **Red Cross** and **Red Crescent Movement** and hosts the United Nations Human Rights Council. The European Broadcasting Union has the official headquarters in the city. Even though Switzerland is one of the most recent countries to have joined the United Nations, the Palace of Nations in Geneva is the second biggest centre for the United Nations after New York, and Switzerland was a founding member of the League of Nations. Apart from the United Nations headquarters, the Swiss Confederation is host to many UN agencies, like the World Health Organization (WHO), the International Telecommunication Union (ITU) and about 200 other international organizations. The World Economic Forum foundation is based in Geneva. It is best known for its annual meeting in Davos which brings together top international business and political leaders to discuss important issues facing the world, including health and the environment.

1.4   Famous Watch Brands Made in Switzerland[1]

Because they are **tabulation process**, the time-consuming human and material resources, is not an ordinary watch can be compared. Professionals said that movement, materials, technology, brands, styles, etc., are all important factors.

Here is the world's top ten list of names:

1. Patek Philippe (Patek Philippe).

2. Vacheron Constantin (Vacheron Constantin).

3. Audemars Piguet (Audemars Piguet).

4. Breguet (Breguet).

5. 10,000 State (IWC).

6. Count (Piaget).

7. Cartier (Cartier).

8. Jaeger (Jaeger LeCoultre).

9. Rolex (Rolex).

10. Girard-Perregaux (Girard-Perregaux).

New Words and Expressions

confederation [kən,fedə'reiʃən]　　　*n.* 联邦

neutrality [njuːˈtræliti]　　　*n.* 中立，中性

FIFA [ˈfiːfə]　　　*abbr.* Federation International de Football Association, 国际足球联盟

Red Crescent Movement　　　*n.* 红新月会(穆斯林国家中相当于红十字会的组织)

Geneva [dʒiˈniːvə]　　　*n.* 日内瓦(瑞士西南部城市)

tabulation process　　　制表工艺

Note

[1] Famous Watch Brands Made in Switzerland：瑞士的制表工艺、耗费人力物力，都不是普通手表所能比拟的。下面是瑞士产世界十大名表：1) 百达翡丽(Patek Philippe)；2) 江诗丹顿(Vacheron Constantin)；3) 爱彼(Audemars Piguet)；4) 宝玑(Breguet)，英国女王维多利亚和英国首相邱吉尔等名人都是宝玑的顾客；5) 万国(IWC)；6) 伯爵(Piaget)；7)卡地亚(Cartier)；8) 积家(Jaeger LeCoultre)；9) 劳力士(Rolex)；10) 芝柏(Girard-Perregaux)。

For more information, you can check out the following link:

http://en.wikipedia.org/wiki/Switzerland

Unit 17   Spain Pavilion and Its Culture

Lead-in: Listening (PPT-51)

Listen to the passage carefully, and answer the following questions:

1. Spain became a global empire during the modern era. How many Spanish speakers are there today, making it the world's second most spoken first language?

_____

2. What function does olive oil has?

_____

Reading

1.1   Spain Unveils Its "Basket" Pavilion

The Spanish Pavilion, fully covered by a skin of 8,500 untreated **wicker panels**, previewed its show for the first time on March 25 in front of hundreds of journalists from all over the world. With the theme of "From the City of Our Parents to the City of Our Children", the three halls in the pavilion will showcase Spanish cities as a **legacy** needing to be **preserved** and improved for future generations. Hall One of Origin presents a journey through time that **highlights** Spain's **identity**. Hall Two of Cities demonstrates the changes seen in Spanish cities from the rural exodus to the present time. Hall Three of Children views the future of the city where our children will live and expresses how cities might be like through the eyes of a child.

1.2   Art Is a Lie That Makes Us Realize the Truth— Pablo Picasso

Analytic Cubism (1909—1912) is a style of painting Picasso developed along with Georges Braque using **monochrome** brownish and neutral colors. Both artists took apart objects and "analyzed" them in terms of their shapes. Picasso and Braque's paintings at this

time have many similarities. **Synthetic Cubism** (1912—1919) was a further development of the genre, in which cut paper fragments—often wallpaper or portions of newspaper pages—were pasted into compositions, marking the first use of collage in fine art.

1.3 Spain Is a Democracy

Spain, officially the Kingdom of Spain, is a member state of the European Union located in southwestern Europe on the Iberian Peninsula. Spain is the second largest country in Western Europe and the European Union after France. Since January 1, 2010, Spain has held the Presidency of the Council of the European Union.

Because of its location, the territory of Spain was subject to many external influences, often simultaneously, since prehistoric times and through the dawn of Spain as a country. Conversely, the country itself has been an important source of influence to other regions, chiefly during the Modern Era, when it became a global empire that has left a **legacy** of over 400 million Spanish speakers today, making it the world's second most spoken first language.

Spain is a democracy organised in the form of a parliamentary government under a constitutional monarchy.

1.4 Olive Oil from Spain Appears on Chinese Market at a Fast Pace

Olive oil from Spain appears on Chinese market at a fast pace. Spanish Embassy in Beijing and Spanish Oliver Oil Association sponsored the promotion activities for their olive oil among Chinese catering circles and customers. The Jingdu Lide Foods Co., Ltd. in Beijing has become the general agent of a Spanish olive oil group in China. Due to its taste and healthcare value, olive oil is gradually well received by Chinese nutrition experts and consumers. Preliminary statistics show that China's average monthly import of olive oil has greatly increased recently.

Persons in the circle hold the view that the rising consumption of olive oil indicates that olive oil has a broad market prospect in China. Scientists point out that olive oil has the function to reduce the incidence of cardiovascular diseases and is conducive to human body **metabolism**.

New Words and Expressions

unveil [ʌnˈveil]	vt.	使公之于众；揭开，揭幕
wicker [ˈwikə]	n.	柳条
	adj.	柳条制的
panel [ˈpænl]	n.	面板，嵌镶板
legacy [ˈlegəsi]	n.	遗赠(物)，遗产(祖先传下来)
preserve [priˈzəːv]	vt.	保护，保持，保存
highlight [ˈhailait]	vt.	加亮，使显著，突出
identity [aiˈdentiti]	n.	身份，特性
Pablo Picasso		巴勃罗·毕加索(西班牙画家、雕塑家)
cubism [ˈkjuːbizm]	n.	立体派
Analytic Cubism		分析立体主义
Synthetic Cubism		综合立体主义
monochrome [ˈmɔnəukrəum]	n.	单色
metabolism [meˈtæbəlizəm]	n.	新陈代谢

For more information, you can check out the following links:

http://en.wikipedia.org/wiki/Spain

http://www.21food.com/news/detail1132.html

Unit 18 Deepened Trade and Economic Cooperation between China and Arab States

Lead-in: Listening (PPT-52)

Listen to the passage carefully, and answer the following questions:

1. What is one of the most powerful and appealing experiences for UAE people?

_____

2. Which two companies are jointly engaged in the natural gas exploration and development, which is the first time for Chinese enterprises to enter into the upper field of energy in Saudi Arabian?

_____

Reading

1.1   United Arab Emirates Pavilion

"One of the most powerful and appealing experiences for UAE people is to travel through our vast desert, and we want to share this experience with Chinese people by building the pavilion," said Salem Saeed Al Ameri, **commissioner** general of UAE's Expo participation.

This photo reminds us of the Chinese Silk Road in the middle ages.

1.2   Deepened Trade and Economic Cooperation between China and Arab States

2006 is the 50th anniversary for China and Arab states launching diplomatic relations. Since China established diplomatic relationship with Egypt in 1956, China signed **bilateral** governmental economic, trade and technological cooperation agreement with 21 Arab states, except Somali, signed investment protection agreement with 16 Arab states, and signed agreement on avoiding double taxation with 11 Arab states.

In 50 years, China and Arab states always kept the principle of equality, mutual benefit, and joint development, and developed trade and economic cooperation. Arab states are China's important destinations for implementing diversified market and going global strategy. China and Arab states have a population of 1.6 billion, with 3.2 trillion USD GDP and 2.2 trillion USD foreign trades. The two parties' economy maintain favorable developing tendency which brings a magnificent opportunity for strengthening trade and economic cooperation.

Trade between China and Arab states increases quickly, Arab states became China's 8th biggest trade partner. China mainly exported mechanical and electrical product, textile and apparel, footwear, tyre, travel items and packages, and imported **crude oil**, chemical raw material, chemical fertilizer and product oil.

In addition, export proportion of high-tech and high value-added product like mechanical and electrical product kept increasing in China's export to Arab states.

1.3   New Achievements Gained in Key Project of Going Global Strategy

Arab states are China's significant markets for implementing going global strategy. As the new turn of infrastructure construction in Arab states, Chinese enterprises should seize the opportunity to get new achievements in communication, electric power and infrastructure construction in Arab states.

The two parties have great complementarities in economy. They would like to explore a new cooperation pattern and field with enthusiasm, utilizing geographical predominance and favorable policy in Arab states to develop investment cooperation in such manufacturing fields as petrochemical, IT, light industry, textile and household appliance, as well as attracting Arab states to invest in China in energy resources, finance and manufacture.

China and Arab states will keep strengthening talks and cooperation in trade and convenient investment, so as to provide politic ensure for expanding and deepening trade and economic cooperation. Cooperation among chambers of industry and commerce will also be **boosted**, cooperative mechanism among promoting organizations of trade and investment will be established. We should better use trade and economic exchanging platform under Sino-Arabic Cooperation Forum and Sino-African Cooperation Forum, provide more communicating and cooperating ways and boost the cooperation to a new level.

1.4 Jointly Engaged in the Natural Gas Exploration and Development

Sinopec and Saudi Arabian Aramco Oil Company are jointly engaged in the natural gas exploration and development[1], which is the first time for Chinese enterprises to enter into the upper field of energy in Saudi Arabian. The picture shows the drilling rig of the exploration site.

New Words and Expressions

United Arab Emirates	阿拉伯联合酋长国(=UAE)
commissioner [kəˈmiʃənə]	*n.* 委员，专员
bilateral [baiˈlætərəl]	*adj.* 双边的
crude oil	原油
boost [bu:st]	*v.* 推进

Note

[1] Sinopec and Saudi Arabian Aramco Oil Company are jointly engaged in the natural gas exploration and development：中石化与沙特阿美石油公司从事天然气勘探开发，这是中国企业首次进入沙特能源上游领域。图为勘探现场的钻机。

For more information, you can check out the following links:

http://english.mofcom.gov.cn/aarticle/newsrelease/significantnews/200702/20070204388030.html

http://www.ccpitgx.org/en/news_show.asp?id=1091&CataID=49

Unit 19   Israel Will Highlight Innovation in Its Pavilion

Lead-in: Listening (PPT-53)

Listen to the passage carefully, and answer the following questions:

1. The Arab League **boycott** of Israel is a **systematic** effort by Arab League member states. What's their purpose?

_____

2. Arab countries suffer economically from the boycott as well. How much worth of goods have they lost the opportunity to export?

_____

Reading

1.1 Israel Will Highlight Innovation in Its Pavilion Along with Putting a Spotlight on Ancient Jewish Culture[1]

It is the first time Israel has committed to building a national pavilion at a World Expo.

The pavilion consists of three areas—Whispering Garden, Hall of Light and Hall of Innovations.

The **Whispering Garden**[2] is a green **orchard** that greets visitors as they enter the building. Some facilities will be installed to make the trees begin to "whisper" in both English and Chinese when visitors walk close to them, Haim Z. Dotan, chief designer of the pavilion, told _Shanghai Daily_.

The **Hall of Light**[3] includes a 15-meter high screen. It will display films highlighting the country's innovations and technological achievements.

The **Hall of Innovation**[4] is the centerpiece of the Israel Pavilion. A special audio-visual show

will allow visitors to talk with Israeli children, scientists, doctors and inventors via hundreds of screens.

1.2   Arab League Boycott of Israel[5]

The Arab League boycott of Israel is a **systematic** effort by Arab League member states to **isolate** Israel **economically** in support of the Palestinians to prevent Arab states and discourage non-Arabs from providing support to Israel and adding to Israel's economic and military strength. Historically, the boycott was also designed to **deter** Jewish immigration to the region.

1.3   Organized Boycott of Israel

Officially, the Arab League boycott covers three areas:

1. Products and services that originate in Israel (referred to as the primary boycott and still enforced in many Arab states);

2. Businesses in non-Arab countries that do business with Israel (the secondary boycott);

3. Businesses shipped or flew to Israeli ports (the **tertiary** boycott).

1.4   Economic Effects

Although it cannot be estimated to what extent the boycott hurt Israel's economy, the boycott cannot be said to have affected it to the extent the Arabs intended.

Arab countries suffer economically from the boycott as well. In its report on the cost of conflict in the Middle East, Strategic Foresight Group estimates that Arab states have lost an opportunity to export $10 billion worth of goods to Israel between 2000—2010. Moreover, the Arab states of the Persian Gulf and Iran together stand to lose $30 billion as the opportunity cost of not exporting oil to Israel in the second half of this decade.

New Words and Expressions

boycott ['bɔikət]	*n. & vt.* 联合抵制，联合排斥某国货物或与某国绝交
highlight ['hailait]	*n.* 最显著(重要)部分
	vt. 加亮，使显著，突出
innovation [,inəu'veiʃən]	*n.* 改革，创新
spotlight ['spɔtlait]	*n.* 聚光灯
ancient Jewish culture	古代犹太文化
orchard ['ɔ:tʃəd]	*n.* 果园，果园里的全部果树

systematic [ˌsisti'mætik]   *adj.* 系统的，体系的

deter [di'tə:]   *v.* 阻止

tertiary ['tə:ʃəri]   *adj.* 第三的，第三位的

Notes

[1] Israel Will Highlight Innovation in Its Pavilion Along with Putting a Spotlight on Ancient Jewish Culture：爱因斯坦曾说过，"以色列只有依靠发展专业科技才能赢得生存的战斗"。现代以色列人的确听取了这位诺贝尔奖得主的建言。此次以色列国家馆展示了改善全世界人们生活的突破性发明，包括太阳能技术及用于医疗诊断的迷你"胶囊内镜"。

[2] Whispering Garden：回音花园象征着人与自然之间的对话。漫步在两旁回音树的隐蔽小道上，观光者避免了太阳的灼热和雨淋，也可以在长椅上休息。观光者可以领略以色列农艺。

[3] Hall of Light：采光展馆。当漫步在流线型的墙壁间，观光者可以领略犹太历史中的创新，从圣经时间到耶路撒冷和爱因斯坦。爱因斯坦是犹太人。

[4] Hall of Innovations：创新展厅是以色列展馆的最大亮点。在观众面前交互的灯光球把创新精神从以色列群众传递给中国观众。

[5] Arab League boycott of Israel：阿拉伯国家联合抵制以色列。

For more information, you can check out the following links:

http://flashtrafficblog.wordpress.com/2010/03/27/nearly-300-members-of-congress-sign-letter-declaring-unbreakable-bond-with-israel/

http://en.wikipedia.org/wiki/Arab_League_boycott_of_Israel

Unit 20 China-Singapore Economic Cooperation Forum

Lead-in: Listening (PPT-54)

Listen to the passage carefully, and answer the following questions:

1. What is the theme of Singapore Pavilion?

_____

2. What is the symbol of Singapore?

_____

Reading

1.1 Theme of Singapore Pavilion

The Singapore pavilion will be a two-story 3,000-square-meter structure with an "Urban Symphony" theme. The pavilion design looks like a huge "music box".

Singapore Prime Minister Lee Hsien Loong said at the groundbreaking ceremony that the World Expo Shanghai will see the largest-scale participation by Singapore yet in any expo. He hoped the miniature of Singapore will bring new experience to the worldwide visitors and further strengthen bilateral ties between Singapore and China.

Singapore Pavilion, titled "Urban Symphony", shows the contribution of Singapore in the field of city planning, water treatment, and environmental services. The harmony of urban and nature, the creativity and diverse-culture will be the key message that Singapore Pavilion tries to deliver.

Lim Sau Hoong, Chair of World Expo 2010 Shanghai China, Singapore Pavilion Advisory Panel said: "We take into account of an ancient Chinese saying that 'the one with the harmony of heaven and earth will be truly happy'. So what we hope to achieve is to let all the audience to feel the 'music', to experience the 'He' of the harmony elements on every spot of our pavilion."

As a world-famous garden city, orchid is Singapore's national flower. Singapore breeds a special kind of orchid for Shanghai Expo, named "Singapore Shanghai Expo Dendrobium", to symbolize the **vitality** of Singapore and Shanghai in their way to international **metropolis**.

1.2   A Statue of the Merlion, a Symbol of Singapore

A statue of the Merlion, a symbol of Singapore[1], is seen **illuminated** at dusk overlooking the Marina Bay area in Singapore November 8, 2009. Singapore will host the Asia-Pacific Economic Cooperation (APEC) meetings from November 11 to 14.

This is a must-see attraction in Singapore. It is nothing more than a statue at the end of the river but the views of the city and river from the observation platform next to the statue are very good. It is also the **icon** of Singapore so you can't really say you've seen the city without seeing the famous Merlion statue.

It's situated at the mouth of the Singapore river and in a nice area with shops and restaurants within easy reach. If you take one of the city tours, especially the river tours, you will see the Merlion but it's worth returning to so you can get up close to it. It's a nice place to sit and relax too and just people watch or enjoy the scenery.

1.3   China-Singapore Economic Cooperation Forum[2]

Singapore International Enterprise Development Board Executive Director Liyixian (Lee Yi Shyan) President: "We are very pleased with our friends in China and Shanghai and partners in this grand event gathered. As foreign investors, we have brought China capital, technology, management experience and international network of relations, the Chinese rich resources, talent and huge market provide for the operation and functioning of the foreign opportunities, have become mutually beneficial win-win partnership. Singapore International Enterprise Development Board's mission is to help Singapore companies internationalization development, the forum is to strengthen cooperation and **liaison** enterprises of the two countries rare opportunity."

New Words and Expressions

Urban Symphony	城市交响曲主题
vitality [vai'tæliti]	n. 活力，生命力；生动性
metropolis [mi'trɔpəlis]	n. 主要都市，都会
illuminate [i'lju:mineit]	vt. 照亮
icon ['aikɔn]	n. 图标，肖像，偶像
liaison [li(:)'eizɑːn, -zən]	n. 联络

Notes

[1] A statue of the Merlion, a symbol of Singapore：鱼身狮头的雕像是新加坡的标志，鱼尾狮是新加坡的象征。

[2] China-Singapore Economic Cooperation Forum：中国-新加坡经合论坛，为中新经济、商务合作提供交流平台和投资商机。

For more information, you can check out the following links:

http://www.chinadaily.com.cn/china/apec2009/2009-11/09/content_8934433.htm

http://www.tripadvisor.com/ShowUserReviews-g294265-d644919-r20975504-Merlion_Statue-Singapore.html

Unit 21   China and Japan's Relationship

Listen to the passage carefully, and answer the following questions:

1. What theme will the country's exhibit feature?

2. Why did China and Japan jointly launch the Sino-Japanese high-level economic dialogue mechanism at Vice Prime Minister level?

Reading

1.1   Japan Pavilion

Japan will highlight the role of advanced ecological technology in helping humans achieve a more comfortable life and confidence in the future with its huge "breathing organism" pavilion at World Expo 2010 as the country signed a participation contract with organizers today in Shanghai.

The country's exhibit will feature a theme on the harmony between the human heart and technology. Technologies can contribute to a cleaner world and a better life so that people may gain **tranquility** and confidence, but it should be guided by our love of the earth, people and our children, said Hiroshi Tsukamoto, Commissioner General of the Japanese Section Expo Shanghai 2010, after the ceremony.

The country's **semi-circular** pavilion will make efficient use of natural resources with solar energy collection batteries and a double-layer membrane that can **filter** sunshine to **coincide** with its **interpretation** of how technology can better our lives.

Visitors will be able to experience some Chinese elements at Japan Pavilion, which will involve Chinese characters and traditional Chinese architectural styles. The history of Japanese diplomatic envoys visiting China will also be part of the exhibit.

1.2　China and Japan Jointly Launched the Sino-Japanese High-level Economic Dialogue Mechanism

China and East Asia keep good economic and trade relation and the level of their cooperation has been upgraded continuously. In order to bring a new era for the Sino-Japanese economic and trade cooperation, China and Japan jointly launched the Sino-Japanese high-level economic dialogue mechanism at Vice Prime Minister level in April 2007. In December 2007, the first Sino-Japanese high-level economic dialogue was held.

1.3　Toshodai Temple and Ganjin

This temple was built by Priest Ganjin in 759, who came to Japan from China, invited by the Emperor. Ganjin arrived in Japan in 754, on his sixth trial.

The Kon-do, which has pillars of beautiful entasis, is the representative architecture of the Tenpyo era. If you step in the silent precinct, you will feel as though the time has stopped. The buildings such as the Kon-do, Kodo, treasure house, and scripture house standing in line, gives people some ideas of its former splendor. The precincts still remains most of its appearance, and the arrangement of the buildings tells the magnanimous Tenpyo era's culture. After the capital transferring to Heian-kyo, the temple once lost its power, but in the Kamakura era, Kakusei Shonin revived the temple. In the Edo era, the temple was repaired again. The temple's name comes from Ganjin from the country Toh (China).

1.4　Culture Interchange with China

Heijo-kyo in this time, was more international than Japan was before the war. Probably, through the Silk Road, nomads such as the Turks, and Persians had come to Japan. Japan did not develop its own culture from ancient times, nor was influenced only by the Chinese or Korean culture. Japan was always connected with the continent by the people's interchange.

This temple transmits the feeling of ancient times, and is surrounded by a strange atmosphere as if we are in rapport with the ancient people. There still remains the vestige of the unique Tenpyo culture's powerful and free culture.

Ganjin arrived to Japan, experiencing many shipwrecks and sufferings. He even lost his eyesight in the end. He provided the first Saidan-in in Todai-ji temple.

New Words and Expressions

tranquility [træŋ'kwiliti]	*n.* 安静，安宁
semi-circular ['semi'sə:kjulə]	*adj.* 半圆的
filter ['filtə]	*n. & vt.* 过滤，渗透，用过滤法除去
coincide [ˌkəuin'said]	*vi.* 一致，符合
interpretation [inˌtə:pri'teiʃən]	*n.* 解释，阐明；口译，通译
Toshodai Temple	日本奈良的唐招提寺
Ganjin	唐代高僧鉴真

For more information, you can check out the following link:

http://library.thinkquest.org/29295/toshodaiji.htm

Examination on Chapter Three

Name _____ **No.** _____

I. Fill in the blanks: 60%

1. The Flag of _____ is the flag and emblem of the European Union (EU) and Council of Europe (COE) (it is also used to indicate the euro or Euro zone countries). It consists of a circle of 12 golden (yellow) stars on a _____ background. The blue represents the west, the number of stars represents completeness while their position in a circle represents unity.

2. The theme of the exposition will be *"Better City, better _____"* and signifies Shanghai's new status in the 21st century as a major economic and cultural center. Its design features a traditional style red architecture called "_____ crown". Organizers said the project is a significant milestone in the countdown to the 2010 event, signaling the beginning of full-scale construction of the Expo's core projects.

3. The theme of the _____ Pavilion is "Rising to the Challenge." The shape of the USA Pavilion shadows that of an _____, a creature that is uninhibited by boundaries. It also serves as the national emblem for America, a country that offers limitless opportunities.

4. Canada's relationship with China has certainly flowered during the 2000s. China is now Canada's _____ trading partner, trailing only to the US. In the _____ Canada-China Business Forum, held in 2005 during a visit by President Hu Jintao to Canada, the two governments set a target to increase bilateral trade to USD30 billion by 2010. That goal was met in 2007, when trade between the two countries climbed to USD30.38 billion.

5. _____ was the first Latin American country to sign a _____ trade agreement in the Expo 2010 and is the second-largest trading partner with China in the region.

6. Chinese Premier Wen Jiabao shakes hands with British Prime Minister _____ _____ during the dinner Brown hosts for him at the British prime minister's official residence on the outskirts of London Jan. 31, 2009. Chinese Premier Wen Jiabao arrived in London on Jan. 31 for a three-day visit to Britain.

7. Siemens Confident of _____ Train Deal with China. The Shanghai Maglev Train connects the Pudong international airport to the Shanghai subway. The 30km (18-mile) trip takes just over seven minutes. Trains can travel at speeds of up to 430 kph (268 mph). _____ Siemens and ThyssenKrupp co-developed the technology.

8. The pavilion will take a _____ outer skin in red and white colors, which represent the colors of the Austria national flag. The _____ color also takes on Chinese meaning of the color of good luck.

9. _____ is home to more nationalities than any other city in the world and Dutch dredging companies and dike builders operate on a global scale. When people think of the Netherlands, a

low lying country with numerous dams, _____ and clogs come to mind. At the upcoming World Expo in Shanghai, the country will demonstrate that it has far more to offer.

10. Luxemburg, _____ Heart of Europe. The idea "forest and _____" comes from the literal meaning of the Chinese term for Luxembourg. The EXPO pavilion, built from steel, wood and glass, will be an open fortress around with greenery. The 15-meter-high main structure will resemble an ancient castle with large openings surrounded by medieval towers.

11. The whole building is a loop, and you get to ride it on one of 1,500 fucking city bicycles they brought over from the DK. You know what else they are bringing? A "little mermaid" statue that has been a symbol of _____ and _____ for almost 100 years.

12. A replica of the 18th century wooden _____ ship *Gotheborg*, which reached the southern Chinese city of Canton several times in the late 1730s and early 1740s, is an important symbol for the friendly exchanges between China and _____.

13. Switzerland, famous for its chocolate, _____ and natural _____, revealed its detail plan after signing the participation contract with the Bureau of Shanghai World Expo Coordination.

14. Israel will highlight innovation in its pavilion along with putting a spotlight on ancient _____ culture. It is the first time _____ has committed to building a national pavilion at a World Expo.

15. Lim Sau Hoong, Chair of World Expo 2010 Shanghai China, Singapore Pavilion Advisory Panel said: "We take into account of an ancient Chinese saying that 'the one with the _____ of heaven and earth will be truly happy'. So what we hope to achieve is to let all the audience to feel the '_____', to experience the 'He' of the harmony elements on every spot of our pavilion."

II. Translate the following phrases into English: 20%

1. 圣母玛利亚(耶稣基督之母) _____
2. 拥抱挑战 _____
3. 桑巴舞(一种源自非洲的巴西舞) _____
4. 探戈 _____
5. 伦巴舞(由古巴黑人民间舞蹈发展而成的一种交际舞) _____
6. 中美洲和南美洲联合展示馆 _____
7. 阿拉伯联合酋长国 _____
8. 回音花园 _____
9. 城市交响曲主题 _____
10. 中国-新加坡经合论坛 _____

III. Translate the following phrases into Chinese: 20%

1. Regional Economic Cooperation to Seek Mutually Beneficial Win-win Situation, and to Build a

Harmonious Region.

_____

2. The Economic and Trade Cooperation between China and the American and Oceanian Region.

_____

3. Joint Statement between China and Denmark on Establishment of Comprehensive Strategic Partnership.

_____

4. Sinopec and Saudi Arabian Aramco Oil Company are jointly engaged in the natural gas exploration and development, which is the first time for Chinese enterprises to enter into the upper field of energy in Saudi Arabian.

_____

5. China and Japan jointly launched the Sino-Japanese high-level economic dialogue mechanism.

_____

CHAPTER *F*OUR

Intercultural Business Communication and Commercial Achievements

Unit 1   America Is Seeing a Challenge from China[1]

Lead-in: Listening (PPT-56)

Listen to the passage carefully, and answer the following questions:

1. Why is America seeing a challenge from China?

_____

2. According to the statement of White House, what is Obama's decision?

_____

Reading

1.1   China Not Manipulating Currency[2]

According to a latest report from the US Treasury, China did not **manipulate the currency** (CNY) and has made remarkable contribution to world economy in 2009. This is very rare and sort of unexpected from US government, who has been one of the biggest complaints of the under-valuation of CNY. According to the report, CNY has appreciated against USD for about 21 percent since 2005, reflecting the true picture of what is needed in real economy. IT would be interesting to see whether there is any follow up of criticism from US on RMB exchange rate after this report.

1.2   China's Foreign Reserve Amounts to 2,273 Billion[3]

China's **Foreign Reserve** in Sept. 2009 has increased by about 63 billion USD from August and reached 2,273 billion USD. Due to the strong recovery in China's export, particularly in low cost goods and low value chain, "Made in China" continues to dominate world export market. China's foreign reserve has surpassed 1 trillion USD in Jan. 2007 and 2 trillion USD in April 2009. The Chinese government has expressed concerns on the "safety" of the reserve (believed to be 90% in USD) for several times since the financial crisis unfolded in 2008. China's foreign reserve is now world's No. 1.

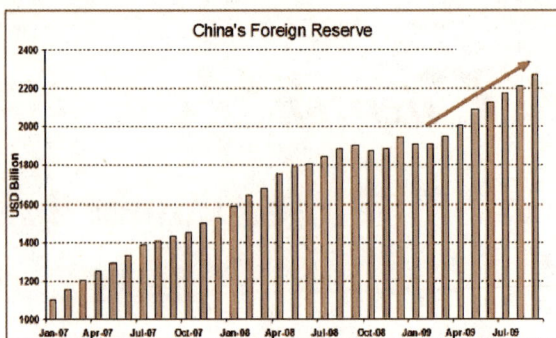

1.3   Export Growth Starts to recover[4]

Sept. is the third consecutive month that China's monthly export growth exceeds that of last year. In Sept. 2009 China's export grew a 116% compared to Sept. 2008, following a healthy growth in July and August. China's export has benefited from the low labor cost in the country, focus on the low value chain and an arguable undervalued RMB. Despite the three months of positive growth, China government

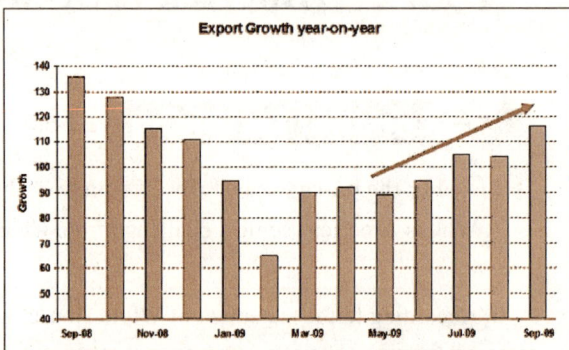

sticks to the view that the current recovery is still very fragile and there is a risk for fall again when the stimulus program is not followed up with further excitement. Therefore it is unlikely that RMB will be revalued any time soon.

1.4   China's Trade Surplus Continues to Grow[5]

China's Trade Surplus continues to grow despite both China and US governments' effort to "rebalance" the world economy. China's world record trade surplus has been criticized as one of **culprits** for the current financial crisis. Both China and US government agree that one of the keys to reverse the current **recession** is for China to consume more, save less, export less and for US to consume less and save more. However, it seems that such a rebalance has not taken place on any significant scale yet.

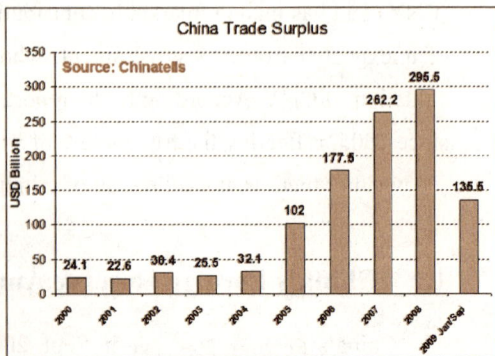

1.5　America to Learn from British Lesson[6]

Wall Street Journal: About 100 years ago, the British Empire has reached its apex. There are British colonies all over the world and British fleet controlling the world's major oceans and trade flows. British pound was the world's currency. Since then, a history of British Empire's fall has been witnessed. American empire, through two world wars, took the leading position and replaced GB as the world's dominant power. Now, **America is seeing a challenge from China**, which might put them in a similar situation as Britain. How to avoid America becoming another Britain becomes the central topic for all the western politicians who are still obsessed with the American system, democracy, freedom of speech, McDonald's and Coca-Cola.

1.6　Obama: China Is Neither Friend Nor Enemy[7]

Fortune: Obama is the first American president in the last 20 years to use WTO Section 421 to penalize China. All the former presidents are well aware of such a section but all opt to pass for the "bigger picture". According to the statement of White House, Obama's decision is to show that the government is determined to **enforce** the trade laws and encourage open policy for free trade. Therefore the government chooses a "million dollar sector" to avoid any sizable mess, even though there are still American companies who own tire factories in China being hurt. According to Mr. Obama, China is not a friend, nor an enemy. China is a competitor. Such a mentality might dominate the American policy towards China in the coming four years.

New Words and Expressions

challenge ['tʃælindʒ]	*n.* 挑战
	vt. 向······挑战
manipulating currency	操纵汇率
foreign reserve	外汇储备
culprit ['kʌlprit]	*n.* 犯人，罪人
recession [ri'seʃən]	*n.* 工商业之衰退，不景气
enforce [in'fɔːs]	*vt.* 强迫，执行；坚持，加强

Notes

[1] America Is Seeing a Challenge from China：美国似乎感觉到了来自中国崛起的威胁和挑战。

[2] China Not Manipulating Currency：《中国日报》报道，美国财政部最近在向其国会递交的一份报告上声称，中国政府没有操纵人民币汇率。

[3] China's Foreign Reserve Amounts to 2,273 Billion：中国外汇储备 9 月份又增加 630 亿美元，达到 2.2 万亿。

[4] Export Growth Starts to Recover：出口增长有恢复，中国 2009 年 9 月出口额相对于 2008 年 9 月增加了 116%，是今年连续第三个月连续正增长。

[5] China's Trade Surplus Continues to Grow：贸易顺差有增无减。

[6] America to Learn from British Lesson：大英帝国衰落的教训。《华尔街日报》曾评论说，在 20 世纪的 100 年中，美国成功地从英国手中夺取了世界霸主的地位。这样的过程绝非一朝一夕能完成，其中也经历了两次惨绝人寰的世界大战。21 世纪的今天，美国似乎感觉到了来自中国的威胁和挑战。如何继续维持美国和美元的强权霸主地位，成为美帝国主义政客们朝思暮想的课题之一。

[7] China Is Neither Friend Nor Enemy：非友非敌的中美关系。

For more information, you can check out the following link:

http://crossick.blogactiv.eu/2010/02/09/china%E2%80%99s-challenge-to-american-hegemony/

Unit 2   EU—Comprehensive Strategic Partner of Cooperation

Lead-in: Listening (PPT-57)

Listen to the passage carefully, and answer the following questions:

1. Since China's Reform and Opening-up, who is China's largest accumulated technology and equipment supplier?

2. At present, within 27 members of the EU, which five countries are the top five trading partners of China?

Reading

1.1   EU—Comprehensive Strategic Partner of Cooperation[1]

Since China's Reform and Opening-up, **EU is China's largest accumulated technology and equipment supplier**. Germany, France, UK, Italy and Netherland rank at the top 5 respectively in technological transfer to China.

EU is the fourth largest actual investor of China. In all the members of EU, as far as the actual investment is concerned, UK, Germany, Netherland, France and Italy rank at the top five.

At present, within 27 members of the EU, Germany, Netherland, Britain, Italy and France are the top five trading partners of China.

China-Europe economic and trade relationship is an important part of China-Europe Comprehensive Strategic Partner Relationship and the important economic base to remain China-Europe bilateral relationship. In recent years, under the great attention paid by the leaders of both parties and with their active promotion, China-Europe economic and trade relationship has developed rapidly and achieved great success. Nowadays, EU becomes the first largest trading partner, export market, resource of technology introduction of China and the fourth largest actual investor of China. And China becomes the second largest trading partner of EU.

1.2 The All-around Development of China-Europe Economic and Trade Relationship[2]

By the end of June 2008, European investment projects in China had exceeded 33,000 with the contract price of 120 billion US dollars and actual use of foreign capital of 64.4 billion US dollars. The amount of single investment project of the European ries is higher than the average of that of other ries and regions, which means the quality of the European investment project is generally better.

The map of Europe 52 ries and regions as well as 2 regional organizations in Europe have established economic and trade relationship with China. The total area of Europe is more than 27 million square kilometers. Its population exceeds 800 million. The ries of European Union (EU) and West Europe belong to developed economies with mature markets, high extent of integration and **stable policies**. The ries of the dle and East Europe with fast economy transition entered into EU successively. The CIS ries all belong to transition economies. In the economic and trade cooperation with European ries, ries of West Europe are important trading partners and resources of capital and technologies of China while ries of CIS as well as the dle and East Europe are the important areas for China to implement the **market diversification** and the strategy of "Going Global".

1.3 European Unemployment and Hopes of an Economic Recovery

The Federal Open Market Committee (FOMC) maintained its extraordinarily **accommodative** monetary policy following its meeting on Wednesday. The communiqué had no surprises and said that the committee expected to keep the fed funds rate target in the 0—0.25% range "for an extended period". As expected, the European Central Bank (ECB) and the Bank of England (BoE) also kept interest rates unchanged at 1% and 0.5% respectively.

"A hesitant **economic recovery**, tame **inflation** and severe credit headwinds suggest that monetary policy will need to stay very easy for at least another year. Liquidity trends will not be a constraint on higher prices for risk **assets** for a while," said BCA Research.

The jump in the unemployment rate to a 26-year high of 10.2% in October—an increase of 0.4 of a percentage point—reminded **pundits** of the challenges in the labor market and broader economy. While investors' hopes of an economic recovery might have got ahead of reality, the **cartoonists** continually reminded us of **worrisome issues**.

New Words and Expressions

strategic [strəˈtiːdʒik]	*adj.* 战略的，战略上的
stable policy	稳定的政策
market diversification [daivəːsifiˈkeiʃən]	市场多样化
accommodative [əˈkɔməˌdeitiv]	*adj.* 善于适应新环境的
economic recovery	经济复苏
inflation [inˈfleiʃən]	*n.* 通货膨胀，(物价)暴涨
asset [ˈæset]	*n.* 资产
pundit [ˈpʌndit]	*n.* 博学者
cartoonist [kɑːˈtuːnist]	*n.* 漫画家
worrisome issues	令人不安的问题

Notes

[1] EU—Comprehensive Strategic Partner of Cooperation：全面战略合作伙伴——欧盟。目前，欧盟是中国第一大贸易伙伴和出口市场、最大技术引进来源地及第四大实际投资方；中国是欧盟第二大贸易伙伴。

[2] The All-around Development of China-Europe Economic and Trade Relationship：全面发展的中国-欧洲经贸关系。

For more information, you can check out the following link:

http://en.wikipedia.org/wiki/European_Union

Unit 3 Regional Economic Cooperation[1] to Seek Mutually Beneficial Win-win Situation

Lead-in: Listening (PPT-58)

Listen to the passage carefully, and answer the following questions:

1. Why is Asia-Pacific Economic Cooperation (APEC) the largest-scaled and highest-level regional economic cooperation forum China has participated in?

2. What policies do the Region of America and Oceania for China utilize?

Reading

1.1 Asia-Pacific Economic Cooperation (APEC)

In recent years, regional economic cooperation is **flourishing** at the global level. Regional economic cooperation is not only an important way for both China and regional members, neighboring ries in particular, to mutually open up, seek common development, share benefits and risks, but also a major approach to promote economic growth in Chinas border areas, and **coordinated** development among different regions in China.

Asia-Pacific Economic Cooperation (APEC) is the largest-scaled and highest-level regional economic cooperation forum China has participated in, which provides an **arena** for China to display its achievements of reform and opening-up and promotes China's further opening-up process. China attaches great importance to the role of APEC and actively participates in its cooperation.

1.2 The Region of America and Oceania for China to Utilize Its "Two Resources" and "Two Markets"

The Region of America and Oceania is an important region for China to utilize its "two resources" and "two markets", in order to carry out its strategies of "Going Global" and "Bring in". In the meantime, two-way investment, overseas project contracting, labor services and design consultations between China and the region have also developed expeditiously. The statistics the Ministry of Commerce shows that by the end of 2007, turnovers of USD 15.573 billion, USD 3.291 billion and USD 68 million were respectively realized in American and Oceanian region for project contracting, labor service cooperation and technical consultation, respectively taking up 7.5%, 6.9% and 3.1% of the total value. In the

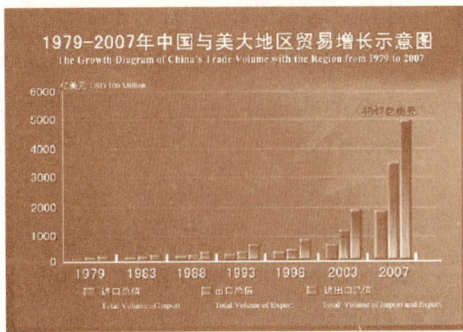

1979-2007年中国与美大地区贸易增长示意图
The Growth Diagram of China's Trade Volume with the Region from 1979 to 2007

year of 2007, China's non-finance FDI outflow to American and Oceanian Region was USD 6.101 billion, constituting 48% of the amount of China's non-finance FDI outflows to the globe that year (USD 12.72 billion). By the end of 2007, the accumulated actual investment American and Oceanian Region to China reached USD 174.099 billion, acing for 22.8% of the whole accumulated actual investment to China (USD 763.015 billion).

1.3 A Contrast of China's Trade Volumes with the Region and with the World in the Past Thirty Years

The statistics the Ministry of Commerce shows that in the year of 2007, China's non-finance FDI outflow to American and Oceanian region was USD 6.101 billion, of which outflows to North America, Latin America, and Oceanian & Pacific Islands respectively reached USD 3.049 billion USD 1.893 billion and USD 1.159 billion. The above mentioned outflow constitutes 48% of China's total non-finance FDI outflows to the world (USD 12.72 billion) in 2007.

By the end of 2007, the actual investment in China American and Oceanian region was USD 174.099 billion, taking up 22.8% of the actual input to China the globe (USD 763.015 billion). The investment the top 6 investors in the region acts for 94.9% of total investment the region. The top 6 are Virgin Islands (USD 74.146 billion), the United States (USD 56.706 billion), the Cayman Islands (USD 13.362 billion), Samoa (USD 9.765 billion), Canada (USD 5.828 billion), and Australia (USD 5.409 billion).

2007年中国对美大地区非金融类对外直接投资分布
Geographic Distribution of China Non-finance FDI Outflows to the American and Oceanian Region

1.4 Economic and Trade Cooperation Mechanism between China and the American and Oceanian Region[2]

During 30 years of opening up, China and the American & Oceanian ries have established the dialogue mechanism of economic and trade cooperation, which mainly includes joint commissions and forums between China and ries in the region. Such mechanism has been an important platform for widening economic and trade cooperation, coping with issues in bilateral economic and trade cooperation, and promoting healthy and steady development of economic and trade relations between China and the American and Oceanian ries.

At present, MOFCOM is taking the lead in coordinating 23 multilateral or bilateral economic and trade cooperation mechanism above vice ministerial level between China and the American and Oceanian ries, of which two are vice prime minister level, 5 ministerial level, 16 vice ministerial level, and 3 others.

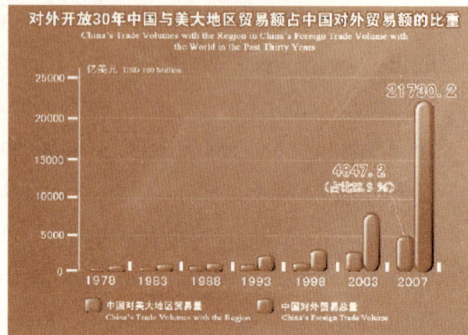

New Words and Expressions

flourishing [ˈflʌriʃiŋ]	*adj.* 繁茂的，繁荣的，欣欣向荣的
coordinate [kəuˈɔːdinit]	*n.* 同等者，同等物；坐标(用复数)
	adj. 同等的，并列的
	vt. 调整，整理
arena [əˈriːnə]	*n.* 竞技场，舞台
mechanism [ˈmekənizəm]	*n.* 机械装置；机构，机制
Oceanian	*adj.* 大洋洲的

Notes

[1] Regional Economic Cooperation：区域经济合作。

[2] Economic and Trade Cooperation Mechanism between China and the American and Oceanian Region：中国和美大地区经贸合作机制。

For more information, you can check out the following link:

http://en.wikipedia.org/wiki/Asia-Pacific_Economic_Cooperation

Unit 4 Multilateral Cooperation in Disaster Relief to Express Humanitarian Care[1]

Lead-in: Listening (PPT-59)

Listen to the passage carefully, and answer the following questions:

1. How many people did the Indian Ocean tsunami kill?

_____

2. Being the only foreign rescue team to run medical-aid stations in quake-ravaged Haiti, what are Chinese rescuers providing quake victims with?

_____

Listen to "Timothy Shiver's Speech at the Closing Ceremont of the Special Olympics"[2] carefully, and answer the following questions:

1. President Rogge also thanked the people of China, all the volunteers and the Beijing Organizing Committee of the 29th Summer Olympics. What did he say?

_____

2. Where will the 30th summer Olympic Games be held?

_____

3. How long did the 29th Summer Olympics last?

_____

Reading

1.1 Assistance to the Earthquake-hit Areas in Pakistan

A major earthquake rocked Pakistan in October 2005. After the earthquake, China immediately provided，through United Nations Development Programme, a large quantity of emergency disaster relief assistance to the earthquake-hit areas in Pakistan.

The picture shows that relief supplies provided by China through multilateral agencies were sent Shijiazhuang Airport to the earthquake-

hit areas of Pakistan on October 12th, 2005.

1.2   China Has Donated Nearly 1.3 Billion RMB to the Indian Ocean Tsunami Disaster-hit Ries

The picture shows the porters moved disaster-relief supplies China in Jakarta airport on January 7th, 2005. Through multilateral and other channels, China has donated nearly 1.3 billion RMB to the Indian Ocean tsunami disaster-hit ries.

In December 2004, the **Indian Ocean tsunami** killed nearly 300,000 people; millions of victims were in urgent need of relief. China donated USD20 million through the United Nations Office for the Coordination of Humanitarian Affairs, the United Nations Development Programme, the World Health Organization and other agencies under the UN system. The donation was used for emergency relief, post-disaster rehabilitation and reconstruction.

The picture shows the school bags procured with China's donation for the affected children in Indonesia.

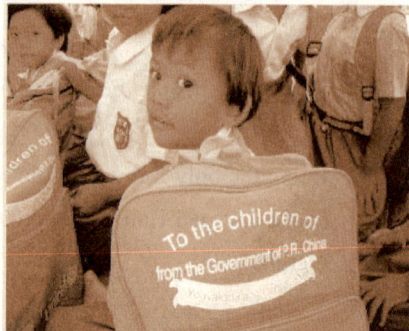

1.3   Chinese Rescuers Provide Much-needed Medical Assistance in Haiti

1.3.1   China's Relief Materials Leave for Quake-hit Haiti

Emergency **humanitarian aid cargo** is seen before being loaded on a plane at the Beijing Capital International Airport in Beijing, **Jan. 16, 2010**. A Boeing-747 jumbo jet carrying 90 tons of Chinese government's emergency humanitarian aid cargo took off from Beijing Capital International Airport to quake-hit Haiti.

In all, Beijing has provided 48 million yuan ($7.1 million) in materials and medical services, as well as $3.6 million in cash to Haiti, according to the Chinese Foreign Ministry.

A second shipment of Chinese goods arrived at the **Port-au-Prince Airport** on January 26. The 65 tons of supplies included **portable** power generators, water purification devices, tents, clothes and medicine. The third shipment, consisting of 25 tons of medical aid, reached Haiti on February 8.

1.3.2   Medical Assistance to Quake-ravaged Haiti

In this photo, a Chinese doctor treats Haitian patients at a shelter for earthquake victims in Port-au-Prince on February 1.

Being the only foreign rescue team to run medical-aid stations in **quake-ravaged** Haiti, Chinese rescuers are giving quake victims what they desperately need: medical assistance.

1.3.3 Peacekeeping Police Officers to Haiti

In this photo, a member of the Chinese anti-riot peacekeeping police team in Haiti cares for an injured Haitian baby at an orphanage in Port-au-Prince on January 30.

In addition to medical workers, China has deployed four more peacekeeping police officers to Haiti. Among the eight Chinese police officers killed in the earthquake, four were members of the Chinese peacekeeping police force in Haiti.

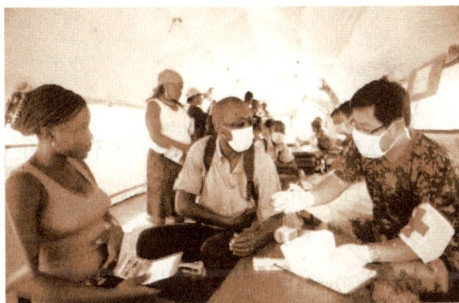

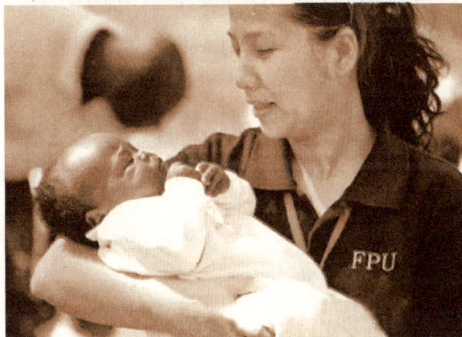

1.4 China Ready to Deliver Quake-relief Assistance to Chile

After the catastrophic earthquake, Chinese President Hu Jintao on Saturday sent a message of **condolence** to his Chilean **counterpart Michelle Bachelet**[3] over the **casualties** and property losses.

Hu, **on behalf of** the Chinese government as well as in his own name, extended sincere condolences to Bachelet, the Chilean people and government as well as deep sympathies to the earthquake victims.

New Words and Expressions

Indian Ocean tsunami [tsjuːˈnɑːmi]　　印度洋海啸
Indonesia [ˌindəuˈniːzjə]　　*n.* 印尼(东南亚岛国)
aid cargo　　援助货物
Port-au-Prince　　太子港(海地的首都，是海地最大的港口)
portable [ˈpɔːtəbl]　　*adj.* 轻便的，手提(式)的，便携式的
quake-ravaged　　地震灾区
condolence [kənˈdəuləns]　　*n.* 哀悼，吊唁
counterpart [ˈkauntəpɑːt]　　*n.* 同等职位的人，配对物
casualty　　*n.* 人员伤亡
on behalf of　　代表……

Notes

[1] Multilateral Cooperation in Disaster Relief to Express Humanitarian Care, and to Build Blocks of Friendship：多边救灾合作：体现人道关怀，共架友谊金桥。

[2] IPC：残奥会会徽，全称是"国际残疾人奥林匹克委员会"(International Paralympics Committee)。

[3] Michelle Bachelet：智利历史上第 1 位女总统巴切莱特。2006 年 1 月 15 日，智利执政联盟总统候选人巴切莱特参加大选并获胜。

For more information, you can check out the following link:

http://www.nytimes.com/pages/world/worldspecial4/

Unit 5   Current Global Economy

Lead-in: Listening (PPT-60)

Listen to the passage carefully, and answer the following questions:

1. What does "a global view of the housing bubble" indicate?

2. The price of gold has broken out to another new high, what did India's Central Bank react?

Reading

1.1   Tentative and Fragile Global Economic Recovery

"Global business confidence has remained largely unchanged during the past two months through mid-October. Sentiment is **consistent** with a very **tentative** and **fragile** global economic recovery," according to the results of the latest Survey of Business Confidence of the World by Moody's Economy.com. "Businesses…are more upbeat about the outlook into next year…South Americans are the most positive, and North Americans generally the most negative."

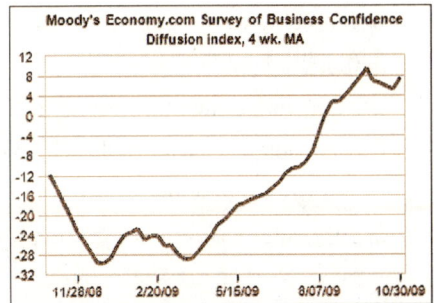

Moody's Economy.com Survey of Business Confidence
Diffusion index, 4 wk. MA

1.2   Improved Employment Prospects in the US, Europe and Asia

"Signs of recovery after a torrid year **reverberated** around the world on Monday as manufacturers reported rising output and improved employment prospects in the US, Europe and Asia," reported the Financial Times. The JP Morgan global composite purchasing managers' index (PMI) rose to 54.4, up from 53 in September, the highest value since July 2004. The recovery in manufacturing was strongest in Asia, where economists said the PMI figures were consistent with pre-crisis growth rates, but also reached multi-year highs in France, the UK and the US.

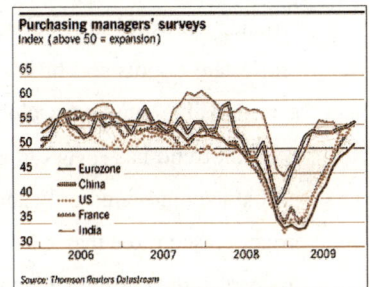

Purchasing managers' surveys
Index (above 50 = expansion)
— Eurozone
— China
— US
— France
— India
Source: Thomson Reuters Datastream

1.3 Unemployment Rate and "Real" Unemployment Rate in US Rose in October

On the US unemployment rate hitting 10.2% in Oct., Clusterstock said: "Worse yet, the 'real' unemployment rate, which adds in things such as discouraged workers who have dropped out of the labor force, hit 17.5%. Ouch."

"Yet there's some light at the end of the tunnel. While the unemployment rate and 'real' unemployment rate rose in October, the rate of deterioration (year-over-year change) for both measures kept falling, as shown below. Thus we're still bleeding jobs and it hurts, but the blood loss is slowing rapidly and starting to come under control. Hopefully the patient still has a pulse by the time the blood stops," said the report.

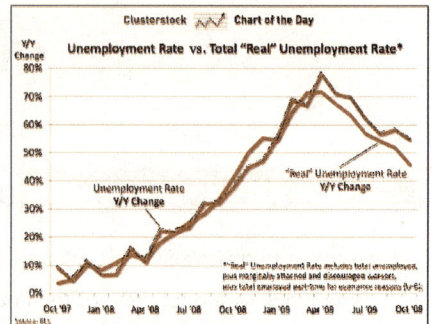

1.4 Commission Raises EU Growth Forecasts

"The European Commission on Tuesday raised its forecast for European economic growth next year, but said the recovery from **recession** would come at the price of record-high **budget deficits** and public debt.

"In its six-monthly economic outlook, the Commission predicted that the 27-nation European Union would grow by 0.7% next year and 1.6% in 2011, after a **slump** of 4.1% in gross domestic product this year.

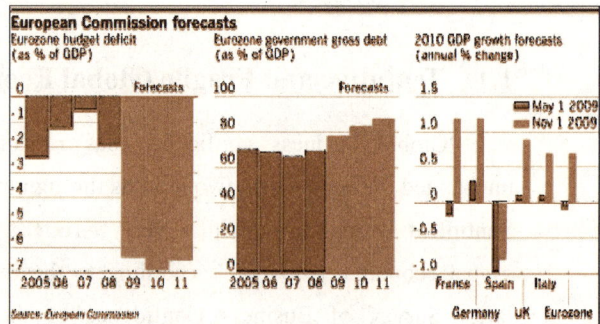

1.5 A Global View of the Housing Bubble

"Although the current crisis started with the bursting of the US housing bubble, other economies around the world are feeling the effects of their own real-estate booms and busts. From 2000 through 2007, a remarkable run-up in global home prices occurred. But that trend has **reversed abruptly**. In 2008, the value of US residential real estate fell 10%; the global average fared only somewhat better, declining by almost 4%. We estimate that falling home prices erased more than $3.4 trillion of household wealth in 2008. And because home prices are slow to correct, the current slide may persist for some time, which could depress global **consumption**."

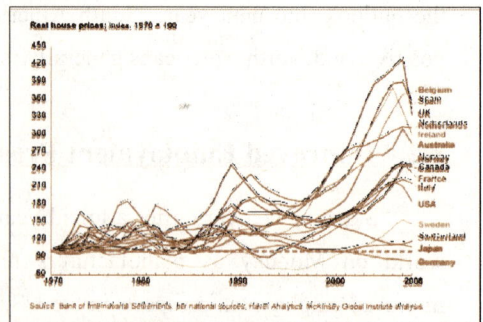

(Source: *McKinsey Quarterly*, October, 2009)

1.6   Gold Soars to New Highs

Gold Future: Last Six Months

"The price of gold has broken out to another new high this morning following news that India's Central Bank **purchased** 200 tons of the metal from the IMF. Previously, the IMF had announced that it would sell around 400 tons, raising speculation that the planned sale would cause a glut of gold in the market. Based on India's $6.7 billion 200-ton purchase, the market may have an easier time digesting the increased supply than previously thought. The average price per ounce for the Indian Central Bank's purchase works out to around $1,045. With gold now trading at $1,079, they have already made $218 million (3.25%). Not bad for a few days work!"

New Words and Expressions

consistent [kən'sistənt]	adj. 一致的，调和的，坚固的	
tentative ['tentətiv]	adj. 试验性的，试探的，尝试的，暂定的	
fragile ['frædʒail]	adj. 易碎的，脆的	
prospect ['prɔspekt]	n. 景色，前景，前途，期望	
reverberate [ri'və:bəreit]	v. 反响	
budget deficit	预算赤字	
slump [slʌmp]	n. (物价)暴跌；消沉，衰退	
	v. (物价)暴跌，跌落；失败，消沉	
recession [ri'seʃən]	n. 工商业之衰退，不景气	
bubble ['bʌbl]	n. 泡沫，幻想的计划	
reversed [ri'və:st]	adj. 颠倒的	
abruptly [ə'brʌptli]	adv. 突然地，唐突地	
consumption [kən'sʌmpʃən]	n. 消费，消费量	
purchase ['pə:tʃəs]	vt. 买，购买	

For more information, you can check out the following link:

http://en.wikipedia.org/wiki/Real_estate_bubble

Unit 6 Mandarin Is Bound to Increase Its Global Influence

Lead-in: Listening (PPT-61)

Listen to the passage carefully, and answer the following questions:

1. Based on a government-financed survey, how many American public and private schools are teaching Chinese?

2. Why is Mandarin Africa's next language?

Reading

1.1   Chinese in USA: Mandarin 3rd Largest Foreign Language in US

In this photo, a board saying "Please speak only Mandarin. If you have to speak English, whisper!" was hung on the door of Yu Ying charter school in Washington, D.C., the United States on January 20, 2010.

Mandarin will surpass German to become America's third largest foreign language, according to an educational report from the *New York Times* on Wednesday.

Based on a government-financed survey cited in the report, about **1,600** American public and private schools are teaching Chinese, up from 300 or so a decade ago. And the numbers are growing **exponentially**.

Among America's approximate 27,500 middle and high schools offering at least one foreign language, the proportion offering Chinese rose to four percent, from one percent, from 1997 to 2008, according to the survey, which was done by the Center for Applied Linguistics, a research group in Washington, and paid for by the federal Education Department.

To prepare the survey, the Center for Applied Linguistics sent a questionnaire to 5,000 American schools, and followed up with phone calls to 3,200 schools, getting a 76 percent response rate.

The results, released last year, confirmed that the number of students taking the Advanced

Placement Test in Chinese, introduced in 2007, has grown so fast that it is likely to pass German this year as the third most-tested A.P. language, after Spanish and French, said Trevor Packer, a vice president at the College Board.

Meanwhile the location of schools that offer Mandarin lessons has also extended from coastal areas to heartland states, including Ohio and Illinois in the Midwest, Texas and Georgia in the South, and Colorado and Utah in the Rocky Mountain West.

"The mushrooming of interest we're seeing now is not in the heritage communities, but in places that don't have significant Chinese populations," said Chris Livaccari, an associate director at the Asia Society.

Experts say several factors are fueling the **surge** in Mandarin. As well as the support of the Chinese government, American parents, students and educators' awareness of China's emergence as an important country and believe that fluency in its language can open opportunities.

1.2 Mandarin is Africa's next language

The Independent UK[1]: The trade volume between China and Africa has increased **dramatically** from 6 billion USD to 60 billion USD recently. However, Africans who can speak Mandarin are very scare and difficult to find. With the inter-relationship between China and Africa improving, Mandarin is bound to increase its influence in the continent of Africa. At the moment there are thousands of oversea African students studying in colleges in China—some of them are expected to become the important bridge between the two regions. On the other hand, China's **venture** in Africa is far from being smooth. Western media has continuously attacked China government on the "ignorance of human rights" in Africa, despite the fact that their own governments are not anywhere better. However, such a humane pressure will continue to push China government to amend its policy in Africa in **exploring deeper trade relationship**.

New Words and Expressions

Mandarin ['mændərin]	*n.* 中国的官话，普通话
exponential [ˌekspəʊ'nenʃəl]	*n.* 倡导者，演奏者；例子；[数]指数
	adj. 指数的，幂数的
surge [səːdʒ]	*n.* 巨涌，汹涌，澎湃；振荡
the Independent UK	《英国独立报》
dramatically [drə'mætikəli]	*adv.* 戏剧地，引人注目地

For more information, you can check out the following link:

http://en.wikipedia.org/wiki/Standard_Mandarin

Examination on Chapter Four

Name _____ No. _____

I. Fill in the blanks: 30%

1. Since China's Reform and Opening-up, EU is China's _____ accumulated technology and equipment supplier. Germany, France, UK, Italy and Netherland rank at the _____ 5 respectively in technological transfer to China.

2. EU is the _____ largest actual investor of China. In all the members of EU, as far as the actual investment is concerned, UK, _____, Netherland, France and Italy rank at the top five.

3. _____ Economic Cooperation (APEC) is the largest-scaled and highest-level _____ economic cooperation forum China has participated in, which provides an arena for China to display its achievements of reform and opening-up and promotes China's further opening-up process. China attaches great importance to the role of APEC and actively participates in its cooperation.

4. Mandarin will surpass _____ to become America's _____ largest foreign language, according to an educational report from the *New York Times* on Wednesday.

5. *The Independent UK*: The _____ volume between China and Africa has increased dramatically from 6 billion USD to 60 billion USD recently. However, Africans who can speak Mandarin are very scare and difficult to find. With the inter-relationship between China and Africa improving, _____ is bound to increase its influence in the continent of Africa.

II. Translate the following into Chinese: 40%

1. America is seeing a challenge from China, which might put them in a similar situation as Britain. How to avoid America becoming another Britain becomes the central topic for all the western politicians who are still obsessed with the American system.

_____

2. America to Learn from British Lesson.

_____

3. Obama: China is neither friend nor enemy.

_____

4. EU—Comprehensive Strategic Partner of Cooperation. Nowadays, EU becomes the first largest trading partner, export market, resource of technology introduction of China and the fourth largest actual investor of China. And China becomes the second largest trading partner of EU.

_____
_____

5. The All-around Development of China-Europe Economic and Trade Relationship.

_____

6. Regional Economic Cooperation.

_____

7. Economic and Trade Cooperation Mechanism between China and the American and Oceanian Region.

_____

8. Multilateral Cooperation in Disaster Relief to Express Humanitarian Care, and to Build Blocks of Friendship.

_____

III. Writing:

Part One (10%)

Mr. Lee is going to buy a large amount of electronic components from your company. He also shows an interest in your company's PCX phone machine, which is in the charge of Mr. Angus Beard, your colleague. Mr. Lee would like to bring 10 samples and some brochures back home to make a trial sale.

- Write a short note to Mr. Angus Beard, one of your colleagues.
- Tell him the fact that Mr. Lee is interested in PCX phone machine.
- Mention the number he wants to have.
- Suggest their direct contact.
- Write 30—40 words on your Answer Sheet.

Part Two (20%)

You are a clerk in Lucky Tourism Company. You are responsible for arranging travelling lines. One day, you received the data as follows:

Read the following table which shows the changes in the way people spend their holidays. The table divides the tourism business into four parts, telling the different percentages in 1980 and in 1990, from which you will notice the trend of current tourism business.

- Use the information in the table to write a short report (about 100—120 words) emphasizing changes of the main business for your company.
- Write on your Answer Sheet.

Where people spend their holidays	1980	1990
Travelling abroad	12%	23%
Going to seaside	38%	32%
Camping	9%	35%
Staying at home	41%	10%
Total	100%	100%

Appendix I

Keys to Listening Comprehension

Chapter One

Unit 1
1. They found the ancestors did cooking nearby.

2. Yes, Pagans, partygoers from far and wide greeted solstice at Stonehenge.

3. Because the excavations show that people once lived there.

Unit 2
1. Because Caesar abandoned the Republic System. If he became dictator for life, Roman people would be degraded into slaves.

2. He said: "Not that I loved Caesar less, but that I loved Rome more. Had you rather Caesar were living and die all slaves, than that Caesar were dead, to live all free men?"

Unit 3
1. King Arthur was a patriotic national hero.

2. Because he defeated the foreign invasion many times.

Unit 4
1. Yes, I agree. When Alfred the Great was king of Wessex in 871, the Vikings were threatening to overrun his kingdom. Alfred fought nine battles against them in one year alone. To prevent the new invaders from landing, Alfred built Britain's first naval force.

2. King Alfred, however, was even greater in peace than he was in war. Alfred was a lawmaker, a scholar and a just king.

Unit 5
1. The Normans were Danish overlords who lived in Normandy from 900 onwards.

2. In 1066, the Normans coquetted England by force.

Unit 6
1. King Richard the Lionheart was an ambitious king.

2. Their purpose was to recapture Jerusalem.

Unit 7
1. It was an infectious disease.

2. It resulted in the death of around a third of the population of the Middle East and Europe. In 1381.

Unit 8
1. She escorted the new but uncrowned king, Charles VII, to Reims to be crowned. However, Joan was soon defeated at Paris and captured by the Burgundians. They sold her to the English, who burned her at the stake as a witch in 1431.

2. This had been a kings' war, but it was the people who had paid the price. Joan of Arc was a patriotic national hero of France.

Unit 9
1. Mistakenly, the planned land reinforcement of Spain did not arrive in time. The exposed fleet of Invincible Armada was driven to the north and hit by vicious storms. The Spanish fleet had to retreat via Ireland's west coast. During this withdrawal, most ships and their crews were lost. In

all, 63 Spanish ships were lost, only 4 in battle.

2. Because Britain defeated their worst and most powerful enemy, the Spanish Invincible Armada.

Unit 10   1. His belief in the rights of the king was disliked.

2. He was unpopular in England because he made mistakes, and because he was Scottish and his Danish wife, Anne, was Catholic. This fact caused religious disputes.

Unit 11   1. Because of the disputes between supporters of King Charles I and supporters of parliament.

2. King Charles I and Cromwell. At last, the king was tried and executed.

Unit 12   1. Chinese silk and porcelain were the finest in the world and their cotton goods were cheap and of high quality. Huge quantities of Chinese tea were sold abroad when tea-drinking became fashionable in Europe during the 18th century.

2. Trade with China was profitable, yet the Chinese government didn't want "barbarian" influences introduced.

Unit 13   1. The Maoris.

2. The Maoris were skilled sailors and craft-workers. They lived a natural life. As the Europeans moved into their land, they resisted.

Unit 14   1. The native people of Africa were captured and shipped to America, then were sold to the white owners of plantations.

2. When they were taken away from their homeland and sold as slaves, they were sad and angry.

Unit 15   1. In 1901.   2. The national emblem was a kangaroo and an emu.

Unit 16   1. By the middle of the 19th century.

2. Many women gained independence by earning a wage for themselves after the Industrial Revolution.

Unit 17   1. Because the empire covered both hemispheres it was known as "the empire on which the sun never sets". Colonies in the Caribbean, Africa, Asia, Australia and the Pacific were ruled from London and were all united under the British monarch.

2. The Trade Union Act of 1871 legalized the trade unions and gave them financial security, allowing them to collect money in support of strike action. Compulsory education was adopted, and universities started to enroll women students.

Unit 18   1. Because Jewish terrorists to attack both the Arabs and the British. Growing demands for a separate Jewish state and the flood of refugees from Europe forced the British to withdraw from Palestine.

2. In 1949.

Unit 19   1. In 1931.   2. Many colonies started to clamor for independence.

Unit 20   1. It is made up of Great Britain and, Northern Island, and a number of smaller islands around them. Great Britain is traditionally divided into three countries, or political regions: England in the south, Scotland in the north, and Wales in the southwest.

2. They are: (1) Buckingham Palace; (2) No. 10 Downing Street.

Chapter Two

Unit 1   1. Maya Civilization.   2. No, it is only a fictional film.

Unit 2   1. Spanish Queen Isabella.   2. The French and Spanish.

Unit 3   1. Yankee Doodle refers to the American soldiers.

2. The background is the American Independent War.

Unit 4   1. It refers to the Mississippi River.   2. They felt rather depressed under the slavery.

1. Five score years ago.   2. Abraham Lincoln.

Unit 5   1. From this point onwards, the south's chances of winning the war declined.

2. In November, 1863.

Unit 6   1. The background of the song is the "American Westward Movement".

2. The song was well-known during the American "Gold Rush" in California.

Unit 7   1. It meant that as immigrants from different regions and cultures came to live in the United States, their old ways of life melt away, and they became part of the American culture.

2. Yes, the United States of America has greatly benefited from this policy, but the undesirable people suffered greatly.

Unit 8   1. The song's background is World War I.

2. Because of the war, many people lost all their savings as the value of money collapsed. Thus the Great Depression occurred.

Unit 9   1. On April 25, 1945.

2. The United Nations was established to keep international peace and solve problems by international cooperation.

Unit 10   1. They felt depressed, deceived and angry.

2. The theme of song: though they felt lost, depressed, yet they were always in the pursuit of truth and justice.

Unit 11   1. light   2. gleaming   3. watched   4. free   5. breeze   6. stream   7. home

Unit 12   1. In 1990.

2. The Multinational Force, including US, Britain and other Middle East forces drove Saddam out in February 1991.

Unit 13   1. The legislative, the executive and the judicial.

2. The White House is the official residence of the US President.

Unit 14   1. No.

2. Seventeen years later he did go to college. But he naively chose a college that was almost as expensive as Stanford, and all of his working-class parents' savings were being spent on his college tuition.

3. Because it was the decision of the company board.

Chapter Three

Unit 1   1. They refer to European Union and Council of Europe respectively. It consists of 12 golden stars on a blue background.

2. No, it represents completeness while their position in a circle represents unity.

Unit 2   1. It is called "oriental crown".   2. The domestic hall.

Unit 3   1. The soaring skyscrapers, the bustling streets and entrepreneurial activity.

2. He concluded as follows: "Shanghai, of course, is a city that has great meaning in the history of the relationship between the United States and China."

Unit 4   1. As it is mentioned in Chapter one Unit seventeen: The British taking of Quebec in 1759 meant the beginning of the end of New France. The French lost their military leadership, and thus lost control of Canada.

2. 啊! 加拿大!

我们的家园与故土!

你的儿女, 忠诚爱国。

雄心万丈, 国势昌盛,

强大、自由的北方之邦!

万众一心, 啊加拿大!

我们挺立护防!

上苍祝幸, 国泰民安。

啊加拿大, 我们挺立护防!

啊加拿大, 我们挺立护防!

Unit 5   1. Because Latin America was once ruled by Spain.

2. It means "the beautiful island" in English.

1. dreamt   2. breeze   3. played   4. Spanish   5. through   6. sting

Unit 6   1. It is an international fresh fruit corporation.   2. Yes.

Unit 7   1. Since establishments of bilateral ties at the ambassador-level in March 1972, Sino-British relations has overcome a variety of challenges and achieved steady progress.

2. Economic ties are particularly strong in the fields of energy, chemicals and the environment.

Unit 8   1. It will present France's contribution in the sustainable urban development for one of the biggest economic metropolises in the planet.

2. (Free talk.)

Unit 9   1. Giuseppe Castiglione, born in Milan, Italy, entered the Jesuit order at the age of 19, came to China in 1715, and was appointed court painter at the Imperial Palace in Beijing. He served in this position under three emperors (Kang Xi, Yong Zheng and Qian Long).

2. Castiglione painted in European style, but featured many Chinese themes.

Unit 10   1. It will showcase German urban life and how the country's design and products can help solve urbanization problems.

2. Siemens Confident of Maglev Train Deal with China.

Unit 11   1. Tourism.   2. Salzburg.

Unit 12   1. Vincent Willem van Gogh.

2. This display is to call on a worldwide concern over the remaining 1,600 pandas remaining in the wild.

Unit 13   1. In 1972.   2. 115.

Unit 14 1. "Little mermaid" statue. 2. A Comprehensive Strategic Partnership.

Unit 15 1. It is designed to show a perfect balance between Swedish cities and forests, as well as its timber industry that has been developing in a sustainable way.

2. Alfred Bernhard Nobel.

Unit 16 1. Chocolate, watch and natural scenery. 2. In Geneva.

Unit 17 1. Over 400 million.

2. Reduce the incidence of cardiovascular diseases and is conducive to human body metabolism.

Unit 18 1. To travel through the vast desert.

2. Sinopec and Saudi Arabian Aramco Oil Company; Sinopec is the first enterprise to enter the upper field of energy in Saudi Arabian.

Unit 19 1. Their purpose is to isolate Israel economically in support of the Palestinians to prevent Arab states and discourage non-Arabs from providing support to Israel and adding to Israel's economic and military strength.

2. Arab states have lost an opportunity to export $10 billion worth of goods to Israel between 2000—2010.

Unit 20 1. Urban Symphony. 2. A statue of the Merlion.

Unit 21 1. A theme on the harmony between the human heart and technology.

2. In order to bring a new era for the Sino-Japanese economic and trade cooperation.

Chapter Four

Unit 1 1. Because this challenge might put them in a similar situation as Britain.

2. His decision is to show that the government is determined to enforce the trade laws and encourage open policy for free trade.

Unit 2 1. EU. 2. Germany, Netherland, Britain, Italy and France.

Unit 3 1. Because it provides an arena for China to display its achievements of reform and opening-up and promotes China's further opening-up process.

2. Its "two resources" and "two markets".

Unit 4 1. 300,000 people. 2. What they desperately need: medical assistance.

1. Thank you to the people of China, all the wonderful volunteers and BOCOG!

Through these Games, the world learned more about China, and China learned more about the world. Athletes from 204 National Olympic Committees came to these dazzling venues and awed us with their talent.

2. In London. 3. Altogether 16 glorious days which we will cherish forever.

Unit 5 1. A remarkable run-up in global home prices occurred.

2. India's Central Bank purchased 200 tons of the metal from the IMF.

Unit 6 1. About 1,600 American public and private schools.

2. In order to explore deeper trade relationship.

Appendix II

Keys to Examinations

Examination on Chapter One

I. Multiple choice: 30%

1	2	3	4	5	6	7	8	9	10
B	A	B	A	A	C	D	D	D	C
11	12	13	14	15	16	17	18	19	20
D	D	C	B	A	D	A	A	D	A
21	22	23	24	25	26	27	28	29	30
A	B	D	A	A	D	A	A	C	C

II. Select the letter of the answer that best matches each term at left: 10%

1	2	3	4	5	6	7	8	9	10
f	h	a	b	c	i	d	j	g	e

III. Match English version with their Chinese equivalence: 10%

1	2	3	4	5	6	7	8	9	10
i	e	a	g	b	j	c	d	h	f

IV. Translate the following terms: 20%

1. 亚瑟王
2. 巨石柱
3. 北欧海盗
4. 北爱尔兰
5. 《末日审判书》
6. 外来词
7. 皮克(特)人(Pict= Picture 早期苏格兰人，他们喜画脸)
8. 七国集团
9. 裘力斯·凯撒(罗马帝国统帅，曾入侵英格兰)
10. 无形贸易(科技知识和旅游)
11. 增值税
12. 白厅
13. 主要政党
14. 大选
15. 沉默的权利
16. 苏格兰场
17. 多数裁决
18. 最高刑罚
19. 独立候选人
20. 拉选票

V. True (T) or False (F): 10%

1	2	3	4	5	6	7	8	9	10
F	F	T	F	T	T	F	T	F	F

VI. Fill in the blanks: 20%

1. Scotland; Wales
2. No. 10, Downing Street

3. the House of Lords; the House of Commons

4. prime minister

5. Conquest; William the Conqueror

6. Conservative; Labor

7. parliament and the king

8. French; Revolutionary

9. Treaty of Paris

10. James Cook

Examination on Chapter Two

I. Fill in the blanks: 12%

1. Maya civilization

2. Spanish, Queen

3. Asia, Bering

4. French, Spanish

5. gloried labor

6. Declaration, Independence

7. Enlightenment, Liberty

8. four, Congress

9. buffalo, Spanish

10. Ellis, harbor

11. melting pot

12. mosaic, Chinatowns

13. Crash, depression

14. peace, 1945

15. iron curtain

16. Shanghai Communiqué

17. oil, Saddam, multinational, Americans

18. separation, legislative, executive, judicial

19. 435, two

20. 100, six

21. Vice-President, Chairman

22. four, 35

23. moral, character

II. Translation the following phrases into Chinese: 20%

1. 葛底斯堡演讲

2. 三 K 党

3. 爱丽斯岛

4. 北大西洋公约组织

5. 政权分离

6. 民主

7. 联邦共和国

8. 国会

9. 联邦法律

10. 参议院

11. 众议院

12. 弹劾权

13. 司法机构

14. 内阁

15. 国务卿

16. 白宫

17. 国会大厦

18. 联合国

19. 落基山脉

20. 新教徒

III. Select the letter of the answer that best matches each term at left: 15%

1	2	3	4	5	6	7	8	9	10	11	12	13	14	15
i	j	h	a	b	d	e	c	f	g	k	l	m	o	n

IV. True (T) or False (F): 15%

1	2	3	4	5	6	7	8	9	10	11	12	13	14	15
F	F	F	F	F	F	F	T	T	T	F	T	T	F	T

V. Reading Comprehension: 20%

1	2	3	4	5	6	7	8	9	10
B	A	A	C	B	C	A	C	A	A

VI. Paragraph Translation: 5%

受托马斯·杰斐逊思想及启蒙运动的影响，1776 年《美国独立宣言》正式发表："我们认为下述真理是不言而喻的：人人生而平等，造物主赋予他们若干不可让与的权利，其中包括生存权、自由权和追求幸福的权利。"

美国独立战争爆发于 1775 年。除了要离家 5 千千米，英国人在战争初期是胜利的。但美国人有一个优势，即在本土作战，而且他们相信一定会取得成功。战争爆发 6 年后的 1781 年，英国军队包围了弗吉尼亚州的约克镇，但被乔治·华盛顿的军队击败了。1783 年，英国最终签订了《巴黎条约》，承认了美国的独立。

Examination on Chapter Three

Ⅰ. Fill in the blanks: 60%

1. Europe, blue
2. *Life*, oriental
3. USA, eagle
4. second-largest, first
5. Chile, free
6. Gordon, Brown
7. Maglev, Germany's
8. porcelain, red
9. Amsterdam, tulips
10. green, fortress
11. Copenhagen, Denmark
12. merchant, Sweden
13. watch, scenery
14. Jewish, Israel
15. harmony, music

Ⅱ. Translate the following phrases into English: 20%

1. Virgin Mary
2. Rising to the Challenge
3. Samba
4. Tango
5. Rumba
6. Central and South American Joint Pavilion
7. United Arab Emirates
8. Whispering Garden
9. Urban Symphony
10. China-Singapore Economic Cooperation Forum

Ⅲ. Translate the following phrases into Chinese: 20%

1. 区域经济合作：谋求互利共赢，构建和谐区域。

2. 中国与美大地区经贸合作。

3. 中国和丹麦之间的关于建立全面战略伙伴关系的联合声明。

4. 中石化与沙特阿美石油公司从事天然气勘探开发，这是中国企业首次进入沙特能源上游领域。

5. 中国和日本共同建立中日高层经济会谈机制。

Examination on Chapter Four

Ⅰ. Fill in the blanks: 30%

1. largest, top
2. fourth, Germany
3. Asia-Pacific, regional
4. German, third
5. trade, Mandarin

Ⅱ. Translate the following into Chinese: 40%

1. 美国似乎感觉到了来自中国崛起的威胁和挑战。如何继续维持美国和美元的强权霸主地位，避免成为第二个"英国"，成为美帝国主义政客们朝思暮想的课题之一。

2. 大英帝国衰落的教训。

3. 非友非敌的中美关系。

4. 全面战略合作伙伴——欧盟。目前，欧盟是中国第一大贸易伙伴和出口市场、最大技术引进来源地及第四大实际投资方；中国是欧盟第二大贸易伙伴。

5. 全面发展的中国-欧洲经贸关系。

6. 区域经济合作。

7. 中国和美大地区经贸合作机制。

8. 多边救灾合作；体现人道关怀，共架友谊金桥。

III. Writing: (Sample for reference)

Part One

Dear Mr Beard,

Mr. Lee, one of my old clients, has interest in our PCX phone machine. He would like to bring 10 samples and some brochures back home to make a trial sale. You may contact him directly on Tel 3108881.

Part Two

Nowadays, less people like to spend their holidays at home. More people go camping outside or even travel abroad. The changes are caused mainly by three factors. First, people become more open. Instead of staying at home, they visit foreign countries to know the different races. Secondly, in the 1990s, house wives are more free from the heavy housework with more and more household utensils. Families are very happy to spend holidays outside with mothers or wives. Thirdly, travelling abroad can also mean enjoying comfortable weather in another country. Therefore less people go to crowded seaside, they turn to other ways.

References

[1] Basil, Hatim. *Communication across Cultures—Translation Theory and Contrastive Text Linguistics*. Shanghai: Shanghai Foreign Language Education Press, 2001.

[2] Eugene, A. Nida. *Language and Culture—Contexts in Translating*. Shanghai: Shanghai Foreign Language Education Press, 2001.

[3] Halliday, M.A.K. *Language as Social Semiotic: The Social Interpretation of Language and Meaning*. Edward Arnold (Publishers) Limited, Foreign Language Teaching and Research Press, 2001.

[4] Jessica, Rawson. *The British Museum Book of Chinese Art*. London: British Museum Press, 1999.

[5] Kramsch, Claire. *Context and Culture in Language Teaching*. Oxford: Oxford University Press; Shanghai: Shanghai Foreign Language Education Press, 1999.

[6] Miranda, Smith. *The Concise History Encyclopedia*. London: Kingfisher Publications Plc, 2001.

[7] Samovar, Larry A., Richard E. Porter, and Lisa A. Stefani. *Communication between Cultures*. Belmont: Wadsworth Publishing Company, 1998.

[8] Susan, Bassnett & Andre Lefevere. *Constructing Cultures—Essays on Literary Translation*. Shanghai: Shanghai Foreign Language Education Press, 2001.

[9] 陈国明. 跨文化交际学. 上海：华东师范大学出版社，2009.

[10] 樊葳葳. 跨文化交际视听说. 北京：高等教育出版社，2009.

[11] 高春丽. 新编剑桥商务英语证书考试模拟考场. 北京：经济科学出版社，2009.

[12] 顾日国. 跨文化交际. 北京：外语教学与研究出版社，2003.

[13] 胡文仲. 跨文化交际面面观. 北京：外语教学与研究出版社，1999.

[14] 来安方. 英美文化与国家概况. 上海：复旦大学出版社，2008.

[15] 张爱琳. 跨文化交际. 重庆：重庆大学出版社，2007.

[16] 周汉民. 上海世博会用语词典. 上海：上海辞书出版社，2008.

[17] 庄恩平. 跨文化商务沟通案例教程. 上海：上海外语教育出版社，2004.

图书在版编目(CIP)数据

欧美概况与跨文化商务交际视听说 / 郑张敏，陆金英编著. —杭州：浙江大学出版社，2010.8(2017.7 重印)
高职高专商务英语、应用英语专业规划教材
ISBN 978-7-308-07871-9

I. ①欧… II. ①郑… ②陆… III. ①欧洲—概况②美国—概况③商务—英语—听说教学 IV. ①K95②K971.2③H319.9

中国版本图书馆 CIP 数据核字(2010)第 152147 号

(本教材配有 PPT 课件，请需要的老师登陆我社网站免费下载，网址：http://www.zjupress.com；或向作者索取)

高职高专商务英语、应用英语专业规划教材
欧美概况与跨文化商务交际视听说
European and American Studies and Intercultural Business Communication
郑张敏　陆金英　编著

丛书策划	张　琛　张颖琪　樊晓燕
责任编辑	张颖琪
封面设计	俞亚彤
出版发行	浙江大学出版社
	（杭州天目山路 148 号　邮政编码 310007）
	（网址：http://www.zjupress.com）
排　　版	杭州中大图文设计有限公司
印　　刷	杭州丰源印刷有限公司
开　　本	787mm×1092mm　1/16
印　　张	14
字　　数	431 千
版 印 次	2010 年 8 月第 1 版　2017 年 7 月第 2 次印刷
书　　号	ISBN 978-7-308-07871-9
定　　价	28.00 元